Modern Legal Scholarship

Modern Legal Scholarship

A Guide to Producing and Publishing
Scholarly and Professional Writing

Christine Coughlin
Sandy Patrick
Matthew Houston
Elizabeth McCurry Johnson

CAROLINA ACADEMIC PRESS
Durham, North Carolina

Library of Congress Cataloging-in-Publication Data
Names: Coughlin, Christine Nero, author. | Patrick, Sandy, author.
    Houston, Matthew T., author. | Johnson, Elizabeth M., author.
Title: Modern legal scholarship : a guide to producing and publishing
    scholarly and professional writing / by Christine Coughlin, Sandy
    Patrick, Matthew Houston, Elizabeth McCurry Johnson.
Description: Durham, North Carolina : Carolina Academic Press, LLC, 2020.
Identifiers: LCCN 2020012537 (print) | LCCN 2020012538 (ebook) | ISBN
    9781531010270 (paperback) | ISBN 9781531010287 (ebook)
Subjects: LCSH: Legal composition. | Academic writing.
Classification: LCC KF250 .C684 2020 (print) | LCC KF250 (ebook) | DDC
    808.06/634--dc23
LC record available at https://lccn.loc.gov/2020012537
LC ebook record available at https://lccn.loc.gov/2020012538

Carolina Academic Press
700 Kent Street
Durham, NC 27701
Telephone (919) 489-7486
Fax (919) 493-5668
www.cap-press.com

Printed in the United States of America

To Caroline, Lynn, Susannah, and Sylvia—
our laughs are limitless, our memories are countless,
and our friendship is endless.

CNC

To three of my greatest teachers in the law:
The Honorable David H. Welles and Professor Judy Cornett,
who taught me how to write as a lawyer and advocate, and
the extraordinary, indomitable Dean Deborah Leonard Parker,
who taught me how to teach legal writing.

SP

To Brooke, whose support helped make this a reality.

MH

To my greatest gifts from God—
Mom, Dad, Seth, Sarah, and Susanne.

EMJ

Contents

Acknowledgments

So much of what we do in any kind of legal scholarship is to build upon the work of others. In truth, this book could not have been written without the work of so many other authors, colleagues, and students. We wrote this book in large part to help students and new lawyers find inspiration, competency, and fulfillment in different kinds of legal writing. As we wrote, however, we often found that *we* were the ones inspired by the wide range of interesting scholarship kindly shared by authors across the country.

We would like to thank so many professional colleagues and students who shared their work, insights, feedback, and time as we crafted each chapter. First and foremost, we would like to thank Adam Messenlehner, former law student and now gifted public school teacher, for his extraordinary contributions to this book. This book is better because of his ideas and expertise.

The following individuals generously shared their work with us and provided permission to use excerpts from their scholarly contributions to help train future scholars. Thank you to:

Kate Acosta, Anna Baitchenko, Kelsey Benedick, Michael Blumm, Jack Bogdanski, Meghan Boone, Robin Boyle Laisure, Elizabeth Sargeant Buttrick, Kami Chavis, Brandon Chirco, Lawrence Cunningham, Lanee Danforth, Danielle Elefritz, Daniel Fan, Miki Felsenburg, Marie-Amélie George, Russell Gold, Laura Graham, Rachel Gurvich, Catherine Hammack, James Huffman, Mark Huffman, Steve Johansen, Stephen Kanter, Aliza Kaplan, Douglas Keith, Robert Klonoff, Anjana Kumar, Brian Larson, Nancy Levit, Douglas Linder, Susan Mandiberg, Ellie Margolis, Cyd Maurer, Andrew McClurg, Ruth Ann McKinney, Adam Messenlehner, Sarah Morath, Anne Mullins, Ellen Murphy, John Parry, Abigail Perdue, Joan Rocklin, Ruth Anne Robbins, Michael Robinson, Jennifer Romig, Allen Rostron, Suzanne Rowe, Rebecca Sandefur, Jessie Schuh, Shaun Spencer, Genevieve Steel, Janet Steverson, Juliet Stumpf, Hadley Van Vactor, Andrew Verstein, Leti Volpp, Daryl Wilson, Ron Wright, Logan Wyont, and Kenji Yoshimo.

We endeavored to acknowledge your work where it appears in each chapter. We have done our best to credit each of you as well as the entity that published your work. To the extent that any errors or omissions exist, we apologize.

Many scholars reviewed various chapters and provided us with gracious critique and thoughtful content and ideas. Again, this book is better because of your feedback and we thank you. These individuals include: Robin Boyle Laisure, Mari Cheney, Christopher Culbert, Marie-Amélie George, Russell Gold, Laura Graham, Rachel Gurvich, Mark Hall, Michael Hyde, Ana Iltis, Adam Kadlac, Nancy M.P. King, Chris Knott, Brian Larson, Lance Long, Mary Susan Lucas, Adam Messenlehner, John Moskop, Ellen Murphy, Richard Robeson, Michael Robinson, Jennifer Romig, and Andrew Verstein.

We would respectively acknowledge the following entities and individuals for their support:

Coughlin thanks Wake Forest School of Law for its support, particularly Dean Emerita Suzanne Reynolds, Dean Jane Aiken, Associate Executive Deans for Academic Affairs Jonathan Cardi and Wendy Parker, and Associate Deans for Research and Development, Andrew Verstein, Gregory Parks, and Kami Chavis. Professor Coughlin also thanks her other Wake Forest legal analysis, writing, and research colleagues who inspire her daily with their scholarship and teaching and are always generous in sharing their scholarly ideas and materials: Lance Burke, Tracey Coan, Luellen Curry, Russell Gold, Laura Graham, Heather Gram, Sally Irvin, Catherine Irwin-Smiler, Chris Knott, John Korzen, Hal Lloyd, Mary Susan Lucas, and Abigail Perdue. In addition, Coughlin would like to thank her Administrative Assistant, Ms. Cynthia Ring, for her extraordinary help and patience. Coughlin would also like to thank the many Wake Forest students who assisted with research and provided other related support for this project: Madison Alligood, Jordan Artrip, Hannah Frye Burgin, Meghan Capps, Hailey Cleek, Ashley Collette, Christopher Culbert, Katie Horton, Sarah Orwig, Sara Kathryn Mayson, Emily Stratmeyer, and Hannah Weiss. It certainly takes a village!

Patrick thanks Lewis & Clark Law School faculty and staff, particularly Dean Jennifer Johnson, Associate Dean John Parry, Associate Dean Libby Davis, and Assistant Director of Library Research and Instruction Mari Cheney. Special acknowledgement should go to professors who have so kindly shared their guidance on scholarly writing: Michael Blumm, Bill Chin, Susan Mandiberg, Jan Neuman, Janet Steverson, and Chris Wold. Professor Patrick also thanks her other Lewis & Clark colleagues who so freely share their ideas, assignments, and scholarship every day: Lawyering colleagues Steve Johansen, Toni Berres-Paul, Bill Chin, Judith Miller, Aliza Kaplan, Hadley Van Vactor, Robert Doeckel; librarians Mari Cheney and Rob Truman; and Writing Specialists Lora Keenan and Hillary Gell. Finally, thank you to the research assistants, Daniel Fan, Stephanie Keys, Sadie Normoyle, and Alexis Baello, who helped throughout the project.

Houston would offer sincerest gratitude to his co-authors for the opportunity to collaborate on this book and for spearheading the effort.

McCurry Johnson would like to give sincere thanks to Christine Nero Coughlin: "My friend; you are a professional and personal inspiration to me and many other women." Thank you to my other co-authors for all your guidance as I embarked on my first endeavor in book publishing. McCurry Johnson would like to thank the firm of Crosswhite, Crosswhite and Johnson for welcoming her and teaching her so many new things over the last few years. The unconditional support has meant so much.

Together, we all acknowledge the help and support we received from our family and circle of friends. We appreciate your patience with us as we were finishing this manuscript. We know there were far too many late nights and weekends, and your support means the world to each of us.

Special thanks to our publisher, Carolina Academic Press. CAP is a pleasure to have as our publisher. We could not ask for a more patient, caring, and competent group of people to guide us on this journey.

And, finally, special thanks to the students who inspire us daily—we hope these words may likewise inspire you to put your ideas out there.

Introduction

"The secret of getting ahead is getting started. The secret of getting started is breaking your complex overwhelming tasks into small manageable tasks, and then starting on the first one."

—Mark Twain

In today's modern world, legal scholarship can take many forms. Traditionally, legal scholarship was relegated to a few main forms—books, treatises, and scholarly articles such as those found in law reviews and law journals. As law study and practice have evolved, so have our methods of communication. Today, legal scholarship appears in many places, from blogs to monthly legal magazines to law review articles. Whether academic or professional in nature, legal scholarship has moved beyond traditional parameters. Lawyers (and, in particular, academics) tend to be people with strong convictions, and many opinions exist on what is or should be included in the diverse world of legal scholarship. Most, however, would agree that the goal of legal scholarship is to contribute to the discourse on topics of law or the general study of the law.

Scholarly writing in any form can be a rewarding form of self-expression in law school and beyond. Researching and writing scholarly works fosters professional development, improves analytic skills, and advances knowledge and understanding of a legal doctrine in a manner far greater than, for example, if you had simply studied the concept for a law school exam.[1] Writers gain "a sense of what it means to be an *expert* in a field—to know its history and literature, its issues and solutions; to synthesize all that is currently known on a subject [and] to see how it fits together."[2] For these reasons, you should select a topic you care about,[3] especially if that topic encompasses an area of law in which you would like to practice or intend to specialize eventually.

On the other hand, without a plan in place, the process of scholarly writing can feel more overwhelming than rewarding. The purpose of this book is to get you started and guide you through the full scholarly writing process, from topic selection to publishing. This book breaks down that process into understandable and manageable tasks to help you get started and complete the project.

Individuals learn best when they understand the context and purpose of a project. To provide as much context as possible for the tasks ahead, and so that you understand both how and why to complete each task, this book walks you through the process of producing a range of quality scholarship both efficiently and effectively.

Notes

1. Claire R. Kelly, *An Evolutionary Endeavor: Teaching Scholarly Writing to Law Students*, 12 J.L. WRITING INST. 285, 285 (2006).

2. Elizabeth Fajans & Mary R. Falk, *Comments Worth Making: Supervising Scholarly Writing in Law School*, 46 J.L. EDUC. 342, 344 (1996).

3. *See* Andrew Yaphe, *Taking Note of Notes: Student Legal Scholarship in Theory and Practice*, 62 J.L. EDUC. 259, 296–97 (2012).

Modern Legal Scholarship

Chapter 1

Exploring Topics and Establishing a System

The first step in any academic or professional scholarship project is finding a topic. Like bungee jumping or riding a zip line, that first step can be the most challenging—one filled with a mixture of curiosity, fear, self-doubt, and exhilaration. As the *Introduction* explained, the goal of legal scholarship is to contribute an original idea to the discourse surrounding a legal topic, preferably a topic you care about or at least one you find interesting. Choosing the best-fitting topic for your interests and crafting a solid thesis that can generate engaging discussion is the best route to contributing that original idea. Getting from an interesting topic to a final, polished product will take a plan. This chapter will help outline the first steps of finding a topic and establishing a workable plan.

1.1 Finding a place to start

With any topic, you can add a creative or original idea; all you really need is a place to start. At first, finding a topic, especially a "perfect" topic, may feel daunting. To overcome any intimidation factor you may be feeling, first, just take a breath. Most likely you have been writing for years, especially in law school. This project, whatever its form, will allow you to build upon the skills you already possess. In training to become a lawyer, you have been taught to assert your thoughts and ideas with each research assignment or legal document you have drafted, so have confidence that you can do the same when writing a scholarly work.

3

Think of the process as a way to engage the creative parts of your mind and simply apply that creativity to an area of legal scholarship. You may not be able to escape the dry content of some textbooks for law school courses, but when crafting legal scholarship, *you* get to chart the course your legal analysis will take. You get to show your creativity. In fact, with the strategies discussed in this book, your creative process can shine. Finding a topic by bringing discreet legal doctrines, disciplines, or concepts together; rethinking the policy implications of a case, statute, or regulation; or critiquing a traditional way of viewing a legal doctrine can be intellectually energizing.

The good news is that potential ideas for topics are everywhere. You can find ideas by listening to the news, volunteering in the community, exploring course syllabi, examining the notes that follow the cases featured in course casebooks (which often discuss unanswered legal issues ripe for a writing project), reading legal blogs, following law professors and attorneys on social media,[1] and conversing with professors, peers, or others.

If you have already identified a particular topic and potential thesis, you are ahead of the game. If not, a place to start is by identifying topics that interest you. As possible topics arise, start narrowing the precise points that interest you. Ask yourself these questions:

- What am I curious about?
- What legal topics do I find thought-provoking or evocative?
- How does a particular legal doctrine or law work? Is that doctrine or law effective? Should something be changed?
- Has the law been changed? If so, does that change help or harm society? What was the catalyst for that change?
- Does this area of the law present an injustice or inequity that does not sit well with me?

Thinking about questions you may have on a particular topic can help winnow down a broad idea. As the answers to these questions appear and as new ideas emerge, you will need an organized way to capture your thoughts. Completing a chart like the one on the next page can help define your areas of interest and ensure you will not forget good ideas.

Using a chart like this one to capture ideas can launch the project (and your thinking) by helping you see the ideas that resonate with you the most. You can then start perusing the various sources that might answer the questions generated by your ideas. (See Chapter 2, *Diving into Research*, for more information and a checklist on how to conduct the important preemption check at the start of the research process.) With your questions in mind, sometimes reading even one or two law review articles on a topic can help you find the issue that interests you the most. If you remain unsure about which topic to choose, keep exploring.

Identifying potential topics for a project

Broad area of interest	Narrower points of interest	Possible topics within those narrow points
Public health law	Quarantine of healthcare workers returning from service in other countries	How do quarantine practices affect healthcare workers returning to the United States?
		Do quarantine practices impact males and females differently?
Criminal law	Reliability of eyewitness identifications	When are eyewitness identifications reliable?
		Are identifications made in court reliable? Does the law ever limit when those identifications can be made?
		Has any research assessed the number of erroneous identifications made over the last decade?
		Why are such identifications problematic?
Sex trafficking laws	Laws or policies to help victims of child sex trafficking	What laws exist?
		Do states have different rules?
		How are these laws geared to help children, specifically those under age sixteen?
		Do the laws go far enough?
		How often are children who are trafficked charged with crimes like prostitution? What kind of resources do these children receive to get them out of harm's way?
		Can victims avail themselves of reentry programs similar to defendants who come out of prison?

1.2 Exploring potential topics

As you explore potential topics, keep in mind that some of the best topics for a scholarly piece investigate conflict—where the rule of law, a policy, a rule, or a right goes too far; where it does not go far enough; or where it clashes with another law, policy, rule, or right. If you have a general idea for your topic, but do not know specifically what to write about, look for the conflict.

Several resources can make the search for a topic easier. Examining the nature of the assignment, reading legal news articles, searching through circuit court split websites, reading journal articles, or even scanning your casebooks can yield a bounty of ideas. The following table may give you some guidance on where to look.

Identifying scholarly topics

Method	Explanation
Nature of the assignment	Are you writing a paper for a particular class that has an assigned topic? If so, what points of law within that specific topic interest you?
Legal news	Track hot topics in the news for an area of practice or interest. Look to specific newspapers covering the legal industry and focus on discrete areas of law across many jurisdictions. Many of these legal newspapers can be found on Westlaw, Lexis, or Bloomberg Law, and your law librarian can help you find such sources.
Circuit splits	Check out circuit splits (divisions or contradictions among the courts) in the different U.S. Circuit Courts of Appeals and examine these divisions. (Charts that track splits among the circuits are available on Bloomberg Law and on Seton Hall's Circuit Review.) As you review the circuit splits, ask yourself: • Where do courts from different circuits diverge on a topic? • Are circuits evenly divided on the issue? • Does the split revolve around a timely legal issue? • How different are the diverging viewpoints? • What is the difference—the courts' rationales or just the outcomes of the decisions? • Has one circuit taken an entirely opposite or "rogue" approach? • Which way should the court rule, in your opinion? • How many litigants have petitioned for certiorari to the Supreme Court, and what has the Supreme Court said in those petitions? (Set up alerts to keep tabs on any potential granting of certiorari.)
Law journal articles — "outside the scope" topics	In law journal articles, look for related or tangential issues that the article does not address. Look for issues that the article's author considers to be "outside the scope" of that article.
Notes and questions from casebooks	Many casebooks include a "Notes and Questions" section after the case. These sections contain unanswered doctrinal questions, any one of which may be the basis of a scholarly article.
Future professional plans	In the legal specialty you see yourself practicing in the future, are there legal issues that interest you? What topics have you explored in classes, clinics, externships, and summer positions that are intriguing? Talk to attorneys who practice in the field—do they mention particular conflicts in the law they would like to see resolved?

The following sections expound on the above table and may help you find those areas of conflict more easily.

1.2.A Legal news

News about new developments in federal, state, or local laws frequently contains topic ideas. Sources providing such news may help identify trends in topics or may spark an interesting question to which you can propose a solution. Specific news outlets cover the legal industry and sub-industries within it. These publications may focus on discrete topics of law across many jurisdictions (such as *The Antitrust Counselor* and *Consumer Bankruptcy News*) or may cover many topics within one jurisdiction (such as *North Carolina Lawyers Weekly*). Most of these legal newsletters can be found on Westlaw, Lexis, Bloomberg Law,[2] or in print in your law library.

1.2.B Circuit splits

Oftentimes, writers can find interesting topics by searching for divisions or conflicts among the various circuits in the U.S. Courts of Appeals. These divisions are known as "circuit splits" and occur when different circuits of the U.S. Courts of Appeals either interpret federal law differently or issue contradictory opinions based on a law. Three sources provide easy ways to search circuit court splits and identify "hot topics" ready for discussion:

> **Caution!**
>
> Be aware that if you decide to write on a circuit split, the U.S. Supreme Court could decide the case, thus making your article moot. Take a moment to see whether the high court has taken your issue on appeal or if any recent petitions for certiorari are pending.

- *Seton Hall Circuit Review.* This publication categorizes circuit splits by topic, from administrative law to statutory interpretation.
- *U.S. Law Week* **by Bloomberg Law.** This publication contains a column dedicated to case alerts and legal news, including weekly updates on circuit splits throughout the United States. For example, the platform categorizes decisions that are split across circuits under a particular topic, such as "Local Government." It also provides a brief description of the legal issues upon which the courts disagreed.
- **Commercial database providers (such as Westlaw or Lexis).** If you have a sense of a topic of interest, commercial databases may provide tools to research circuit splits on specific topics through Boolean, that is, "terms and connectors," searches or through advanced search tools. If you are not prolific in legal research using terms and connectors, ask for help from your law librarian or from the commercial provider's reference support staff.

When conflicts arise between two or more circuits, the U.S. Supreme Court may step in to resolve the conflict. Searching "Petitions for Certiorari" (the written requests attorneys make asking the U.S. Supreme Court or the highest court of any state jurisdiction to review the decision of a lower court) may help pinpoint those areas of conflict. Most commercial research providers typically have tools writers can use to search this area.

These resources are just a few ways to pinpoint where conflicts exist among different federal courts. Keep in mind the expertise of law librarians when researching circuit splits. Law librarians are well versed in the rapidly changing legal research front, and they can help you with resources and queries.

1.2.C "Outside the scope" of law journal articles

Another search strategy to find interesting and emerging topics is to see what scholarly authors have decided *not* to address in their articles. Many law review articles include statements from the author about issues that an article does not address or what the author indicates is "outside the scope" of the paper. These statements can provide ideas on novel topics or substantial ideas for writing about an existing topic in a new way.

After locating one of these "outside the scope" references and reading the underlying article, start thinking through the other issues (or even the proposed solutions) the author raised but did not address. By addressing these related questions or unresolved issues, you can continue the scholarly conversation on this topic.

Once you have selected a topic, you are ready to start the process in earnest. Before you jump in, be kind to your future self and take just a moment to get yourself organized. Consider your goals for the research and writing process, your timeline, and how you will keep up with the vast amount of resources you might be reviewing. Organization saves time and promotes efficiency.

1.3 Establishing a workable system

How valuable is your time? For most of us, our time is our most valuable commodity—we certainly do not want to waste it. When we fail to have articulated goals or to implement workable systems to meet those goals, we may find ourselves wasting time. After all, "goals are simply dreams with deadlines."[3] To meet your scholarly goal, you will need to create a system that incorporates manageable tasks with deadlines so that you can measure your progress.

Creating a workable system that accounts for both long-term goals and the incremental tasks that make up those goals help you in a few ways. First, assessing your major deadlines and the tasks that must be completed before each deadline is met can keep you focused on the topic and prevent you from wandering into black holes.[4] Second, starting from scratch without any type of system can lead to the paralysis of inaction or the frustration of disorganization. With a system, however, as you get things done, your project will gain momentum and you can move forward through the project without getting stuck for days or weeks in an early stage. Finally, by fashioning a system, you can create a deliberate method for organizing your thoughts, your notes, and your research findings, thus allowing you to work more efficiently and to finish the project faster.[5] The following sections will guide you through a few strategies to create a timeline, assess incremental tasks, formulate a plan, and control your time. Whether writing a short blog post on a recent state court decision or a fifty-page scholarly article on a nuance of complex federal law, start by setting up a workable system for your process.

1.3.A Creating a timeline

The linchpin of a workable system for scholarly writing is the schedule, or timeline, for the project. No matter what kind of project you are writing—in school or in practice—time constraints are inevitable. Getting things done within the time you have is pivotal to your success.

The most useful timelines will incorporate major milestones in the project and then set out the incremental tasks that need to be completed to reach those milestones. Setting up target dates to complete those incremental tasks will make the timeline even more helpful.

To get dates on your timeline, first, think about the final due date for your project. Working backwards from the final deadline, identify target dates for completion of the major milestones. Those major milestones will include researching, outlining, writing the down draft (where the words just get written down on paper), revising the draft, meeting with professors or supervisors for review, polishing the final draft, and finally, submitting the work. For example, if the project is due December 1, you likely will need to have a full draft ready for editing by November 1, which means the research should begin in early September, and your outline and first draft should be ready by the first part of October.

To be really useful—and to shield you from the inertia that can accompany a large writing project—do not stop with your major milestones. Instead, take your planning one step further and think about the tasks that need to happen for a milestone to be met. Along with the major milestones, add these incremental tasks to your timeline.

1.3.B Setting interim deadlines for smaller tasks

Breaking up a large project into smaller pieces by assessing smaller tasks and their deadlines can help you see what actually needs to be done. Is a broad goal like "finishing research" or "writing the Discussion section" sufficient? Although each of those milestones should make up part of your project's timeline, those tasks are probably still too broad. Instead, try crafting the tasks in such a way that you can actually know what you should be doing, see your progress, and measure your success.[6]

You can analogize this process to that of a video game. When gaming, you may want to get to the highest level or score the most points, but likely those goals will take time, and if achieving those goals is too hard, you might stop playing altogether. In most games, the game makers want to keep you playing, so they give you smaller ways to score points as you move up level by level. Essentially, by including incremental tasks that you can complete, you feel like you are making progress. An added benefit is that your brain is getting dopamine hits with each success. Without those small hits of success, many people would probably just give up. You can, however, structure your writing project like a video game. While you are working toward that top level in which you can submit a finished paper, give yourself a chance to get those hits of success along the way by meeting interim tasks. These smaller successes will help you stay motivated and keep moving forward.

When setting interim tasks, identify the task in a specific way. By defining tasks concretely, you will have a clearer grasp of what needs to be done, and you can prioritize the tasks to maximize your time. The more concretely you frame the task, the easier it is to measure your progress.

To define the components of a milestone task, think through what you want to accomplish, what limits are involved, and what incremental steps you should take.[7] While most writers are good at establishing a general workable system, you must intentionally create specific interim tasks that can help you measure your progress toward your overall goal. Thinking through each interim task will help you use time efficiently and will keep you from getting bogged down in a jumble of research and notes. Look at the difference between general goals and specific tasks in the following table.

Examples of specific interim tasks and deadlines

Not Specific	Conduct research and read about my topic.
Specific	Find ten to fifteen articles or secondary sources that are relevant to my topic within the first two weeks of research. Highlight and take notes on the relevant portions. Organize the primary legal points into a broad outline.
Not Specific	Write a rough draft of my article.
Specific	Dedicate two hours (10 a.m.–12 p.m.) three times a week (M, W, Th) during weeks four and five to create a detailed outline of main points I, II, and III in the discussion section.

Specific, measurable tasks not only function like a "to-do" list, but they also can function like route markers that guide you from one task to the next.[8] These markers, in turn, provide a workable system that will show which tasks are completed and which tasks remain.

1.4 Putting your plan in writing

After brainstorming the goals of a particular project and identifying your system for completing them, put that system in writing by using a written chart (like the one shown below) or even a linear timeline.[9] People who write down their plan are more likely to achieve their goals than their counterparts who do not.[10] Post your proposed plan in a place where you will routinely see it—perhaps on the first page of an outline, on a calendar, or even on piece of paper taped to your front door. The form or the location of your system does not matter, as long as you can see the tasks daily. Below is a sample timeline for a seminar paper. (See Chapter 8, *Seminar Papers and Capstones Projects*, for more details on drafting these types of papers. Other chapters, in which you may find more detailed information about the various tasks, are noted in blue.)

Scholarly paper with a one-semester timeline

Week 1	• Identify topics in which you are interested. (Chapter 1) • Think about the form of your final product—what kind of scholarship do you want to write? (See Chapters 7–13) • Draft a timeline of major milestones for your paper. Start assessing the interim tasks that must be completed to meet each milestone. (Chapter 1) • Start getting your research and writing process organized; think about your weekly schedule and how you will manage your sources. (Chapter 1)
Week 2	• Conduct a preemption check and survey the field of available research. (Chapter 2) • See if your topic needs to be broadened or narrowed. (Chapter 2) • Start crafting a thesis statement. (Chapter 3) • Meet with professor or supervisor for approval of thesis and timeline. • Finalize the list of incremental tasks necessary for completion of each major milestone. (Chapter 1)
Weeks 3–4	• Conduct research. (Chapter 2) • Organize research as you go with a research chart or other system of organization. (Chapter 2) • Take careful notes on your research. (Chapter 5) • Create a broad outline. (Chapter 6)
Weeks 5–6	• Refine your thesis if necessary. (Chapter 3) • Use your notes to create a detailed outline. (Chapter 6) • Review any points of analysis that are not supported or developed, and research those analytical holes. (Chapter 2, Chapter 4, and Chapter 6) • Once holes are filled in your detailed outline, start writing the working draft (also called the down draft or zero draft) of the paper. (Chapter 6) • Schedule an appointment with professor or supervisor to discuss progress.
Weeks 7–9	• Complete a draft. (Chapter 6) • Revise and edit initial draft, making sure organization is sound and analytical points are supported. (Chapter 4 and Chapter 6) • Meet with professor or supervisor to review draft.
Weeks 10–12	• Revise and polish the paper, integrating the reviewer's comments. (Chapter 6) • Proofread for substance. (Chapter 6) • Proofread for grammar, punctuation, and style. (Chapter 6) • Correct citations in proper format according to your preferred citation manual. (Chapter 6)

1.5 Controlling interruptions

Reaching your writing goals often means learning how to work without interruptions.[11] The world today is full of interruptions—from emails to text messages to working in environments that garner interactions (whether a coffee shop, the law library, a study carrel, or your own dining room table). Your most difficult challenge may be finding time to unplug from those interruptions and complete the task. As noted previously, your time is your most valuable commodity. Distractions make us accrue a time debt that eventually must get paid. Too much debt and you may default on completing the project by its deadline.

The good news is this: You have the power to choose how accessible or inaccessible you are to others. For truly effective time management, you must determine the boundaries you need and then implement systems or strategies to enforce those boundaries. Here are some strategies for avoiding interruptions while working:

- **Minimize distractions from devices.** Technology does come with an "off" button, so use that button during the times you are thinking, reading, and writing. You can put your phone in airplane mode, use the "Do Not Disturb" function, or keep the phone out of sight and reach while working. On tablets or laptops, while you may need the internet to conduct online research, you can minimize distractions by turning off email, text, or social media notifications. You can also install a browser extension that allows you to block distracting websites for a defined period of time.

- **Plan for the distraction.** If you cannot work for long without checking email or texts, try working in fifty-minute intervals, with ten-minute breaks, to catch up on communications. Hold yourself to the time limit you set for working and catching up.

- **Refocus after an interruption.** Transitioning from an email or phone call can take several minutes, so learn to refocus more efficiently. To refocus, try reviewing the last page of notes or quickly skim your "to do" list for the goals you want to complete for the day.

- **Choose your work spot wisely.** Often, writers will know the best place to go for their solo work; it may be a quiet spot on the top floor of the library or in a coffee shop that has some background noise. Try to find whatever type of spot works best for you and use it wisely.

Ultimately, *you* are in control of the schedule, and you must set firm boundaries to protect your valuable time. With a workable system in place for your project and a realistic timeline for the project's completion, you will be on your way to creating an efficient process.

1.6 Holding yourself accountable

Having a workable system with firm deadlines is an excellent strategy for producing work. Even so, you may be tempted to miss a deadline from time to time, especially when school, work, or home life becomes busier. To fend off these temptations, implement a strategy to help you maintain accountability.

You can hold yourself accountable in countless ways. For example, you can schedule regular appointments with a professor, teaching assistant, or colleague to explain the work. These one-on-one meetings can focus your attention on the task at hand and help you clarify arguments and processes along the way. Another option is to require yourself to frequently check in with a peer who is also working on a writing project and pledge to keep each other on track.

Yet another strategy for maintaining accountability is to plan something positive when a milestone is completed. For example, once you have written a particular section of a paper, reward yourself with something you enjoy—a short hike, your favorite dark chocolate, or a shiny new ink pen. Remember the dopamine hits one gets from playing video games? Rewarding yourself with small treats when tasks or milestones are accomplished can function in much the same way.

No matter what strategy you use, having a system of accountability will help you reach your milestones and complete the project. With your topic in hand and a workable system to manage yourself and your time, you are ready to tackle the next big step—starting the research.

Notes

1. Telephone Interview with Professor Rachel Gurvich, University of North Carolina, Chapel Hill (Dec. 4, 2019).

2. Because commercial databases frequently change their names when upgrading their search platforms, we use the general database name throughout the book.

3. Attributed to author Napoleon Hill (1883–1970).

4. *See generally* MINDTOOLS, *SMART Goals: How to Make Your Goals Achievable*, mindtools.com (last visited Apr. 16, 2019) [hereinafter "*SMART Goals*"].

5. Art Markman, *To Achieve a Major Goal, First Tackle a Few Small Ones*, hbr.org (Feb. 24, 2017).

6. *See id.*

7. *See id.*

8. *See* Shawn Doyle, *6 Daily Habits of Highly Productive People*, Inc.com (Oct. 20, 2016).

9. *See SMART Goals, supra.*

10. *Id.*; *see also* Markman, *supra.*

11. KATHLEEN ELLIOTT VINSON, SAMANTHA A. MOPPETT, SHAILINI JANDIAL GEORGE, MINDFUL LAWYERING: THE KEY TO CREATIVE PROBLEM SOLVING 9–21 (2018).

Chapter 2

Diving into Research

"Research is not about luck, it is about strategy"[1]

Now that you have a general topic and a framework for your process of research and writing, you are ready to start researching that topic, assessing its viability, and drilling down to the main point you will make with your writing: the thesis. Researching for a scholarly or professional paper may be a bit different than researching for memos or briefs. Scholarly research may require you to cast a wider net and analyze and synthesize a multitude of secondary sources, but remember, the same techniques that you learned to research memos and briefs effectively and efficiently still apply.

The first major task to complete once you decide on a topic is the preemption check, which is a search of all of the literature on your topic. The goal with the preemption check is to ensure that your idea has not been fully addressed or preempted by previous articles. This chapter will walk you through how to plan your research, manage the information that you find, and complete the all-important preemption check.

2.1 Planning your research

When working on a big project, most tasks can be done more efficiently if you see where each task fits into the larger process. Research is no different. Researching for a scholarly or professional article—whether it is a full-length law review article or a relatively short blog post—requires a sound, methodical strategy for finding and selecting sources, weighing those sources, and managing your information. The scholarly research process may be broadly broken down into the following phases:

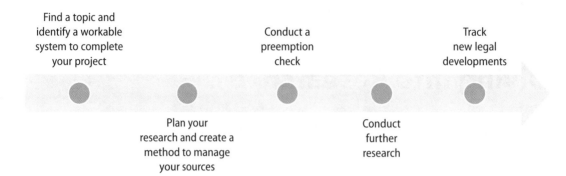

A sound research strategy can yield fruitful results efficiently. Without a strategy, research can be like trying to find a perfect seashell on the beach while blindfolded at night. Understanding from the outset what sources you will need to support your argument, having a methodical plan on how to find those sources, and keeping track of what you have found will ensure that you efficiently retrieve the relevant sources. Your time—whether you are in law school or law practice—is a valuable commodity.

Finding a topic and identifying a workable system to complete your project were discussed in Chapter 1, *Exploring Topics and Establishing a System*. As you can see from the graphic below, the next phase is to plan your research and create a method to manage your sources.

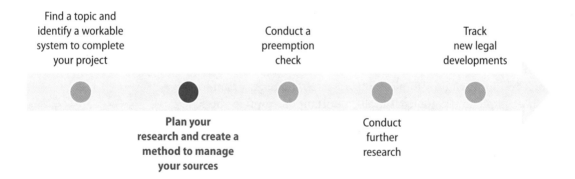

Research plans will necessarily differ depending on the topic, the issue, your baseline knowledge of the topic, and the unique parameters of the project. However, you should consider the following factors as you think through possible sources of primary and secondary law.

A time frame for the project and any internal deadlines

Any potential issues or sub-issues

Any relevant jurisdictional limitations

Relevant search terms

Relevant social, historical, political, or economic factors

A list of scholars with expertise in the area

A list of other academic disciplines that address similar issues or sub-issues

Thinking through how each factor above affects your particular topic will help you organize your thoughts and pinpoint where to begin your research. You might want to have a simple brainstorming session in which you list possible sources for each factor listed. Having a focused process will get your research off to a good start and help you research efficiently and effectively as you go.

2.2 Managing your sources

You will need to have a process for managing the sources you locate. Beyond merely tracking research, you will also want to consider how you will save, organize, and store information, including versions of your work in progress. Having a system for managing your research sources will help you remember the sources' origins and the research path you took to find the information. In addition, a management system will have ancillary benefits like helping you keep track of your citations and preventing unintentional plagiarism.

2.2.A The research log

The best way to track research is to use a research log (sometimes called a "research trail"), which is essentially a running account or checklist that shows where you researched, the queries used, a summary of your findings, and notes to yourself. A research log has no set format but should work for your particular style. A log can be organized digitally in a chart or spreadsheet format or by hand in a running narrative. It should also note additional, helpful sources that you come across and might want to use later.

Research Tip: Stay focused on your topic

You may find yourself losing time by reading interesting materials that are not directly relevant to your project. If you think they may be useful later, make a note of them in your research log. That will allow you to easily retrieve the source if it becomes relevant.

No matter the form of your scholarship (whether a traditional law review article or a short blog or social media post), always track your sources. A research log typically contains the name and full citation to the source along with how it may be relevant to your work product. You may also want a place to note that you have reviewed the subsequent history of any primary source so that you know it is still good law. The following chart shows a student's preliminary research on the topic of how municipalities increase homelessness by using exclusionary zoning to prevent the construction of affordable housing.[2] You may notice its informality—this research log is a strategy document for *your* reference, so you can use shorthand and perhaps not worry that your citations are not yet properly formatted.

Sample research log

Date	Database/ Source	Research Terms/ Queries	Results	Helpful sources	Next steps with this source	Done?
9/17	WL	All secondary sources: "affordable housing"	10,000 ==>"legal restrictions" = 49 secondary sources	Nothing helpful		
	WL	All sources: "litigation" and "affordable housing"	1801 ==>just states = 209 sources	*The Mount Laurel Doctrine: A 25 (Plus)-Year Personal Perspective* 188 N.J. Law 8		✓
				Oregon's Housing Crisis Or. St. Bar Bull 18 (July)		✓
	WL	All cases: "affordable housing" and "exclusionary zoning"	139 ==>State only = 122 sources	*Southern Burlington Cty NAACP v. Mount Laurel*, 456 A.2d 390 336 A.2d 713	Need to read.	
	Lexis	Secondary Sources: "Exclusionary zoning" and "affordable housing"	Good search	#7: Great Source: *How the courts should fight exclusionary zoning* 32 Seton Hall L. Rev. 1 (2001)	Read relevant cases from article: • *Berenson v. Town of New Castle*, 341 N.E.2d 326 (NY 1975). • *Mt. Laurel I and II* (see pp. 48–55) • *Robert E. Kurzius, Inc. v. Incorporated Village of Upper Brookville*, 414 N.E.2d 600 (NY 1980) [pp. 45–46]. From FNs • Blay and Blay, *The Cost of Inequality: Metropolitan Structure and Violent Crime*, 47 Am. Soc. Rev. 114 (1982). • Oliver, *The Effect of Metropolitan Economic Segregation on Local Civil Participation*, 43 Amer. J. Pol. Sci. 186 (1999). • Laura Padilla, *Reflections on Inclusionary Housing and a Renewed Look at its Viability*, 23 Hofstra L. Rev. 539 (1995).	✓ ✓ ✓

If keeping a digital log feels too difficult, you can always record your searches by hand. That same log, written longhand, might look like this:

Research Log
Friday, 9/14

Westlaw

1. All Content: "affordable housing"
    - 10,000 Secondary sources
    - Search within: "legal restrictions"
      49 secondary sources (nothing helpful)
2. Secondary sources: "litigation" and "affordable housing"
    - 1801 Sources
    - Jurisdiction: Limit to state
    - → 209 secondary sources
    - Possible helpful source: "The Mount Laurel Doctrine: A 25 (Plus) Year Personal Perspective" 188 N.J. Law. 8 (Nov.) (read this and look for other sources)
3. Cases: "affordable housing" and "exclusionary zoning"
    - 139 results—too many results. How to narrow?
    - State-only jurisdictions: 122 results
    - Possible hits:
    - Southern Burlington County NAACP v. Mount Laurel, 456 A.2d 390 [AND] 336 A.2d 713
4. Secondary sources: "affordable housing" and "exclusionary zoning"
    - Source 7: Great hit!
    - "How the Courts Should Fight Exclusionary Zoning," 32 Seton Hall L. Rev. 1 (2001).
    - Section A: "The Courts" found relevant case law.
    - pp. 44–45: Berenson v. Town of New Castle, 341 N.E.2d 236 (NY 1975)
    - pp. 48–50: extensive write-up on Mt. Laurel I and II
    - pp. 45–46: Robert E. Kurzius, Inc. v. Inc. Village of Upper Brookville, 414 N.E.2d 680 (NY 1980). [need to read this case—sounds on point]
    - FN 25: Judith R. Blau and Peter Michael Blau, "The Cost of Inequality: Metropolitan Structure and Violent Crime," 47 Am. Soc. Rev. 114 (1982) (may provide more relevant cites)

Since your log is for your eyes only, it should note your findings and your thoughts about those findings in whatever style or format you choose. Although perfect citations are not required for the log, make sure to include enough information so that you can easily use the citations to find the exact location of a source again.

Keeping up with the queries and the results will take a little more time on the front end, but a research log will save you time in the long run. Consider the following scenario: Let's say that after a few days of researching the topic, the student in the prior example is finding too many resources. She makes an appointment to meet with the supervising professor to discuss the best way to narrow the topic. The professor will likely ask the student what steps she has taken to complete the project. By having a research log that details her process and progress, she can more accurately explain her path and get more detailed feedback from the professor on other possible primary or secondary sources.

Creating a research log can also be quite practical for your own workflow. Rarely will you have the time to research a project without any interruptions. A research log will help you stay mindful of the different paths you have researched and the relevant sources—or dead ends—you have found so far. When returning to the research, you will not then waste time running the same searches that you have already conducted.

2.2.B Other research management tools

In addition to creating a research log (and taking notes), a few online programs can help both manage your research and generate citations as you write. Several online programs provide research tools that help you organize, analyze, and store research. Other programs may also automatically create citations for the sources you are researching; be aware, however, that many citation manager programs are not geared toward legal research and may not format citations in accordance with legal citation style. Rather, these citation manager programs were created to work broadly with any type of research. Programs such as EndNote and Evernote allow researchers to create a virtual binder of sources. Programs such as RefWorks, Zotero, and Mendeley work well with the internet and traditional academic databases; however, some of these programs may not work as well with traditional legal databases such as Westlaw or Lexis. Juris M and PowerNotes, on the other hand, seem to work better with legal databases, but you will still need to double check the formatting of citations against *The Bluebook*, the *ALWD Manual*, or other applicable legal style guide.

By this point, you have discovered a topic and found a system to manage your research. You may have an idea of a narrow legal question that you would like to write about, or you may not. Either way, the next step is to see what has already been written about your topic and to verify that your precise paper has not already been written (thereby preempting your paper). As you can see from the graphic below, this next phase is called the preemption check.

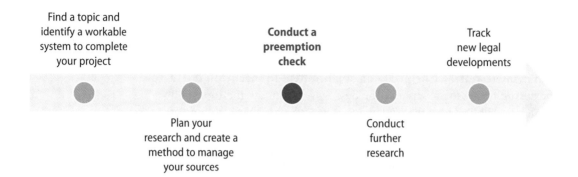

Find a topic and identify a workable system to complete your project

Plan your research and create a method to manage your sources

Conduct a preemption check

Conduct further research

Track new legal developments

2.3 Conducting the preemption check

After selecting an initial topic, you must make sure the topic is not preempted—in other words, has not been squarely addressed by another scholar. To do so, you will want to conduct a "preemption check" by thoroughly searching scholarship similar to your intended topic.[3]

Preemption checking requires you to carefully investigate what literature and legal authority is out there and how your topic (or thesis) fits into the larger body of research. If multiple sources have already addressed your topic or answered your questions, it is better to know now before you have invested too much time and effort into the project.

The first goal of preemption checking is essentially to prove a negative—specifically, that another scholar has not directly addressed a topic in a manner indistinguishable from the way you intend to address it. A preemption check is not a linear progression but is a nuanced process involving the careful evaluation of primary and secondary sources. More directly, a preemption check involves more than simply running a few key words in Westlaw, Lexis, or Google. Instead, you will likely find a web of primary and secondary sources addressing various aspects of your topic, and you will need to sort through those sources to make sure that your exact legal questions have not already been answered.

If you find that your topic is ripe for discussion and has not been preempted by other scholarly works, the preemption check will help you with a second goal: discerning how to situate your personal contribution within the broader scholarly narrative. In other words, the preemption check may help you find the thesis or specific legal point that you want to write about. Your specific point must find its own original place within the web of scholarly work by either building off existing strands of thought or by trailblazing a new path with an original thought. As part of the preemption check, you should read and parse other scholars' important points to see how each piece of scholarship adds something novel to the conversation and how each legal authority or piece of legal scholarship fits into the topic's narrative. In reviewing the background literature, think about how your own scholarship may connect with previous works. By the end of this process, you should be able to answer the essential question: What original thought does my work contribute to the discussion?

While starting a preemption check may seem daunting, like most things in life, it is best done with a plan. To make the preemption check easier, consider walking through the following steps (adjust them as necessary for your unique topic):

Conducting a preemption check

Step #	Explanation	Completed?
Step 1	Meet with a law librarian — librarians are amazing resources who can help shepherd you through the research process. They can often guide you to databases that you have not used before and provide you with other helpful advice.	
Step 2	Look at your law library's list of databases to see if a subject-specific database or library guide is available for your topic.	
Step 3	Create broad and narrow Boolean searches relevant to your topic and search in databases such as Westlaw, Lexis, Bloomberg Law, HeinOnline, or Google Scholar.	
Step 4	Search different legal periodical indices that catalog law reviews, law journals, and bar journals for additional articles that may be relevant. Some popular indices include Current Index to Legal Periodicals, Gale's LegalTrac, EBSCO's Legal Sources, and the Index to Foreign Legal Periodicals (available on HeinOnline).	
Step 5	Search for books and book chapters on sources such as WorldCat and Index to Legal Periodicals & Books.	
Step 6	Check with your law school's library catalog to identify applicable print sources including treatises, loose-leaf, and monograph titles.	
Step 7	Locate any relevant primary sources for which you have the citation.	
Step 8	If your subject is interdisciplinary, search for articles from other disciplines on academic databases. (Hint: Many times, you may find links to these sources on your own law school's library website or an undergraduate university's library website.)	
Step 9	Check out the Legal Scholarship Blog, which posts announcements for upcoming conferences and symposia in law schools and the Law Professor Blogs Network for entries on your broad topic.	
Step 10	Search for working papers on sources such as the Social Science Research Network (SSRN) and bepress Legal Repository.	
Step 11	Look at Twitter or other social media sites for conversations and links posted by law professors, lawyers who practice in your area of interest, and even judges.	

The benefit of a preemption check is twofold. First, after finding and reading all of these materials, you can verify that your topic is not preempted. As a bonus, a preemption check should also provide you with a sound grasp of the relevant scholarship and the central arguments other scholars are making. Through the preemption check, you may find a majority of your sources.

If, however, your topic is preempted, what should you do? Do not give up automatically, at least not before you consider whether you may be able to shift the focus of your paper. To shift the focus, consider whether you can use one of the following options:[4]

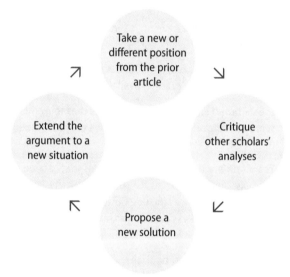

Thus, even if your initial thesis is preempted, you can probably change tack to approach the same or similar issue in an alternative way by taking a new and different position than the prior article, critiquing other scholars' analyses, proposing a new solution, or extending the argument to encompass a new situation.

The preemption check also provides information about whether the depth and breadth of your research universe are manageable. Once you have gone through this initial research, you may find that the topic is either too broad, yielding too much information to manage within the scope of one paper, or too narrow, not yielding enough information to write about.

If a topic is too broad or generates too many sources, you may not be able to successfully limit the supporting sources or explain the topic in anything short of a tome. For example, if your topic of interest is employment discrimination based on gender, the preemption check will likely yield an unwieldy amount of resources. You would then want to narrow the topic to one aspect of gender discrimination. In the following table, notice a few ways in which a broad topic can be narrowed.

Ways to narrow your topic[5]

Idea	Explanation
Limit the jurisdictions	Instead of covering all of U.S. law, choose one, two, or a few states. Or, instead of covering an issue in a global manner, focus on one country or compare two countries.
Focus on only one issue	If your topic has several issues, focus on only one or two. For instance, instead of analyzing all of the possible challenges to a new statute, focus on a single challenge.
Focus on a sub-issue within the broader legal issue	Find a small issue within your general area of interest. For instance, if you are researching issues in the public health administration of quarantine and isolation, focus on the effects on a certain population, such as undocumented immigrants.
Narrow your time span	Instead of analyzing all that has happened with respect to a legal issue since its inception, focus on a specific time span (e.g., a particular era or only more recent years).

On the other hand, if your topic is too narrow, you may not be able to find sufficient background sources from which to engage in a deep and thoughtful analysis. For instance, if your topic explored drug rehabilitation policies in eastern Oregon for minors accused of sex trafficking, that topic is likely to be far too narrow for a full article. The topic might still be too narrow if expanded to examine policies in the state as a whole. You would likely need to employ strategies to widen the scope of the topic. The following table provides strategies to broaden a narrow topic.

Ways to broaden your topic[6]

Idea	Explanation
Add one or more jurisdictions	For example, instead of analyzing only Texas law for an issue, you may want to survey other states in the Southwest or consider a national survey of state law.
Add a global perspective	Instead of analyzing only U.S. law, compare how other countries treat the issue.
Increase your time span	Instead of discussing how a legal doctrine developed over the last several years, analyze how it developed over many decades.
Define the issue more broadly	Instead of dealing with a discrete sub-issue, consider adding other sub-issues or examine the broader legal issue generally.
Add a theoretical framing	In addition to discussing the legal doctrine, add a discussion based on a different theoretical framing like feminism, critical race theory, or law and economics. (See Chapter 7, *Law Review and Law Journal Articles*, for more details on incorporating a theoretical framing into your scholarly article.)
Add a perspective from another academic discipline	In addition to discussing the legal doctrine, add perspective from a discipline such as economics, philosophy, or public health.

Although you will want to avoid a topic so narrow or arcane that sufficient background sources are not available, narrow topics typically are easier to research and manage. Further, if a topic is narrow, you may more easily contribute meaningfully to the scholarly dialogue. In other words, the narrower the topic, the deeper the dive you will be able to take into the analysis and the more likely you can contribute a new idea. In any event, your hope is to find the "sweet spot"—that is, a topic narrow enough that it can be discussed in a reasonable number of pages but broad enough to be supported by a sufficient array of primary and secondary sources.

In addition to assessing the appropriate broadness or narrowness of the topic, you should also evaluate whether the scope of your topic is actually manageable given any time constraints and project requirements. To do so, ask yourself questions such as the following:

- Can you research this topic thoroughly in the time available?
- Will this topic allow you to demonstrate a high level of understanding of a complex issue and underlying theories?
- Are you motivated to complete this project?
- Do you have support from a law librarian, professor, or someone knowledgeable in the field?

Research Tip:

Remember to consider non-legal sources as well. For instance, if you are writing about the intersection of feminist theory with laws that directly affect the rights of women, you may want to consult *Researching Gender,* a four-volume encyclopedia set by Christina Hughes that contains a comprehensive compilation of feminist methodologies. Although not a traditional secondary source for legal research, the compilation would provide countless relevant sources.

Once you feel comfortable that your topic is not preempted, that the scope of your topic will provide you with sufficient background materials for your project's requirements, and that you have the time, support, and motivation you need to successfully produce a quality work product, you will want to focus on crafting your thesis. Put simply, the thesis is a concise statement or assertion that the work will prove—in other words, the thesis is your contribution to the scholarly debate. (Chapter 3, *Crafting Your Thesis*, will walk you through the process of developing an initial thesis and honing your thesis as you conduct further research and throughout the writing process.) Although the preemption check will give you a good basis for research, you will likely find yourself rolling up your sleeves and conducting further research as you unearth new information or new realizations during the writing process. As you can see from the following graphic, the next section provides you with some guidance for conducting further research.

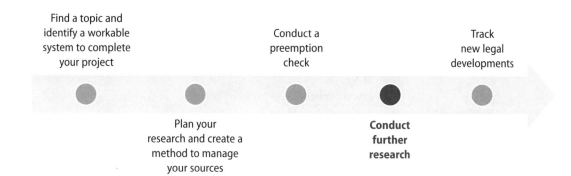

2.4 Conducting further research

While the preemption check will have uncovered sufficient material so that you will feel confident that your topic or thesis (if you have one at this point) is viable and not preempted by another work, further research will be needed to support your analysis fully. In addition, you will want to ensure that you not only have sufficient sources to bolster your position but that the sources you are relying upon are credible. Finally, you will want to be sure that you have reviewed all background sources that may provide an alternative or opposing view to the stance your article is planning to take—after all, a position without an opposing side is probably not all that interesting or unique. (For more information on how to analyze opposing viewpoints, see Chapter 4, *Developing Critical Legal Analysis.*)

Although you will likely complete each phase in sequence, the recursive nature of research and writing means that you may need to revisit phases of the process. As you continue to research, you will likely revise and refine your topic, particularly after you construct a clear thesis. Your broad research may uncover areas in which you need to dive more deeply. Researching within a narrow subtopic may help you recognize tangential ideas that need to be examined in a more comprehensive context. You may also discover that another discipline has relevant information and sources that can inform your thinking on your topic and thesis.

At this stage, it may be helpful to review more secondary sources to determine whose voices—and which doctrine and theories—are most influential for the issue you are researching. Depending on your topic, you may want to consult one or more of the following common secondary sources. Your law librarian can also help you pinpoint additional secondary sources that may be useful.

Common secondary sources for research

- American Law Reports (ALRs)
- Bar Journal Articles
- Blogs
- Law Dictionaries
- Law Review Articles
- Legal Encyclopedias
- Legal Periodicals
- Looseleaf Services
- Monographs
- On-line Resources
- Relevant Social Media
- Research Bibliographies
- Restatements
- Specialty Databases
- Specialty Research Guides (LibGuides)
- Treatises
- Uniform Laws and Model Acts

Secondary sources will help you dig deeper and locate additional primary sources as well as other relevant sources that will help you find, develop, and hone legal arguments relevant to your thesis.

Some additional resources you may want to consult:

J.D.S. Armstrong, Christopher Knott & R. Martin Witt, Where the Law Is: An introduction to advanced Legal Research (5th ed. 2018);

Deborah A. Schmedemann, Ann L. Bateson & Mehmet Konar-Steenberg, The Process of Legal Research (9th ed. 2016);

Legal Research Series (a book series published by Carolina Academic Press with each book in the series focused on state- and jurisdiction-specific research instruction);

Amy E. Sloan, Basic Legal Research: Tools and Strategies (7th ed. 2018); and

Eric P. Voigt, Legal Research Demystified: A Step-by-Step Approach (2019).

Using these and other secondary sources will help you find the right research path for your topic. You may consult one of the many excellent legal research texts that exist and check out your institution's law library website, which will have myriad resources and links.[7] Remember, one of the best resources will always be a law librarian. Law librarians can help you chart a path through the many sources, and they can also help you find good information from sources with which you might not be familiar.

Remember, however, that research is not a static process. Whatever research path you take, as you find, develop, and hone your legal arguments, you will also need to set up alerts to keep abreast of any developments, especially since the law is constantly evolving.

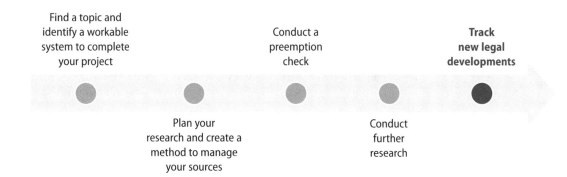

2.5 Tracking new developments

Once the heavy lifting of the preemption check is complete, you will need to continually check for new developments. One of the easiest and most comprehensive ways to check for new developments is by setting up alerts for new cases, laws, news articles, and other sources that relate to your topic. You can set up alerts through Bloomberg Law, Lexis, Westlaw, or through other search engines such as Google Alerts or Yahoo Alerts. All of these search engines have different features available for saving searches or setting up alerts.

In conclusion, one tip bears repeating: Most of the time, the best source to consult is a law librarian—these individuals have not only been to law school, but they have also received an advanced or master's degree. They have a wealth of knowledge and can be an invaluable resource to help you efficiently and effectively research any project.

With a plan for a sound research strategy, and your preemption check behind you, the next stop is crafting and honing your original thesis.

Notes

1. Attributed to Elizabeth McCurry Johnson, attorney with Crosswhite, Crosswhite & Johnson (former professor at the Wake Forest University School of Law).

2. Topic and chart from Cyd Maurer, student at Lewis & Clark Law School (on file with authors).

3. Thank you to Mari Cheney, Assistant Director of Research and Instruction at Lewis & Clark Law School, and Professor Mary Susan Lucas and Dean Chris Knott, Wake Forest University School of Law, for their ideas and contributions to this chapter.

4. Heather Meeker, *Stalking the Golden Topic: A Guide to Locating and Selecting Topics for Legal Research Papers*, 1196 Utah L. Rev. 917, 935 (1996); U. of Wash. L. Sch. Gallagher L. Library, *Shaping Your Topic*, guides.lib.uw.edu (last visited Jan. 10, 2020) [hereinafter "*Shaping Your Topic*"].

5. Adapted from *Shaping Your Topic, supra.*

6. *See id.*

7. *See, e.g.*, U. OF WASH. L. SCH. GALLAGHER L. LIBR., *Writing and Publishing in Law Reviews*, guides.lib.uw.edu (last visited Jan. 3, 2020); GEORGETOWN L. LIBR., *Research Strategies for Seminar Papers*, guides.ll.georgetown.edu (last visited Jan. 3, 2020); LEWIS & CLARK L. SCH. PAUL L. BOLEY LIBR., *Finding & Researching Your Paper Topic: Strategies*, library.lclark.edu (last visited Jan. 3, 2020); COLUMBIA L. SCH., *A Selective List of Guides to Foreign Legal Research*, library.law.columbia.edu (last visited Jan. 3, 2020).

Chapter 3

Crafting Your Thesis

3.1   Originality
3.2   Developing your initial thesis
3.3   Honing your thesis

Your thesis is the specific point you want to make or the problem you want to solve with a paper. Put differently, the thesis is an original thought that targets a specific aspect of the legal issue raised by a case, statute, regulation, policy, or topic. Regardless of the form of legal scholarship you are writing, the thesis will be the backbone of the work. You might have an idea of the thesis at the outset of your research, but often, the thesis emerges while sorting through sources and discussions of your topic during the preemption check. Because the thesis is a concise articulation of your contribution to the scholarly debate, you will want to make sure that it is original, analytical, and honed to be an accurate statement of your assertion.

3.1 Originality

While refining your topic into a workable thesis, first assess the originality of your proposed idea. Judging originality in an article sounds relatively straightforward—engage in a thorough preemptive check to see if anyone has made a similar argument, and if they have not, begin the writing process. We all wish it were that easy.

To be original, your thesis should make some readily discernable contribution (even if small) to the existing body of scholarship. While finding that point of originality may be difficult, curiosity about your broad topic has likely led to questions that have not yet been answered. Your fresh perspective on those questions and their accompanying answers are likely the seeds of an "original" argument.

You can create an original point in several ways. Being the first person to publish a critique of, or a solution to, a certain legal issue will guarantee originality. A second way builds on existing legal scholarship. Scholars and others may have previously addressed many arguments, critiques, or proposals on your topic. Even so, you do not necessarily have to throw out the baby with the bathwater if another article on the subject already exists; instead, you can simply build upon the work of others (with proper attribution, of course). When revisiting prior scholars' analyses, a writer's "original" contribution may be to add a new point, insight, twist, or nuance to the subject. To see how an article can build on previous ideas, consider Professor Joan M. Rocklin's article, *Exam-Writing Instruction in a Classroom Near You: Why it Should be Done and How to Do It.*[1]

Adding a new point to existing scholarship

The articles that document the relationship between practice and feedback, and performance do not, however, provide a method for teaching exam-writing skills. This article adds to those earlier studies by recommending a comprehensive method for teaching exam-writing skills. **It takes as its starting point the cognitive apprenticeship model for learning described in *Educating Lawyers*, the landmark report on improving legal education and better known as the *Carnegie Report*.** Under a cognitive apprenticeship model, learning is most likely to occur when an expert makes key features of a skill visible to the novice so that the novice can appropriate that skill…. **Part III of this article addresses that gap in law students' education. It provides a conceptual model that identifies the key features of an effective exam answer.** It focuses particularly on how to effectively apply the law to facts. It then explains how that conceptual model can be integrated into students' coursework so that professors can better guide their students toward the appropriation of expert exam-writing skills.

> Notice how the author specifically identifies and describes the import of the earlier work, links this existing work to an interdisciplinary model (the cognitive apprenticeship model), and explains how this piece adds a new idea about how to improve student performance on exams.

As you can see, because she adds a new twist on a prior idea, Professor Rocklin acknowledges the landmark scholarship in the area and explicitly addresses how her article adds an original idea to the scholarly discussion on improving legal education.

The bottom line is that originality can be achieved in multiple ways. Now, let's back up a bit and examine a process for developing, evaluating, and honing your original thesis.

3.2 Developing your initial thesis

Somewhere in your thoughts about the broad topic you have chosen lives a thesis. The great master Michelangelo said, "I saw an angel in marble. I carved until I set him free." Crafting a thesis is a little like that but not nearly so hard. Like all of legal scholarship, no magic formula dictates what constitutes an effective thesis. The thesis will vary depending on the type of paper, the number of legal issues, the complexity of those legal issues, and whether your work is theoretical and descriptive or more pragmatic. Using the following step-by-step approach can help guide you in developing your initial thesis statement.

Walking through these steps will help you develop a solid initial thesis statement—one that explores a legal problem and, if possible, identifies a concrete solution or, at the very least, a path forward.

Step-by-step approach to crafting your initial thesis

Step	Question	Example
1	Name the broad topic.	Tax law
2	Ask a question about a topic of interest to you.	Do students face tax consequences when their student loans are bought by a nonprofit as part of a student loan forgiveness program?
3	Research to identify the crux of the problem and to identify the specific legal critique(s) you want explore.	U.S. tax laws may have unintended consequences for certain individuals whose student loan debt is purchased by third parties through a student loan forgiveness program because the loan forgiveness may result in costly tax consequences as the purchase may constitute income.
4	If applicable, add potential solutions.	Education or awareness that students may face negative tax implications when third parties purchase student loan debt.
5	Revise and put it all together.	Although social factors may promote student loan forgiveness programs, when student loan debt is purchased by a third-party debt purchaser, students may face serious tax implications, including possible unintended income and higher tax penalties for the year. Student loan forgiveness programs need to take steps to better educate recipients about the potential tax consequences.

These first two steps—exploring topics and formulating potential questions—are discussed in Chapter 1, *Exploring Topics and Establishing a System*. Once you have explored a topic generally and formulated questions you are curious about, the next step (Step 3 in the above chart) is to identify the legal problem that you want to critique in your paper. At this stage, you want to think deeply about how and why the topic may be problematic or have some

Revisit the thesis:

The final thesis may not be evident to you at the beginning of the writing process. As you review sources and critically analyze your issue, the thesis may need to be broadened or narrowed (as discussed further in Section 3.3, *Honing Your Thesis*). Your thesis will likely evolve with your research and need to be refined as you move through the process.

type of legal or social consequence. You may also want to think about which kind of critique will best identify the problem. To jump-start the process of identifying which type of common critique may be most useful, you may want to consider whether any of the statements below apply and, if so, how. This mental exercise may allow you to adapt one or more of the common critiques as you identify the crux of your original critique.

Common critiques used in scholarly writing

- Faulty analysis led the court to the wrong result because
    - the court failed to apply the law correctly.
    - the court's decision is inconsistent with that of other jurisdictions.
    - the court's decision has unintended consequences.
    - the court's ruling is too broad, too vague, or ambiguous.
- The decision of the court is correct, but
    - the court used the wrong approach.
    - the decision has negative consequences for society.
    - using an alternative approach would lead to more consistency in the law, is more logical, has fewer consequences, or is better supported by social or public policy.
    - the court missed an opportunity to address important issues that other courts may face in the future.
    - the court ignored public policy, public sentiment, or equity.
- The court should not have decided the case because
    - the issue is properly one for the legislative or executive branch.
    - the court lacked the authority because of a jurisdictional issue.
    - an appropriate rule could not be created from the facts of that particular case.
- The legislation is problematic in whole or in part because
    - the legislation is inconsistent with the legislative history.
    - the legislation is too broad, vague, ambiguous, or leads to an absurd result.
    - the legislation violates public policy or has an unintended consequence on a legal institution, society, or certain individuals.
    - the legislation is inconsistent with doctrines, policies, or laws.

Each of these critiques not only identifies the crux of the problem about which you are writing but also follows up with a more detailed exploration of why it is a problem or the consequences of the problem. Identifying the crux of the problem in such a manner is more nuanced and sophisticated than simply asserting that "the court got it wrong" or "the legislation is ineffective."

With respect to Step 4—adding potential solutions—you will need to decide whether you want to propose a solution to the legal problem you are analyzing. In most instances, you will propose some type of solution. Indeed, an important part of your analysis will be explaining how a law or social policy should change to fix the problem you identified.

However, though adding potential solutions can augment the analysis, providing a solution is not *required*. A thesis—and indeed an entire analysis—can be more theoretical and descriptive in some circumstances. Consider the two thesis statements below—one that includes a proposed solution and one that is both theoretical and descriptive (Chapter 4, *Developing Critical Legal Analysis*, and Chapter 7, *Law Review and Law Journal Articles*, discuss the role of theory in more detail). The first thesis statement is an excerpt from Professor Andrew McClurg's article *Preying on the Graying: A Statutory Presumption to Prosecute Elder Financial Exploitation*.[2] After explaining the complexities of elder financial exploitation, Professor McClurg identifies the problem the article addresses, along with his proposed solution.

Example of a thesis that identifies a legal issue and proposes a solution

Proving exploitation in any type of elder fraud case is complicated because the transactions usually occur in secret and victims may make poor witnesses due to cognitive or other impairments, or because they refuse to cooperate with authorities. This Article proposes the adoption of state criminal statutes that create a permissive presumption of exploitation with regard to certain financial conveyances from elders to non-relatives. It sets forth a detailed statute intended as a conceptual framework for states to use in fashioning a permissive presumption statute that fits within their existing elder protection legislative schemes.[3]

As stated above, another option is to set forth an in-depth analysis of your critique, perhaps identifying consequences about the issue but not necessarily proposing a concrete solution. Consider Professor Marie-Amélie George's article titled *The LGBT Disconnect: Politics and Perils of Legal Movement Formation*. In this article, Professor George's thesis describes her concerns that transgender individuals may find their interests at the bottom of the hierarchical ladder within the LGBT movement.

Example of a thesis that is more theoretical and descriptive

These contests highlight a crucial problem that the LGBT movement is currently facing: lesbian, gay, and transgender rights are sufficiently disconnected that many Americans are willing to accept the former (LG) and not the latter (T), and yet the two are integrated enough that one can be deployed against the other. National LGBT rights organizations are transgender inclusive in their legal goals, and yet their strategies unintentionally created an internal hierarchy of interests, with gender conforming gays and lesbians at the top.... [T]his approach has given rise to serious consequences....[4]

While most student papers propose a solution, a theoretical and descriptive thesis, as long as it thoroughly explores a topic in a multidimensional manner (as in the excerpt above), can be an effective way to contribute to the scholarly dialogue and debate and initiate a path forward.

After deciding whether your paper will describe the problem in a theoretical manner or prescribe a potential fix, Step 5 is to pull all the components of your initial thesis together. In this step, you will want to evaluate whether the proposed thesis has enough breadth and depth to describe the problem. You will also want to ensure that it resonates with prospective readers and covers any potential solution you may recommend. Ask yourself the following questions as you evaluate your initial thesis:

- Does the thesis provide the reader with appropriate context or background to fully appreciate the problem addressed by the paper?
- Is the thesis sufficiently detailed so that the reader knows why the legal issue is important and why the reader should care about the issue?
- Does the thesis allow the reader to understand a bottom-line assertion for how either the law or the way we think about the problem should change?[5]
- Does the thesis reflect the paper's original point or addition to the scholarly discussion?

Is the thesis crafted in such a way that the reader knows why the reader should care about the legal issue?

Does the thesis enable the reader to understand how the law or the way the reader thinks about the law should change?

Developing your thesis

Does the thesis provide the reader with sufficient context to understand the crux of the problem?

Does the thesis identify the original point you are contributing to the scholarly discussion?

If your initial thesis does not answer all four of the above questions in the affirmative, then you may need to revise it.

Let's assess the effectiveness of a few sample thesis statements. Assume you are writing an article on revenge pornography (i.e., the display and dissemination of an individual's sexually explicit images without the individual's consent)[6] and how current tort remedies are ineffective in eradicating the problem. The following table shows three different thesis statements for the topic. What kind of information does each thesis provide? Which thesis statement best identifies the problem and the proposed solution?

Evaluating thesis statements

Sample Thesis 1	The current laws for revenge porn provide ineffective remedies for claimants and should be changed.
Sample Thesis 2	Traditional tort law remedies are inadequate for revenge porn claims because the remedies may violate First Amendment protections, and they do not mandate the removal of images from the internet.
Sample Thesis 3	Traditional tort law remedies are inadequate for revenge porn claims because the remedies may violate First Amendment protections, and they do not mandate the removal of images from the internet; instead, revenge porn claims should fall under the umbrella of information privacy laws, which afford greater protection for victims without running afoul of First Amendment laws.

Among the three examples, which thesis statement is the most effective and why?

- Sample Thesis 1 is ineffective because it does not fully identify the problem or its causes and provides only a superficial solution.
- Although Sample Thesis 2 is better because it provides detail about the problem, the sample does not provide sufficient detail about the potential solution proposed.
- Sample Thesis 3 is the most effective of the three samples because it specifically identifies the problem and the specific point of law impacted, and it also identifies a concrete solution.

As you see with Samples 1 and 2, the lack of sufficient detail of the problem or the solution leads to an inadequate thesis that fails to advance the scholarly conversation. Following the step-by-step process outlined above will help you to be as precise as possible with how you frame the crux of the problem and any proposed solutions your paper is addressing. This, in turn, will help ensure your thesis effectively encapsulates your original contribution.

3.3 Honing your thesis

Because the thesis will act as the spine of the article—the central point from which every component of the article derives—you will need to hone your thesis during the writing process. The research and writing process is recursive, meaning that the thesis will likely evolve as you critically evaluate existing law and scholarship through the lens of your own understanding. This tenet is true even when you have a good handle on your topic and your initial thesis seems solid. So, do not be alarmed to find that you need to broaden, narrow, or simply refine your thesis at various points throughout the process.

One way to hone your thesis is to compare it to the main points of your analysis. Using a detailed outline of your analysis or a table of contents for your paper, compare the initial thesis to the main points that have emerged during the writing process. Hone your thesis to make sure that it matches those main points. Consider, for example, the thesis from Professor Andrew Verstein's article *The Misregulation of Person-To-Person Lending*.[7] Professor Verstein informs his readers of the problem and explains his proposed regulatory scheme to fix the problem.[8] His thesis is set forth below and compared to the article's table of contents.[9] Note how the article's entire structure stems from how the thesis is formulated.

Example of how the thesis compares to the article's table of contents

Thesis	Table of Contents
Amid a financial crisis and credit crunch, retail investors are lending a billion dollars over the Internet, on an unsecured basis, to total strangers.	I. Introduction

Technological and financial innovation allows person-to-person ("P2P") lending to connect lenders and borrowers in inspiring ways never before imagined.	II. Person-to-Person Lending
	     A. The Heartland of Person-to-Person Lending
	     B. Core Benefits and Efficiencies of P2P Lending
	     C. Risks: Lender's Money, Borrower's Privacy

However, all is not well with P2P lending. The SEC threatens the entire industry by asserting jurisdiction with a fundamental misunderstanding of P2P lending. This Article illustrates how the SEC has transformed this industry, making P2P lending less safe and more costly, threatening its very existence. The SEC's misregulation of P2P lending provides an opportunity to theorize about regulation in a rapidly disintermediating world.	III. P2P Lending and Problems with the SEC
	     A. Regulatory Overreach
	     B. Perverse Consequences of SEC Regulation
	        1. Formalistic Registration
	        2. Mandatory Disclosures
	        3. Difficulty of Private Enforcement
	        4. No Mandate to Help Borrowers
	        5. The Cliff Effect: Disparate Treatment for Similar Risks
	     C. Understanding Misregulation

Example of how the thesis compares to the article's table of contents continued

Thesis	Table of Contents
The Article then proposes a preferable regulatory scheme designed to preserve and discipline P2P lending's innovative mix of social finance, microlending, and disintermediation. This proposal consists of regulation by the new Consumer Financial Protection Bureau.	IV. Reform Proposal: P2P Lending Under the Consumer Financial Protection Bureau

To determine whether your thesis remains consistent with your analysis or needs to be further honed, it may be helpful to chart your working thesis and a broad table of contents as in the above example as you draft. This tactic can help you understand whether you are veering off course with the paper or whether your thesis needs to evolve as the analysis has evolved.

Now that you have considered how to develop and hone an effective thesis, we next dive into strategies for developing critical legal analysis. Understanding the differences between description and analysis, knowing where and when to describe or analyze, and identifying various types of arguments and data that can support balanced legal arguments are key skills to creating a quality work product.

Notes

1. Joan M. Rocklin, *Exam-Writing Instruction in a Classroom Near You: Why it Should be Done and How to Do It*, 22 J. Legal Writing Inst. 189, 191–92 (2017).

2. Andrew J. McClurg, *Preying on the Graying: A Statutory Presumption to Prosecute Elder Financial Abuse*, 65 Hastings L.J. 1099, 1100–01 (2014).

3. *Id.* at 1105.

4. Marie-Amélie George, *The LGBT Disconnect: Politics and Perils of Legal Movement Formation*, 2018 Wisc. L. Rev. 503, 506 (2018).

5. Elizabeth R. Baldwin, *Freedom in Structure: Helping Foreign-Trained and International Graduate Students Develop Thesis Statements by Component*, 31 (1) The Second Draft 8–14 (Spring 2018).

6. This topic and thesis were derived from Kelsey Benedick, Lewis & Clark Law School student (on file with the authors).

7. Andrew Verstein, *The Misregulation of Person-to-Person Lending*, 45 U.C. Davis L. Rev. 445, 445 (2011).

8. *Id.* at 445–51.

9. *Id.* at 445.

Chapter 4

Developing Critical Legal Analysis

4.1   Reading to write
4.2   Transforming description into analysis
4.3   Thinking critically to write analytically
4.4   Identifying types of supporting arguments
4.5   Using empirical data
4.6   Adopting a balanced approach to your scholarship

Legal scholarship may come in many different shapes and sizes, but at the heart of every piece of scholarship lies one thing: critical legal analysis. Constructing an effective legal analysis, whether for purposes of a legal memo or brief, scholarly article, seminar paper, or blog post, depends upon the writer's goals with respect to the piece, the intended audience, and the issue or doctrine being analyzed. The written product is the recitation of the writer's analysis. So, effective legal analysis begins not when you are actually writing the paper but when you first begin investigating the topic. The following sections provide both theoretical and practical tips for developing the analytical skills necessary to produce the diverse written works that comprise today's scholarly and professional writing.

4.1 Reading to write

In his book *On Writing*, author Stephen King warns that, "if you don't have time to read, you don't have the time (or tools) to write. Simple as that."[1] King is not the first writer to advocate more reading. Famed American novelist William Faulkner once said, "Read, read, read! Read everything—trash, the classics, good and bad, and see how they do it, just as an apprentice studies the master. Read! You'll absorb it! Then write. If it's good, you'll find out. If it's not, throw it out of the window."[2]

Reading for pleasure:

Some law students (and lawyers) complain that law school (and law practice) "sucks the joy out of reading." If this describes you, you may want to consider writing-expert Professor Bryan Garner's advice from *How to regain the joy of reading*:

> Sometimes I'll start reading *The New Yorker* as if it were a typical law report. I have to consciously remind myself to slow down and read every word. Relish the language. Don't rush. Pay attention not just to what's being said but also to how it's being said.... Once I make that mental adjustment, reading becomes pleasurable again — not merely utilitarian.

Bryan A. Garner, *How to regain the joy of reading*, Bryan Garner on Words, ABA JOURNAL (Nov. 1, 2014).

This advice is not solely for aspiring novelists. Reading, particularly *quality* pieces from the genre that you are tackling, improves writing by increasing vocabulary and by broadening and deepening subject matter knowledge both generally and with respect to your specific topic. Reading helps you to absorb the analytical techniques and norms important to the genre.[3] Reading from a particular genre also enables you to understand the range of ideas that are being discussed and debated. It simultaneously helps you understand how to enlarge that set of ideas so that you can contribute your own independent and original analysis to the discussion.

4.2 Transforming description into analysis

One of the primary challenges of scholarly writing is to transform writing from description (what other courts and scholars have said) to analysis (what *you* think). When a writer "describes," the writer essentially regurgitates what others have done in the past by, for example, discussing the case law development of a legal issue, reporting results from an empirical study, or providing a historical background for a legal institution. When a writer analyzes, the writer synthesizes information, connects ideas, and brings forth new ideas based on those connections.

Think of analysis like a geometry proof. A geometry proof is a mathematical argument that begins with known facts. From the description of those facts, the mathematician makes a series of reasoned, logical deductions to explain and prove a conclusion about the geometrical shape at issue. The conclusion often can be reached in different ways, but to correctly solve a geometry proof, all steps must be written down, and not even a small step can be omitted.

The same is true when crafting legal analysis. You may prove your thesis in different ways, but every step of your reasoning must be shown. You may describe past thinking, but you must also go beyond the background sources, either by extending their conclusions or deviating from them.

The chart below sets forth differences between how information is communicated depending upon whether the writer's purpose is either to describe or to analyze.

Description vs. scholarly analysis[4]

Description	Scholarly Analysis
States what happened	Delves into the significance of what happened and identifies potential factual, historical, social (defined broadly), or legal consequences
Tells the story so far	Investigates the impact of how one piece of the story or event affects another
States the order in which things happened	Clarifies why things may have happened in the order in which they occurred
Describes a theory	Justifies why a particular theory is relevant (or not relevant) to a legal doctrine, historical event, or social problem
Explains how a legal doctrine works	Illustrates why a legal doctrine satisfies (or fails to satisfy) legal, policy, and social goals
States when something occurred	Scrutinizes why timing is important or relevant to the legal doctrine
States different factors	Dissects the different factors and probes the weight of the factors singly and collectively
States options	Elucidates reasons for each option and identifies any intended and unintended consequences that may arise
Lists details	Explores why certain details should be given more weight than other details
Gives information	Identifies the relevance of information, draws relevant analogies, and provides well-grounded and legally sound conclusions or solutions

After understanding the differences between description and analysis, you should strategically identify when to describe and when to elevate the writing from mere description to analysis. Sometimes description is appropriate and other times you need to analyze. The table on the next page provides guidance for when to describe versus when to analyze.

When to describe vs. when to analyze[5]

When should the writer describe?	When should the writer analyze?
When introducing the legal issue, a legal doctrine, construct, or theory	When deciding how to organize all of the legal sources, information, and analysis in the work product
When identifying relevant background sources and history	When evaluating the merits of background sources
When describing the methodology in an empirical study	When evaluating the results from a study or criticizing the validity of the methodology
When outlining or summarizing areas of knowledge from different doctrinal areas, disciplines, or jurisdictions	When trying to link similar ideas or theories or make other connections between different doctrinal areas, disciplines, or jurisdictions
When quoting from other scholars, legal or other-wise	When critiquing the conclusions of other scholars
When describing what others have done in the past to remedy the problem	When proposing new remedies that should be employed to solve the problem
When identifying consequences	When evaluating possible intended and unintended consequences

While description is a component of scholarly writing, it is usually only a portion of the analytical framework. You will need to connect the description to the analysis to show how and why the thesis is correct. The end goal is to move the reader in a new direction, away from the past sources and toward your own critical legal analysis, which will add a nuance or even a new dimension to the scholarly discussion as a whole.

4.3 Thinking critically to write analytically

Critical legal analysis begins at the outset of your project when you are researching and reviewing sources. Start thinking critically by (1) asking who, what, where, when, and why; and by (2) questioning what you read.

4.3.A Asking who, what, where, when, and why

To understand the nuances of any legal issue, as well as to enable your creativity to flow, you will need to ask questions about the legal doctrines and the sources of law you are evaluating. The five Ws typically used in investigative analysis apply quite well to scholarly and professional writing. Asking questions, such as those set forth below, will help you to think critically about the legal doctrine(s) at the core of your topic and thesis.

The five Ws of investigative analysis[6]

Who	• Wrote the law, opinion, or other source being examined? • Participated in the debate surrounding the law's passage? • Is harmed? • Has written about the topic? • Is directly impacted? • Are the key stakeholders or constituents? • Benefits from this (law, rule, policy, action)? • Did the writers want to benefit from this (law, rule, policy, action)?
What	• Are the advantages and limitations of the current doctrine? • Is a perspective the authors failed to consider? • Is another alternative explanation? • Is the best- and worst-case scenario? • Is the most important aspect or explanation? • Is the least important aspect or explanation? • Can be done to alter this situation or solve a problem? • May occur if the status quo remains? • Are the intended and unintended consequences of the status quo? • Are the foreseeable consequences of any change? • Implications does this doctrine have for policies readers may think are unrelated to it?
Where	• Do we see this problem in other legal doctrines, jurisdictions, or disciplines? • Have solutions been proposed or tried in other legal doctrines, jurisdictions, or disciplines?
When	• Did this happen, and what else was happening in society at that time? • And how did the timing affect the legal topic? • Did or will the intended and unintended consequences of either the status quo or the proposed change occur? • Are proposed changes going to be debated?
Why	• Is there a problem or challenge? • Is this topic important? • Should readers know more about this? • Is there a need to critique and analyze this issue? • Has policy related to the issue changed or failed to change? • Is this issue disruptive?

Considering the five Ws will provide you with both broad context and concrete information about your thesis. This knowledge will enable you to expand your mind, gain substantive understanding, and even think more creatively about the potential legal issues and possible solutions that should be considered in the paper. More importantly, by answering these questions, you will be developing the critical legal analysis that scholarly work requires.

4.3.B Questioning what you read

The next step in developing critical legal analysis is to intensely question the sources you uncover during your preemption check and research. Effective legal analysis explains the *why* and the *how* for the underlying critique and, often, how to fix it. To understand the *why* and the *how*, you will need to carefully read and critically question each background source. You may want to ask questions such as the following:

- Who wrote the law, opinion, or other primary or secondary source being examined?
- When was it written?
- Who published it?
- What precise legal issue is it addressing?
- Who or what does this issue affect and why?
- What historical, political, social, or economic influences may have affected or contributed to it?
- Why is this issue important?
- Why would someone want to write about this issue?
- What is the evidence to support the claims made?
- How much of the content is rhetorical versus substantive?
- Does the information present a balanced view of the issue?
- Does the source typically present accurate, unbiased information?[7]

After you have critically read each source, you will want to analyze and synthesize the sources collectively. You may want to consider these questions as you engage in that process:

Sample questions to analyze and synthesize sources[8]

The issues or themes raised by the background sources:	Are the issues raised by the various sources consistent? What are the concerns raised by the various authors? What are the implications of any critique or proposed solutions to the issues raised? Is there a majority and minority approach?
Commonalities and differences between the sources:	What do your various sources have in common? How are they different? What time span do they range? Do they share theoretical or empirical frameworks or concepts? Do they share common historical, philosophical, social, political, or economic concerns?

Sample questions to analyze and synthesize sources continued[8]

Alternative or divergent points of view:	What are the authors challenging? What is the other side of the story? Is there a trend among the sources for a certain point of view? What are the intended and unintended consequences proposed for either a critique or proposed solution? Is one point of view more credible and, if so, why? Do historical, philosophical, social, political, or economic factors support an alternative point of view?
Consequences and harms:	Has a vulnerable population been overlooked in the prior scholarship? What are the known short-term or long-term consequences? What unintended consequences did sources predict? Did any unintended consequences occur? Do the sources address whether some institutions or particular populations benefitted while others have suffered?

Questioning the background sources individually and then collectively will help you understand the nuances of the topic at a deeper level. It may help reveal issues and trends you may not have seen during your preemption check. It also helps to present issues in a different light and identifies different schools of thought or approaches that have been used. Since one of the goals of scholarly and professional writing is for the writer to join the discussion with substantive heft, it is imperative that you have a deep understanding of the discussion that has gone on in the past.

4.3.C Assessing the credibility of secondary sources

Another important facet of questioning your sources is to question their credibility. In the era of "fake news," it has become more important than ever to verify that the sources we are relying on are legitimate. To assess the credibility of a secondary source, consider the following factors:

- **Author.** Can you determine the author's affiliation or credentials?
- **Publication place.** Is the publication medium respected in the scholarly community? Does it lean either to the left or the right politically?
- **Publication date.** When was this published? Is the information current?
- **Peer review.** Is the information located in a peer-reviewed journal?
- **Citations to the work.** Has the work been cited by respected scholars in the appropriate field of study? Is it considered mainstream?

These and other factors can help determine whether the information you are relying on in forming your own analysis is credible. But you will also want to consider whether your intended audience will deem the source credible. If you find a source is not credible, however, you can use that to bolster your argument that a contrary position should be taken. No matter what the source, if you plan to use it, verify that the information is timely, the opinions expressed are not overly biased, and that the source is "good law." Sound arguments require credible underlying sources.

4.4 Identifying types of supporting arguments

After analyzing the background sources individually and categorizing them collectively, the next step is to craft supporting arguments. These supporting arguments are the evidence that lawyers use to critique the law. While many schools of legitimate analytic argumentation exist,[9] consider, at the very least, the following three kinds of arguments: (1) textual arguments, (2) normative arguments, and (3) institutional arguments.[10]

4.4.A Textual arguments

Textual arguments are arguments that support the interpretation of text, including text in various types of primary authority and legal documents, such as contracts, deeds, or wills. Textual arguments may use plain meaning, lay usage, dictionary usage, terms of art, or the definition provided for a constitution, statute, or regulation. A textual argument may be used where text is unambiguous, and the plain meaning does not lead to an absurd result. Textual arguments are also helpful where the author is analyzing text that is ambiguous or where the intent of or context surrounding the text supports an interpretation that goes beyond the plain language. Many of the statutory construction techniques you study in law school may be helpful in crafting textual arguments.

Notice how the authors included this term of art in the title of the article, forecasting the importance of this textual argument to their overall thesis.

Below is an excerpt from *"Coordinating" with the Federal Government: Assessing County Efforts to Control Decisionmaking on Public Lands*, where the authors use textual arguments to support their proposition that while "the Federal Land Policy and Management Act and the National Forest Management Act encourage cooperation between local governments and federal land planners, they do not authorize local land-use control on public lands."[11]

An example of a textual argument[12]

III. STATUTORY AND REGULATORY CONTEXT: NFMA AND FLPMA

   The federal agencies managing much of the western public lands — the United States Forest Service ("Forest Service") and Bureau of Land Management ("BLM") — operate under different statutory mandates, which include "coordination" requirements.... The regulations make clear the section should not be read "to indicate that the responsible official will ... conform management to meet non-Forest Service objectives or policies." Neither NFMA [National Forest Management Act of 1976] nor agency regulations require the Forest Service to conduct land planning via government-to-government consultation with counties.... [B]oth versions of the regulations acknowledge the agency's broad discretion in reaching consistency with local plans.... FLPMA and its regulations require BLM to listen to local sentiments on public land management but do not require the agency to ensure compatibility with local government resource plans.

   No federal court has interpreted the "coordination" provisions in either NFMA or FLPMA [Federal Land Policy and Management Act of 1976]. Under the deferential judicial review of the Administrative Procedure Act of 1946 ("APA"), federal courts will likely uphold reasonable agency regulatory interpretations of "coordination." Counties lack authority to interpret the coordination provisions in NFMA or FLPMA to create binding obligations on federal agencies. NFMA and FLPMA require the Forest Service and BLM to consider the views of and attempt to collaborate with local governments in agency planning. But neither the statutes nor agency regulations require the Forest Service or BLM to conduct government-to-government consultation with county governments on public land management.

In the article, the authors use substantive footnotes (which have been omitted for the purpose of this excerpt) to set out the text of the applicable law. This choice allows the authors to focus on the essential textual language in the body of the article, as well as the broader arguments supporting the authors' proposition that coordination does not equate to local control.

4.4.B Normative arguments

   Normative arguments are essentially policy arguments that show how the thesis achieves or undermines a social goal or social values.[13] With a normative argument, the writer creates arguments concerning what the law *should* or *should not* include or what it *ought* or *ought not* to be. Often, normative arguments predict consequences that are likely to result from a certain interpretation or enactment of law and determine whether those consequences are acceptable, given a certain social or policy goal.[14] Some normative arguments go on to offer a possible solution or resolution, and they may also predict consequences that may arise from the proposed solution or resolution.

Three types of normative arguments:

1. **Moral arguments** — a particular rule/theory/thesis should or should not be adopted because it is consistent with generally accepted standards of society.

2. **Social utility arguments** — if society should promote the health and well-being of its citizens, then the rule/theory/thesis at issue either deters or encourages conduct that affects the goal.

3. **Corrective justice arguments** — the party or entity that caused the problem or damage should be responsible to ensure fairness.

See Ellie Margolis, *Closing the Floodgates: Making Persuasive Policy Arguments in Appellate Briefs*, 62 MONT. L. REV. 59 (2001).

Below is an excerpt from a law student's master's thesis, *Addressing the Inequities in Access to Reproductive Healthcare for Gay Male Couples*, where the author uses normative arguments to assert that medical providers' conscientious objections to providing gay male couples with access to reproductive healthcare violates bioethical principles.

An example of a normative argument[15]

The author quotes well-regarded bioethics experts' views to support a policy-based argument that healthcare workers' conscientious objections to providing gay men with reproductive health-care are both unethical and discriminatory.

The bioethical principle of justice is violated when a physician refuses to provide a gay couple with reproductive healthcare based on a conscientious objection. While there are several different theories regarding the bioethical principle of justice, one of the most common is the overall idea of justice developed **by bioethicists Tom L. Beauchamp and James F. Childress, described as "a group of norms for fairly distributing benefits, risks, and costs."** Physicians who only distribute the benefit of their reproductive healthcare to heterosexual couples are doing so in a manner that is unfair to gay couples. Both couples exhibit a need or want for the healthcare the physician is providing, yet by only providing the healthcare to the heterosexual couple, the physician is discriminating against the gay couple for reasons that lie outside of their control. The refusal to provide the care creates the risk that a gay couple may never be able to become parents where one father is biologically related to the child — especially in rural areas where the law allows for no protection, and fertility clinics are separated by hundreds of miles.

After explaining the principle of justice in more detail, the author illustrates his theory that allowing widespread conscientious objection may create gross variation in access by creating an easy to understand hypothetical.

Udo Schuklenk, a Canadian bioethicist, claims that "[p]atients are entitled to receive uniform service delivery from healthcare professionals. They ought not to be subjected to today's conscientious objection lottery." This lottery is one that seemingly any gay couple could be subject to when they walk into a fertility clinic hoping to obtain treatment services. **A gay couple may walk into a clinic and see Dr. A who has no qualms about providing fertility services to them; whereas, another gay couple could walk in at the same time and see Dr. B who subsequently refuses to provide fertility services because the doctor is morally opposed to homosexuality.** On its face, this inconsistency violates the bioethical principle of justice.

In the end of this section, the author notes gay male couples are particularly vulnerable to losing the ability to become legal parents if physicians deny reproductive services. These arguments all provide policy- and theory-based evidence for a later conclusion that "a singular federal law providing that [conscientious objections] cannot be used in a discriminatory manner is needed."[16]

Normative arguments can be supported by legal, social science, or empirical data (see Section 4.5, *Using empirical data*, which discusses data in more detail). They can also be used to bolster a textual argument or institutional argument by fleshing out the social implications of the result one is arguing for or against.[17] The majority of scholarly articles contain normative arguments and claims both in the creation of the thesis and throughout the analysis. Chapter 7, *Law Review and Law Journal Articles*, examines these arguments and their structure in greater detail.

4.4.C Institutional arguments

Institutional arguments are focused on the entity deciding the issue or engaging in the conduct at issue. For example, institutional arguments may concern the relationship between federal and state law, as well as that between the legislative, judicial, and executive branches of government.[18] Institutional arguments also consider the practical effects of certain rules on the administration of justice.[19]

Like normative arguments, institutional arguments are often used to support textual arguments.[20] However, instead of showing the social consequences of a particular legal doctrine, as a normative argument would, an institutional argument may focus on the function of government bodies in applying a doctrine. As Professor Ellie Margolis explains:

> These are arguments about which branch of government (generally the judiciary or the legislature) should address a particular issue. The goal at the heart of institutional competence arguments is the fair and efficient running of the legal system, as well as the maintenance of the constitutional separation of powers....
>
> An argument that an issue is better suited for the courts focuses on the nature of courts as institutions set up for resolving individual disputes and dealing with complex factual issues. The argument would emphasize the court's ability to be responsive to changing circumstances, and to be objective. In addition, the court has a unique ability to entertain witnesses and make objective determinations of credibility. Finally, this argument would emphasize the court's freedom from the political constraints faced by the legislature....[21]
>
> The argument that the legislature is better suited to resolve an issue focuses on similar concerns. This argument asserts that courts are not competent to resolve the issue because resolution involves a change in the law, which is within the legislature's province. The legislature is better able to reflect changes in public opinion, and to hold hearings and gather complex and varied facts that may not be relevant in the context of litigation. Allowing the court to create law on such an important issue would threaten the separation of powers.[22]

> **Some sources you may want to consult to learn more about different types of legal and policy arguments include:**
>
> Wilson Huhn, The Five Types of Legal Arguments (3d ed. 2014).
>
> Ellie Margolis, *Teaching Students How to Make Effective Policy Arguments in Appellate Briefs,* 9 Perspectives 73 (2001).
>
> Kristen Konrad Robbins-Tiscione, Rhetoric for Legal Writers (2d ed. 2016).

Textual, normative, and institutional arguments, while commonly used argumentation techniques, are just a few of the many types of arguments that you may want to consider. Both your intended audience and the genre or type of scholarly or professional project you are drafting will affect which types of arguments you use. However, researching, identifying, and understanding the many different types of legal arguments will help you craft analytical arguments in a manner appropriate for the intended audience.

4.5 Using empirical data

During the twentieth century, legal education shifted from the traditional perspective that law is a stand-alone discipline to the perspective that law is one of many components that make up the fabric of our society.[23] Because legal scholarship is often normative, many scholars believe the law needs to be examined in context with other disciplines such as science, psychology, criminal justice, history, or business theory (just to name a few) as these disciplines so often intersect with and affect legal doctrines, theories, and institutions.[24] However, while most other disciplines in the sciences and humanities use empirical studies, conducting empirical studies is a relatively new practice in the law.[25]

An **Institutional Review Board** or **IRB** is an administrative body that institutional entities establish to protect the rights and the welfare of human subjects who participate in research activities or research studies. To conduct a study that involves human subjects, researchers must first seek permission from the institution's IRB.

Empirical legal scholarship relies on experimentation or observation to remark on the law or its application. Because of the countless combinations of social factors and values that can affect any aspect within the legal process, such information helps us understand the law in a deeper manner.[26] Some law professors (particularly those who have a Ph.D.) may be conducting their own studies. However, some students may have a unique educational background that lends itself to conducting empirical research. Most of the time, law students will either be working with a professor as a research assistant on an empirical study or using empirical data derived from other studies to bolster their analysis. If, as a student, you work on any phase of an empirical study, be sure to consult with faculty members who have expertise in empirical scholarship. Also, be sure to seek any needed permission from your institution's Institutional Review Board (see Sidebar) before engaging in surveys, interviews, or other similar activities.

Whether you conduct a study yourself, work as a research assistant, or use data from another study completed by someone else, empirical data can help readers understand law in its social context and provide evidence of real-world observations. It can provide a more nuanced understanding of interrelated factors that may be at play with a legal issue. It may also help to convey the gravity of a situation. Thus, when considering any type of legal analysis, you should have a basic understanding of the difference between quantitative data (data that can be measured in numbers) and qualitative data (data that can be observed and discussed but not necessarily measured).

4.5.A Quantitative data

Quantitative research identifies patterns that emerge from studying a large, usually randomly drawn sample from a given population. It may also be used to respond to questions such as "what," "how much," or "how many." At its most basic definition, quantitative data use numbers to measure or count a particular sample. As one scholar explains: "Researchers collect quantitative data from the [population] sample and examine the relationship among variables. They quantify the variables through counts, categories, and ratings…and draw conclusions about what the relationships between variables mean."[27]

To break down the process a bit further, the population is the entire group you are studying. A population, for example, could be all law students, all lawyers, or a social category such as teenagers who vape. Representative samples are created through types of probability sampling or randomly selecting individuals from a broader population. A predetermined percentage of the sample is then selected. So, if the study is about lawyers in the United States who currently work as in-house counsel in the business sector, the population would be approximately 104,000.[28] Researchers may be able to then make inferences from the entire population by surveying a smaller group of 1,000 in-house counsel.[29]

Four types of quantitative research:

1. Descriptive research — attempts to describe the current status of an undefined variable.

2. Correlational research — attempts to determine whether two variables are tied together.

3. Causal-comparative research — attempts to explain the cause-and-effect relationship between multiple variables.

4. Experimental research — attempts to mitigate the effect of all other variables except one to test how it affects the dependent variable.

To conduct quantitative research, the researcher must come up with a hypothesis, which is a statement that the research study can support or refute. The researcher identifies dependent variables (that measure the outcome) and independent variables (factors that may influence the outcome). In other words, the independent variable is the consistent characteristic that is controlled to test its effect on the dependent variable. The dependent variable is the outcome that the experiment is trying to explain. Researchers then test the hypothesis to determine whether there is a statistically significant relationship between the variables in the sample.[30]

Is **data** singular or plural? In scientific and scholarly writing the word "data" is plural. The singular form indicating one piece of evidence would be the word "datum." Increasingly, however, especially in everyday usage, the word "data" is used as a collective, singular noun. Newspapers often shift between singular or plural usage depending on the context. When writing about empirical data, be mindful of how you are using the term and the level of formality your audience will expect. When in doubt, err on the side of formality.

For example, in his article *Using Empirical Methods to Study Legal Writing*, Professor Shaun Spencer explains, "in a study examining the correlation between note-taking methods and exam scores, the dependent variable would be the exam score.... [T]he independent variable might be each subject's note-taking method—laptop or longhand."[31] After undergoing statistical analysis of the data from a study of students' exams scores, the researcher may have data that support (or do not support) that there is a statistically significant relationship between exam scores and taking notes by hand.[32]

After gathering results from a representative sample, data are then categorized, measured numerically (often in assigned units), and then analyzed through different types of statistical analysis programs. The resulting statistics or "hard" data (as they are sometimes called), gathered from reliable quantitative studies, can be a powerful tool for your analysis.[33] Data can strengthen an argument by acting as a higher authority; if objective quantitative data validate the writer's concerns, readers are more likely to view the thesis as credible.

With respect to using data to bolster your argument, consider, for example, Associate Provost and Professor of Law Kami Chavis's op-ed in *The Nation* titled *The Supreme Court Didn't Fix Racist Jury Selection*.[34] This op-ed provides a powerful example of how quantitative data can be interwoven with a compelling case-based narrative to support an opinion. (See Chapter 11, *Op-Eds*). In this piece, Professor Chavis explains how the Supreme Court's decision in *Foster v. Chatman*[35] (where the prosecutors wrote a "b" next to all African Americans in the jury pool) was too narrow to prevent the widespread use of race in jury selection, as it only prevents the *explicit* use of race in jury selection. Professor Chavis notes that the rule still provides lawyers the opportunity to use thinly veiled, "race neutral" explanations to strike African American jurors.[36] See how, in the following excerpt, statistics are used to support the author's opinion.

Using statistics to support an opinion

Note the use and placement of multiple studies to convince the reader that race plays a central role in jury selection.

Numerous studies indicate that black jurors are struck more often than white jurors. For example, **a study of 300 felony jury trials in Caddo parish** between 2003 and 2012 shows that prosecutors used peremptory strikes against 46 percent of black jurors, while they used peremptory strikes against 15 percent of other jurors. **Researchers at Michigan State University examined 173 death penalty proceedings** in North Carolina and documented that prosecutors struck 52.6 percent of the eligible black jurors, and only 25.7 percent of all other eligible jurors. **Amnesty International has documented similar phenomena nationwide. Similarly, Ron Wright, Dr. Gregory Parks, and I (all professors at the Wake Forest University School of Law) have conducted a study of all non-capital felony trials in North Carolina from 2011 and 2012.** After reviewing data on 22,000 potential jurors, our preliminary findings indicate that prosecutors strike non-white potential jurors at a disproportionate rate. In these cases, prosecutors struck

16 percent of non-white potential jurors, while they struck only 8 percent of white potential jurors.

Notice that the author identifies the institution conducting the research in the same sentence as each statistic. This connection allows readers both to evaluate the credibility of the source and to locate the referenced information. When using data to support a proposition, however, be sure to consider whether you are using data in a balanced manner. As Professor Anne Mullins explains, "As lawyers, we marshal all evidence in support of our position and minimize contradictory information. Ph.D. programs, on the other hand, challenge students to take their favorite hypothesis and test it every possible way and examine it closely in light of all of the evidence against it."[37] The bottom line is that data should be used thoughtfully and ethically, and never used in a way that is misleading or in which the data's limitations are hidden.

4.5.B Qualitative data

Qualitative data, on the other hand, are descriptive and conceptual and involve the "how" and "why" of various issues. Thus, unlike quantitative data, qualitative data are not measured in hard numbers but are more subjective. Because qualitative data are many times gathered through interviews, observations, or document review, these data can help researchers in understanding underlying attitudes, motivations, trends, or themes in a given population.[38] Regardless of the source, qualitative data (also known as "soft" data), once gathered, properly analyzed, and verified, can provide invaluable information about common themes and categories that can pinpoint the underlying reasons for a certain phenomenon.[39]

For example, in *Beginning Legal Writers in Their Own Words: Why The First Weeks of Legal Writing Are So Tough and What We Can Do About It*,[40] professors Laura P. Graham and Miriam E. Felsenburg surveyed students at various law schools to see if they could uncover reasons why first-year students find the first few weeks of legal writing class so difficult. The surveys showed that a significant percentage of students reported a loss in confidence in their writing during the first semester of law school due to (1) a lack of professional context in which to place their skills, (2) inexperience with difficult analytical thinking, (3) lack of confidence with the new genre, and (4) inability to assess how prior writing strengths and weaknesses will be impacted with the new genre.[41] Analyzing the data from student surveys enabled these professors to note patterns in the students' responses and come up with suggestions to smooth the transition into legal writing. Interestingly, many of their findings are equally applicable to students embarking on a scholarly writing journey.

When qualitative data are derived from document review, a content analysis is usually conducted whereby the textual content of different documents is coded, analyzed, and compared. Some scholars propose that content analysis could form the basis for a "uniquely empirical legal model." *See* Mark Hall & Ron Wright, *Systematic Content Analysis of Judicial Opinions*, 96 CAL. L. REV. 63, 64 (2008).

In addition, many times scholars use qualitative and quantitative data together (a "mixed methods methodology") to examine various dimensions of a legal or social issue. This combination can lead to a deeper understanding of a legal or social phenomenon as "[q]uantitative research may provide information about a pattern, while qualitative research may provide an understanding of why such a pattern exists."[42]

The bottom line is that data can be a powerful tool to bolster your argument. But, in using data to bolster your argument, you will want to know how the data were obtained and what the data show or do not show to make your analysis most compelling to the reader. As Professor Sarah Morath warns: "Regardless of the type of research, however, 'a study can be no better than the data on which it is based and that data need to be properly drawn and defined.'"[43]

> **Further reading:**
>
> This section only skimmed the surface with regard to concepts of quantitative and qualitative data. Students interested in delving further into empirical legal research should contact one of the professors at their institution engaged in empirical legal research or a law librarian who may have specialized training in the area. Other resources you may want to consult include:
>
> Oxford Handbook on Empirical Legal Research (Peter Cane & Herbert M. Krizer eds. 2010);
>
> The Journal of Empirical Legal Studies (through Cornell Law School);
>
> Empirical Legal Studies Blog, elsblog.org;
>
> Shaun B. Spencer, Using Empirical Methods to Study Legal Writing, 20 J. Legal Writing Inst. 141 (2015); and
>
> Sarah J. Morath, It's Not All Statistics: Demystifying Empirical Research 27(1) The Second Draft 24 (Summer 2013).

As you gather your evidence, verify that the data are trustworthy. Think also about which existing resources will best support your ideas while simultaneously being credible to your readers. You can access credible data through many resources, including but not limited to bipartisan organizations, university research programs, and government repositories. Many of these entities provide accessible statistics on a number of contemporary issues that can be effectively used to bolster your legal analysis.

4.6 Adopting a balanced approach to your scholarship

Finally, as you construct your critical legal analysis, pay attention to an important (and sometimes overlooked) aspect—make sure that you consider all the evidence and issues in a balanced light. That is, make sure you consider both—or multiple—sides of the thesis being evaluated, just as you would if writing a memorandum of law or brief. By considering all sides, you will be forced to reckon with opposing evidence and viewpoints in analyzing the problem and coming up with workable solutions.[44]

Lawyers always want to manage adverse authority in a forthright and practical way. For example, under Rule 3.3 of the American Bar Association's Model Rules of Professional Conduct,[45] attorneys practicing law are under an ethical obligation to disclose adverse legal authority to the court. The same principle of disclosure should hold true in scholarly analysis. While lawyers are trained to zealously advocate for clients (and this advocacy naturally bleeds into writing), resist the temptation to consider only the strength of your analysis and ignore its weaknesses. Legal analysis is useful only to the extent that it is complete. Therefore, when you see differing constructions of law or disparate conclusions from other scholars analyzing a particular law, analyze those contradictory sources to see whether a distinguishing factor or error explains the different results or conclusions.

A comprehensive analysis examining all sides of an issue, and that is set forth precisely and accurately, is both credible and professional. An analysis based on "sliding premises" (an inaccurate or imprecise categorization of the opposing side or position used to shift the discussion in a way that is more seemingly favorable to the writer) weakens analysis and can result in the writer's advocating more extreme and unfounded positions.[46]

Analyzing opposing viewpoints does not mean that you need to accept every opposing point of view—indeed, a scholar should freely critique points of view that are distinguishable, weak, inconsistent, or not credible. However, if the opposing positions are an important part of the scholarly discussion, you should work to understand all of the competing arguments and ultimately disclose valid opposing arguments in text precisely and accurately.

Remember that the confidence displayed in acknowledging aspects of an issue that do not support your particular argument can add credence to the aspects that do.[47] In the long run, a balanced approach to information lends credibility. Instead of merely advancing a certain prerogative, or "winning at all costs," a balanced approach *deepens* analysis because the writer is forced to grapple with the issue at a more nuanced level.

In conclusion, legal analysis involves both theory and skill. The ideas and strategies set forth in this chapter should help you intentionally decide when you need to describe versus when you need to analyze. They should also help you to critically analyze your sources and think about which kinds of arguments you should develop and how you may want to use data to support your legal arguments. A writer's ability to engage in critical legal analysis is one that involves time and practice, but the dividends will enhance your credibility and your scholarly work.

Notes

1. STEPHEN KING, ON WRITING: A MEMOIR OF THE CRAFT 147 (2010).

2. A. Wigfall Green & Richard M. Allen, *First Lectures at a University*, in CONVERSATIONS WITH WILLIAM FAULKNER 80 (M. Thomas Inge ed., 1999).

3. *See* Mike Hansky, *Want to Be a Better Writer? Read More.*, huffpost.com (April 22, 2014).

4. Adapted from *Critical Thinking and Reflection*, U. PLYMOUTH (2010).

5. Adapted from U. BIRMINGHAM, *A Short Guide to Critical Writing for Postgraduate Taught Students*, intranet.birmingham.ac.uk (last visited Apr. 17, 2019).

6. Adapted from GLOBAL DIGITAL CITIZEN FOUND., *The Ultimate Cheat Sheet for Critical Thinking*, sacramento.org (last visited Apr. 17, 2019).

7. *See* U. KENT STUDENT LEARNING ADVISORY SERV., *Critical Thinking and Writing*, kent.ac.uk (last visited Apr. 17, 2019).

8. ELIZABETH FAJANS & MARY R. FALK, SCHOLARLY WRITING FOR LAW STUDENTS: SEMINAR PAPERS, LAW REVIEW NOTES AND LAW COMPETITION PAPERS 5 (4th ed. 2011); EUGENE VOLOKH, ACADEMIC LEGAL WRITING: LAW REVIEW ARTICLES, STUDENT NOTES, SEMINAR PAPERS, AND GETTING ON LAW REVIEW 15 (3d ed. 2007).

9. FAJANS & FALK, *supra*, at 37; *see* KRISTEN KONRAD ROBBINS-TISCIONE, RHETORIC FOR LEGAL WRITERS: THE THEORY AND PRACTICE OF ANALYSIS AND PERSUASION 83–98 (2009).

10. *See* FAJANS & FALK, *supra*, at 32–33. For an excellent discussion of the different types of legal arguments, see generally WILSON HUHN, THE 5 TYPES OF LEGAL ARGUMENT (3d ed. 2014).

11. Michael C. Blumm & James A. Fraser, *"Coordinating" with the Federal Government: Assessing County Efforts to Control Decisionmaking on Public Lands*, 2017 PUB. LAND & RESOURCES L. REV. 1, 1 (2017).

12. *Id.* at 17–23 (internal citations omitted).

13. FAJANS & FALK, *supra*, at 31.

14. *Id.*

15. Logan Wyont, Addressing the Inequities in Access to Reproductive Healthcare for Gay Male Couples, 45–46 (2018) (M.A. Thesis, Wake Forest University) (on file with authors).

16. *Id.* at 53.

17. FAJANS & FALK, *supra*, at 33.

18. *Id.*

19. *Id.*

20. *See id.*

21. Ellie Margolis, *Teaching Students How to Make Effective Policy Arguments in Appellate Briefs*, 9 PERSPECTIVES 73, 76–77 (2001).

22. *Id.*

23. Richard A. Posner, *The Decline of Law as an Autonomous Discipline, 1962–1987*, 100 HARV. L. REV. 761, 766–77 (1987).

24. Richard Delgado, *How to Write a Law Review Article*, 20 U.S.F. L. REV. 445, 446 (1986).

25. *See generally* Michael Heise, *The Past, Present, and Future of Empirical Legal Scholarship: Judicial Decision Making and the New Empiricism*, 2002 UNIV. OF ILL. L. REV. 819 (2002).

26. *Id.*

27. Shaun B. Spencer, *Using Empirical Methods to Study Legal Writing*, 20 J. LEGAL WRITING INST. 141, 143 (2015) (internal parentheticals within the text omitted).

28. AM. BAR ASS'N, LAWYER DEMOGRAPHICS, YEAR 2016 (2016); *see also* Spencer, *supra*, at 145.

29. Adapted from Spencer, *supra*, at 145.

30. *See* Spencer, *supra*, at 146–47.

31. *Id.* (citing Pam A. Mueller & Daniel M. Oppenheimer, *The Pen is Mightier Than the Keyboard: Advantages of Longhand over Laptop Note Taking*, 25 PSYCHOL. SCI. 1159 (2014)).

32. *Id.; see also* Kristen E. Murray, *Let Them Use Laptops: Debunking the Assumptions Underlying the Debate over Laptops in the Classroom*, 36 Okla. City U. L. Rev. 185, 186 (2011); Robin A. Boyle, *Should Laptops be Banned? Providing a Robust Classroom Learning Experience Within Limits*, 2 Perspectives 8 (2011).

33. With respect to legal education and legal writing, there are several excellent articles that use quantitative studies to examine the presence of a statistically significant relationship. *See, e.g.*, Lance N. Long & William F. Christensen, *Analysis of Readability in Appellate Briefs and Its Correlation with Success on Appeal*, 12(1) J. of App. Practice & Process 145 (2011) (finding no statistically significant relationship between readability [using the Flesch Reading Ease scale and the Flesch-Kincaid Grade-Level scale] of appellate briefs success on appeal); Shaun B. Spencer & Adam Feldman, *Words Count: The Empirical Relationship Between Brief Writing and Summary Judgment Success*, 22 J. Legal Writing Inst. 61 (2018) (finding that brief readability is significantly correlated to summary judgment success, but that it has a stronger relationship in federal than state courts); Emily Zimmerman, *Do Grades Matter?*, 35 Seattle U.L. Rev. 305 (2012) (using quantitative methods to study law students' expectations and attitudes about grades); Lance N. Long & William Christensen, *Clearly, Using Intensifiers Is Very Bad—or Is it?*, 45 Idaho L. Rev. 171 (2008) (finding a statically significant relationship between the use of intensifiers and success on appeal).

34. Kami Chavis, *The Supreme Court Didn't Fix Racist Jury Selection*, The Nation (May 31, 2016).

35. Foster v. Chatman, 578 U.S. ___, 136 S. Ct. 1737 (2016).

36. Chavis, *supra*.

37. Anne E. Mullins, *Opportunities in the Age of Alternative Facts*, 58 Washburn L. J. 577, 594 (2019) (internal citations omitted).

38. Spencer, *supra*, at 163–64.

39. *Id.* at 165.

40. Laura Graham & Miriam E. Felsenburg, *Beginning Legal Writers in Their Own Words: Why The First Weeks of Legal Writing Are So Tough and What We Can Do About It*, 16 J. Legal Writing Inst. 223 (2010).

41. *Id.* at 226–27.

42. Sarah J. Morath, *It's Not All Statistics: Demystifying Empirical Research*, 27(1) The Second Draft 24, 25 (Summer 2013); *see generally* Joe Fore, *"A Court Would Likely (60–75%) Find …": Defining Probability Expressions in Predictive Legal Analysis*, 16 Legal Comm. & Rhetoric: JALWD 49 (2019).

43. Morath, *supra*, at 24 (quoting Frank Cross et al., *Above the Rules: A Response to Epstein and King*, 69 U. Chi. L. Rev. 135, 137 (2002)).

44. Erwin H. Epstein, *Writing with Authority: Pitfalls and Pit Stops*, in The Handbook of Scholarly Writing and Publishing 91, 100 (Tonette S. Rocco & Tim Hatcher eds., 2011).

45. Model Rules of Prof'l Conduct r. 3.3 (Am. Bar Ass'n 2016).

46. Telephone interview with Professor Emeritus Ruth Ann McKinney, University of North Carolina, Chapel Hill School of Law (Mar. 5, 2018).

47. Epstein, *supra*, at 100.

Chapter 5

Avoiding Plagiarism: Taking Notes Carefully and Attributing Properly

The work of writing an article begins long before the actual writing starts. A successful project, meaning one that you can research and write in a timely manner, starts when those ideas swirling in your head are first committed to paper as notes. Your process in understanding the material you read and capturing the salient points in your notes may be as important as the sentences and paragraphs you compose. Likewise, the method by which you organize the notes can yield bounty or frustration.

Another part of the note-taking process that warrants care is the obligation to avoid plagiarism. Plagiarism occurs when one uses the work, ideas, or materials of someone else without giving credit to the original source. While progressing through high school and college, you have probably been warned to avoid plagiarism at all costs. Taking someone else's work without permission can yield high-stakes consequences and may result in a reprimand or serious punishment. Because lawyers follow additional standards of ethics and professionalism, those stakes may be even higher in law school and beyond. If most everyone knows plagiarism is wrong, then why does it happen and how can it be avoided?

This chapter explains several strategies for taking and organizing notes gathered from your research. It also explains a few common errors that can lead to plagiarism and how you can avoid them in your writing process.

5.1 Taking notes carefully

Taking detailed and accurate notes from the outset of your project is a good idea for many reasons. A large part of your project's success may stem from the notes that captured your thinking from day one. First, taking good notes requires engaging analytical skills, beginning with the first search query and going all the way through the writing phase.

Second, by engaging those analytical skills, you can save time and effort. Taking good notes and organizing those notes by grouping the research into logical topics can save hours of time, particularly on a long article or paper. Additionally, the research and outlining phases of the project will go much more smoothly with some semblance of organization while working. Note taking often occurs over a period of days, weeks, or even months; you will not remember all that you read or where the information came from. Without good notes about prior research (that includes at least rudimentary citations so the information can be easily traced back to its source), you will likely waste time rereading previously identified authorities. Worse, you might also inadvertently use another author's material improperly.

Finally, taking accurate and thorough notes combats plagiarism. In modern legal scholarship, your goal is to add an original thought to the discourse on the law. To do that, however, you will likely build upon others' original ideas. Those original ideas can be packaged in many different ways—written, audio, digital, or online materials. Today, when access to information is a keyboard click away, material can be copied and pasted from any original source quite easily. That ease of access and use can lead to poor notation of the original source, which in turn, can lead to plagiarism, particularly for those who are not careful in the note-taking process.

5.2 Strategies for effective note taking

One trap that writers fall into when researching an article is viewing the "information gathering phase" as a distinct process from outlining—that is, a time when you would naturally think about how the analysis fits together. Gathering pages of information from relevant sources without thinking about how that information fits together has many downsides. One downside is that sitting down with page upon page of unconnected notes can be overwhelming. Another is that having a mass of unconnected notes can waste precious time—they are harder to organize and harder to convert into outline form. This section identifies a few strategies for taking good notes and for organizing information along the way.

Before starting in-depth research, think about the organizational note-taking system that makes the most sense for your project. Do you prefer to take notes by hand on paper or notecards? Or do you prefer to keep digital notes in your files or use a note-taking app? No matter how you take notes, what system do you normally use to organize your notes—organized notecards that are arranged by topic and maybe even color coded? Paper notes kept within folders in an accordion file? Or maybe organization is not your strong suit and you take notes on whatever paper you find available at the time without any real system of organization. Even if you fall into the latter camp, you can get your notes under control.

To begin, think about how you process information and the best organizational system for you. Will you have a color-coding system for different points or ideas, maybe using a particular ink or particular color of notecards consistently for each main legal argument? Will you have different sections of a notebook or different folders (digital or hardcopy) for the main points of your document? As discussed in Chapter 2, *Diving into Research,* several online programs can help you organize and store your research. If you prefer digital files, programs such as EndNote, Evernote, RefWorks, Zotero, or Mendeley may appeal to you. Choose the strategy that makes the most sense to you and that will help you maintain a firm handle on the information you are gathering. Then, commit to that system.

After you have considered the system that will work for you, think about the general framework of your project and where each source of information fits into the overall scheme. What are the main parts of the document you are writing—for instance, are you writing a scholarly article that will have introduction, background, analysis, and conclusion sections? If, on the other hand, you are writing an op-ed, it will contain an opening paragraph stating a claim about a contemporary topic, body paragraphs explaining the author's perspective, a qualifier paragraph acknowledging divergent perspectives, and a takeaway paragraph that challenges the reader to rethink prior assumptions in light of the information in the editorial. From the outset of the project, think about where every piece of information will fit within that general framework. Having folders (again, whether paper or digital) for each section of the document is an effective way to categorize material and will likely save time.

Within that general framework, consider how the notes should be organized within each of those sections. Review your thesis: What main points do you already know will support that thesis? Completing enough preliminary research to choose a topic and develop an initial thesis will provide a sense of the major points for each section. For example, the preemption check will likely help identify the major legal (and non-legal) sources that will need to be discussed. It will also help identify the major points needed to prove the thesis. Even early in the process, see if you can organize by the major legal points supporting your thesis. If so, organize your notes according to the major points or subpoints your article will need to prove or support your thesis. (See Chapter 3, *Crafting Your Thesis*, for more details on crafting an effective thesis).

Although every major point might not be obvious at the outset, several points and subpoints may emerge during the early phases of research. As additional ideas and legal points develop, you will likely find it helpful to categorize your notes according to those major points, keeping all of your notes for a particular point or subpoint together.

Again, you can tweak your note-taking system to suit your personal style; the main point is to start with a system that works for you and stick with it. However, no matter the system, the following strategies can enhance your organizational system:

- **Cite every source used in your work.** Do not expect to remember where the information came from—you probably will not. Every sentence in the notes should be followed by a reference to the source and the page from which it came. Although every citation need not be perfectly formatted at this point, you must make sure that key components of the citation, like the volume, page, website, and date, are in your notes.

- **Use a labeling system.** Create a code for labeling information in your notes. For example, use abbreviations like "DQ" for direct quotations, "P" for paraphrasing, and "M" for "my idea."[1] Consistently coding notes in this way will not only prevent plagiarism, but it may help identify your own original ideas more easily. This system can also increase efficiency in the writing process, saving time that might otherwise be spent looking up every quote.

- **Direct quotes.** When taking language verbatim from an original source, indicate such by using quotation marks in the notes. Be consistent from the outset in marking the exact language taken from the source and the page on which that material is found. Not noting the specific language and page number can lead to accidentally plagiarizing content.

Look at the following example of notes. Notice the amount of detail the writer includes, including the sources of the information for each fact along with a designation noting direct quotes and paraphrasing, and additional questions (noted in blue) that the author has about the source.

1

Section: Background
Topic: History of Quarantine (how and when quarantine laws developed)
Date: 9/14

- From Italian term: *quarantana giorni* (when ship traders had to wait 45 days to go onshore, Rothstein et al., *Quarantine and Isolation: Lessons Learned from SARS*, at 17). **P** (What is the translation of this term?)
- Bible (lepers were quarantined in *Bible NASV*, Leviticus 14:4–8);

Greeks (Hippocrates: "avoid[ ] the contagious") (see Markel, Quarantine: East European Jewish Immigrants and the NYC of Epidemics of 1892 at 2.) **DQ**

According to the system above, this "**P**" indicates the information is paraphrased from Professor Rothstein's article. Notice how the labeling system can help you keep track of your use of sources.

This "**DQ**" indicates the material is a direct quote. Notice also that the researcher provides sufficient information about the cite but doesn't necessarily put it in final citation form.

2

Section: Background
Topic: History of Quarantine
Date: 9/21
Major US laws that changed landscape:

- Late 1700s, local governments had a system to deal with quarantines of ships bringing disease from other countries/continents. Invested with power to quarantine; also had power to treat quarantined people. **P** (What were the powers at this time — did the Crown have powers or just local gov'ts?)
- In 1796, Congress and fed gov't got involved enacted a law directing fed officers to help execute quarantine law in response to yellow fever outbreak in Philadelphia. (Katherine L. Vanderhook, *A History of Federal Control of Communicable Diseases: Section 361 of the Public Health Service Act* 4 (Apr. 30, 2002). **P**
- In 1799 "An Act Respecting Quarantine and Health Laws bill" was passed to authorize gov't to help states with quarantine measures. (Vanderhook, dash.harvard.edu) (Repealed prior act). (What did this change about prior act?)
- After cholera and yellow fever epidemic in 1893, law was expanded. National system of quarantine was then created w/ "National Quarantine Act." (Tyson, *Short History of Quarantine*, NOVA).
  - Gave Congress right to use quarantine practice to prevent contagious and infectious diseases.
  - State and local quarantines still allowed, but national system co-existed and could provide aid. **M**[2]

This "**M**" (for "mine" or "my idea") indicates that this is an idea from the writer, not a source.

Because these notes are detailed and organized, when the writer circles back to the notes weeks later, she will be able to see when the notes were taken, where they came from, where in the paper these notes belong, and what questions arose as she took the notes.

The strategies employed on these notes will not only help ensure your notes are accurate and precise, but they also offer significant protection from plagiarism. The typical causes of plagiarism and other ways to prevent it are explored in the remainder of the chapter.

5.3 What is plagiarism, and how does it happen?

At its core, plagiarism is simply the unauthorized taking of original ideas someone else created without proper attribution. In legal writing, authors must cite all of the authorities they use. In legal writing for law practice, because of *stare decisis* and strength of precedent, the more a lawyer can illustrate that ideas are well-supported by the law or other sources, the more force the work will have. In academic and professional legal scholarship, however, a tension arises between creating original ideas and using authorities to support those ideas. Authors are tasked with creating an original thesis but basing that thesis upon thorough background research.[3] Often, authors directly build upon the work of others—criticizing, supporting, or expanding that work. Combining new ideas with preexisting, original ideas can be complicated.

Below is a table listing some common sources that should always be cited when writing.

Kinds of sources that might be plagiarized[4]

Written materials	Books, articles, treatises, handbooks, magazines, poetry, letters, essays, newsletters, comics, newspaper articles, print advertisements, screenplays, statutes, cases, regulations, legislative materials, rules of procedure, restatements, or journal articles
Visual materials	Charts, tables, diagrams, captions, illustrations, digital advertisements, or drawings
Audio-visual materials	Movies, television shows, podcasts, songs, videos, spoken blogs, newscasts, social media posts, or interviews

When you were in undergraduate school, your professors probably explained the concept of plagiarism while extolling the virtues of creating a paper replete with your own ideas. In modern legal scholarship, original thought is still needed. In legal academia, just as in other forms of scholarship, proper attribution of ideas to their sources—whether a legal scholar's article or a case published by a court—is required.[5] The rigid standards of academia loosen somewhat in legal practice because the concept of *stare decisis* and the value of precedent underpin any writing—we rely on existing primary and secondary authority both to support and to add credibility to our words. Thus, even though judicial opinions and legal briefs may be drafted by multiple people using ideas and phrases borrowed from other sources, proper attribution is still required. Taking another's work, whether from an article or a judicial opinion, without proper attribution is still plagiarism. Even when unintended, plagiarism has consequences.

5.4 Intentional versus unintentional plagiarism

Plagiarism can be intentional or unintentional, but the consequences are often the same. Intentional plagiarism—tantamount to cheating—is usually easy to spot. Examples include purposely using all or parts of a published or unpublished work as one's own original ideas; copying a portion (whether a page or a sentence) from another person's paper and using it within one's own paper; or even taking an idea espoused in another work and using that idea in a very similar way to the original without attribution. The table below illustrates a few examples of conduct that qualify as intentional plagiarism.

Examples of intentional plagiarism

Act	Plagiarism?
Verbatim copying of any written material without attribution	**Yes**
Paraphrasing or building upon an idea of another without attribution	**Yes**
Paraphrasing without sufficiently changing the structure or content of original material	**Yes**
Buying a paper or paying someone to write your paper	**Yes**
Stealing someone else's work either in person or electronically	**Yes**
Downloading work from the web and pretending it is yours	**Yes**

In any type of academic or professional setting, this intentional kind of taking is an egregious offense and can result in serious consequences.

Most often, though, plagiarism occurs unintentionally. Unintentional plagiarism examples include inadvertently forgetting to use quotation marks for a statement, changing too few words of a sentence when paraphrasing, or simply thinking that a note jotted down in the margin of a legal pad was one's own idea instead of information taken from a separate source. The ease with which we can copy and paste from online or digital resources is a leading culprit behind unintentional plagiarism. Sometimes, when copying and pasting an item into a document, writers forget to immediately attribute the source; once that information lives in a document for a while, the writer may forget that the material was not the writer's own original thought.

The best way to avoid unintentional plagiarism is to be mindful of its causes. A few causes of unintentional plagiarism include:

- Not understanding *when* to attribute ideas;
- Lack of clarity on when to quote versus paraphrase an idea;
- Not understanding *how* to properly quote or paraphrase an original idea;
- Failing to document carefully the source of material for every note taken, especially when copying and pasting;
- Waiting until the paper is in final form before citing sources;
- Having a mistaken notion that rules of attribution do not apply to more creative types of scholarship like blogs or essays;
- Being in a rush and letting impending deadlines obscure judgment; and
- Mistakenly expecting to remember what information was borrowed and where it came from.

Even with unintentional plagiarism, the consequences can be dire. Students could fail the class, be charged with academic dishonesty or an honor code violation, have the incident recorded on their transcript, be tried according to the law school's honor code procedures, or be expelled from school altogether. In addition, such a charge will likely need to be disclosed to any state licensing board and may affect admission to the bar. Similarly, professionals can face equally negative penalties. A lawyer[6] or professor who plagiarizes could be fired, sued, or face charges of ethical violations. At the very least, the writer is likely to be embarrassed and have a tarnished reputation.

5.5 Knowing when and how to attribute sources

Knowing when and how to attribute credit to sources will help avoid plagiarism. Of course, the best practice is to give credit for any idea that did not arise in your own head. When unsure whether to cite an idea, such as a general concept, err on the side of caution. Even for an original idea, if that idea builds upon the thoughts of other authors, give those authors appropriate credit. When looking at a source, the more you think, "This idea is perfect—exactly what I wanted to say!" then the more imperative it is to cite that idea. The next few sections explain when and how to attribute sources to avoid plagiarizing.

5.5.A Common knowledge exception

The only exception to the requirement that every idea should be attributed is when that idea is "common knowledge." That means, when an idea is widely known or has existed for many years, you need not cite authority for that idea. Some authorities say that if the same undocumented idea appears in five or more different sources, it need not be cited.[7] For example, using the basic definition of the term common law—"law developed by the courts in the absence of a statute"—would not require citation because the definition is so widely known.

In legal writing, however, the common knowledge rule is not liberally used because assertions without supporting authority are typically not viewed as being very authoritative.[8] Thus, in this genre, we cite. For example, if you were explaining legal standards for obscenity and wanted to use particular phrasing from a Supreme Court justice who said that, while he could not adequately define hardcore pornography, "I know it when I see it,"[9] that material should be cited as the justice's original idea even though the quotation is well known and widely repeated without citation.

Items of common knowledge include information about historical events, legends or myths, urban legends, fables, old wives' tales, folklore, common facts, and so on. Thus, if items from these sources are common knowledge, they technically may need no citation to their original source. In legal writing, however, you might want to cite the source anyway. Citing to a credible source will make your proposition stronger. If you have any uncertainty as to whether the item would satisfy a common knowledge standard, cite it.

5.5.B Direct quotes

Verbatim copying of another's work or idea without attribution always constitutes plagiarism. If an author takes material—whether an idea, phrase, sentence, paragraph, or more—from another work without altering the material, using quotation marks or block quotes to designate the borrowed material, or attributing the work in an appropriate citation, the author has plagiarized that material. Those rules apply in both legal scholarship and in legal practice, even in documents such as briefs or motions.

When directly quoting something, use quotation marks to identify the material and a citation to show where the material originated. Next, carefully ensure that the wording (and punctuation in most cases) is identical to that used in the original. Any omissions or alterations to the words or phrases should be indicated according to the guidelines of the predominant citation or style manual. Making a singular word plural, changing verb tense, or omitting the beginning and ending of a sentence all require appropriate notation. Even correcting a word that was misspelled in the original requires notation.

Remember to use direct quotations sparingly. In most forms of legal writing, authors tend to avoid frequently using direct quotations and long quotations for a couple of reasons. First, use of both direct or long quotations break up the text and can disrupt the flow of information. Second, any legal reader will want to see *the writer's* analysis and how the points being presented are connected. A string of direct quotations may lack cohesion. Moreover, direct quotations, especially when overused, are a poor substitute for the explanation and analysis the reader needs to understand the topic. A better practice is to paraphrase most cited items and to use direct quotes only when something is said in a unique way or the exact phrasing is required for the reader to understand the full significance of the material. The pertinent language of statutes or regulations, for example, is something that should typically be quoted directly. A court's holding from a case or a general principle of law may be something that can be easier to understand if paraphrased and put in your own words.

5.5.C Paraphrasing properly

Because legal readers disfavor a multitude of direct quotes, legal writers frequently turn to paraphrasing to convey ideas. Paraphrasing material can be a little trickier than using direct quotations because standards for proper paraphrasing can vary. Some guidelines say that no more than five words can be taken in the same sequence from the original without using direct quotation marks, while other guidelines may allow no more than three words. When writing for a law school assignment or a particular publication, review the guidelines the assigning professor or the publisher prefers and use those.

Generally, a workable standard is that both the content and structure of the original passage should be changed to reflect one's own thoughts, understanding, and choice of words. Changing a few words in the passage is not enough. To avoid plagiarism, the paraphrased material should be changed significantly. It should not be recognizable as the work from the original.

Even when borrowing from legal authorities like cases, paraphrase properly. Copying and pasting a court's words about a case is easy, but it is also plagiarism. Legal writers must still cite that material and use direct quotes for unaltered phrases, sentences, or paragraphs.

Understanding how and when to cite can cut the risk for impermissibly using material without attribution. Other strategies can help minimize the risk throughout the process as well. The best strategy is to cite as you write (this concept is discussed further in Chapter 6, *Writing, Revising, and Proofreading*). When you take notes from a source, keep the citation with the notes, indicating whether the material is a direct quotation or paraphrased. When outlining or drafting, cite as you go.

The following chart shows you some examples of unintentional plagiarism and how the issues could be fixed.

How to correct inappropriate use of material

Examples of Plagiarism			
Original Material	"In short, the Reagan and Bush Administrations sought to construct a sharp dichotomy between horrific acts that amount to torture and other forms of conduct. Torture would become a category with few gray areas, because it would encompass only the worst of the worst—conduct that everyone assumed was not only already illegal but also almost never practiced in the United States. In the process, more debatable categories of conduct would be shunted aside and apparently relegated en masse to the lesser category of cruel, inhuman, or degrading treatment. At the same time, both Administrations also sought to limit the scope of the cruel, inhuman, and degrading treatment category—which they reasonably viewed as ambiguous. The result of their efforts was to take some of the conduct that arguably would fall within the convention and place it outside, at least under the United States' understanding of its obligations. Put differently, the Executive Branch sought to raise the bar for establishing that either torture or cruel, inhuman, and degrading treatment had taken place." John T. Parry, *Torture Nation, Torture Law*, 97 Geo. L. J. 1001, 1042 (2009).			

Material used in this way:	Plagiarism?	Reason?	The Fix:
At the same time, both Administrations also sought to limit the scope of the cruel, inhuman, and degrading treatment category—which they reasonably viewed as ambiguous. John T. Parry, *Torture Nation, Torture Law*, 97 Geo. L. J. 1001, 1042 (2009).	Yes	Although the writer cited the original source of the material, using the exact language without direct quotation marks is plagiarism.	Add quotation marks to indicate the material is directly taken from the source.
Both the Reagan and Bush Administrations tried to limit the scope of the category known as cruel, inhuman, and degrading treatment because that category was, they believed, ambiguous.	Yes	Here the writer is attempting to paraphrase the material, but this attempt fails because it wrongly appropriates another author's ideas without a citation. Even if the writer had properly attributed the material, too few words were changed when paraphrasing; thus, plagiarism still would have occurred.	First, properly attribute by citing the work. Next, significantly alter the passage's phrasing and quote key phrases that cannot be changed like "cruel, inhuman, and degrading treatment."

How to correct inappropriate use of material continued

Examples of Plagiarism			
Material used in this way:	Plagiarism?	Reason?	The Fix:
Previous administrations existing toward the end of the cold war, specifically those of Presidents Reagan and Bush, sought to draw a strong distinction between the kinds of conduct that could be deemed torture and other conduct, or "enhanced interrogation techniques," that could be bumped down to a lesser category of cruel, inhuman, and degrading treatment. Even with that change, both Administrations simultaneously made it harder for conduct to meet even that lower classification. Thus, President Obama's executive order banning these "enhanced interrogation techniques" evidenced a pivotal turn in policy.	Yes	This attempt is tricky because the writer has made significant changes to the original passage, distilling several points into one main idea and then adding a different point. But the writer makes a fatal error in not citing the original source material upon which the writer's work builds.	Cite the works that provide a foundation for your own analysis.

Plagiarism can be avoided by simply understanding what it is and how to prevent it. Taking careful notes on the sources of information and then citing as you write will ensure that you do not plagiarize someone else's original work.

5.6 Quick reference chart

Since much of your legal scholarship, particularly for any project within the academic realm, will involve citing or building upon someone else's original work, know how to use that work properly. Citation manuals and legal writing style manuals typically set out numerous rules for quoting and citing materials, and they explain how to indicate omissions within direct quotations. The quick reference chart on the next page may give you a sense of how to use the material.[10]

Now that you understand some of the best practices to avoid plagiarism, in the next chapter, we explore additional techniques for efficiently and effectively writing your paper.

Quick reference chart

Referenced material	What to use	How to use it
A sentence or passage from the original source is perfect and you want to use it, or a large part of it, verbatim.	Direct quotation along with a citation to the material.	Use quotation marks around the complete sentence or passage. Include a citation to the original source every time the material is used.
You want to use a term, phrase, or part of a sentence or passage in your work.	Paraphrase the material, quoting any key language from the original.	Paraphrase by changing the content and structure of the original passage to reflect your own thoughts, understanding, word choice, syntax, and grammar. Put quotation marks around any phrase or sentence that is directly taken from the original source. Cite the original source.
You want to quote some original material but omit other parts.	Follow the rules of your citation manual or legal writing style manual for omissions or changes.	Use brackets [ ] to show the omission of or change to a single character such as when required by grammar conventions. Use brackets to show the addition or substitution of a word. Original: "The witness testified plaintiff substantially contributed to the guest's intoxication." Altered: "[P]laintiff substantially contributed to the guest's intoxication." Altered: "[The] plaintiff substantially contributed to the guest's intoxication."
You want to omit words within a directly quoted sentence or phrase.	Follow the rules of your citation manual or legal writing style manual for omissions using an ellipsis.	Original: "A person is visibly intoxicated when the person's intoxication is conspicuous or readily observable by the social host." Altered: "A person is visibly intoxicated when … intoxication is … readily observable by the social host." (Use ellipsis whenever omissions are made, except at the beginning of the sentence.) Altered: "A person is visibly intoxicated when the person's intoxication is conspicuous…." (Use ellipsis, then final punctuation.)

Notes

1. *Safe Practice,* Purdue Online Writing Lab, owl.english.perdue.edu (last accessed Oct. 2, 2019).

2. The "M" in this example is made for purposes of illustrating a coded note-taking system. Many public health scholars have made this point.

3. *Overview and Contradictions,* Purdue Online Writing Lab, owl.english.purdue.edu (last accessed Oct. 2, 2019).

4. *Types of Sources,* Purdue Online Writing Lab, owl.english.purdue.edu (last accessed Oct. 2, 2019).

5. *But cf.* Brian L. Frye, *Plagiarism is Not a Crime,* 54 Duq. L. Rev. 133 (2016).

6. *But see, e.g.,* Andrew Carer, *The Case for Plagiarism,* 9 U.C. Irvine L. Rev. 531 (2019).

7. *Is It Plagiarism Yet?,* Purdue Online Writing Lab, owl.english.purdue.edu (last accessed Oct. 2, 2019).

8. Posting of unknown author to *Quoting, Paraphrasing, & Plagiarizing,* LWI Online Listserv (2003) (on file with authors).

9. Jacobellis v. Ohio, 378 U.S. 184, 197 (1964) (Stewart, J., concurring).

10. Posting of unknown author to *Quoting, Paraphrasing, & Plagiarizing,* LWI Online Listserv (2003) (on file with authors).

Chapter 6

Writing, Revising, and Proofreading

6.1   Moving from research to a working outline

6.2   Using efficient drafting techniques

6.3   Revising and polishing your draft

6.4   Perfecting citations

Almost all good writing begins with terrible first efforts. You need to start somewhere. Start by getting something—anything—down on paper. A friend of mine says that the first draft is the down draft—you just get it down. The second draft is the up draft— you fix it up. You try to say what you have to say more accurately. And the third draft is the dental draft, where you check every tooth, to see if it's loose or cramped or decayed or even, God help us, healthy. —Anne Lamott[1]

The writing process can be a time of great creativity and productivity, but it can be riddled with challenges as well. Staring at that blank screen while imagining the fantastic piece of scholarship you want to produce can be exhilarating. On the other hand, the pressure of producing a great paper, coupled with the sheer stamina required to produce a lengthy paper, can lead to writer's block. Moreover, because writing tends to be a recursive process, you may feel like you are taking one step forward and two steps back as you circle back for more research yet again. Although the process of writing a piece of legal scholarship can be daunting when viewing the whole thing at once, you can reduce stress and anxiety by breaking down the drafting process for a paper or article into its component parts. As the writing process progresses, remember the key goals of legal, professional, and academic scholarship: disseminating ideas, creating a scholarly dialogue, and enhancing professional credibility and reputation. This chapter will show you how to meet those goals in an efficient way.

As with any scholarship, you want to disseminate ideas and create a scholarly dialogue in a way that highlights new concepts or thoughts and explains how those new ideas relate to established concepts. Above all, as discussed in Chapter 5, *Avoiding Plagiarism: Taking Notes Carefully and Attributing Properly*, any scholarly writer must properly attribute any ideas that come from another source. Keeping those concepts in mind, this chapter will walk you through the next big steps of the writing process: moving from research to a working outline, using techniques for efficient drafting, spending most of your time revising, and saving some time for polishing the very final draft.

| Moving from research to a working outline | Using techniques for efficient drafting | Spending most of your time revising | Saving some time for proofreading the very final draft |

Within each step, you will learn that the time you invest up front when researching and outlining reaps rewards in efficiency that allow you to work smarter, not necessarily harder, to produce a quality work product in a timely manner.

6.1 Moving from research to a working outline

For most legal writers analyzing complex ideas, outlining is a helpful precursor to the drafting process. In general, outlining serves three main intersecting purposes:

Outlining helps produce a linear, easily readable product that makes sense to the audience.

Outlining helps the writer evaluate the sufficiency of information that the audience will need.

Outlining helps determine the appropriate beginning, middle, and end of the writing.

The most effective outline actually occurs when all three of these purposes intersect in the concept map above. Outlining facilitates linear thinking by helping determine whether the proposed topics make sense in proximity to each other, whether headings are properly descriptive, and whether successive chapters or sections are conceptually connected.[2] In the same way, outlines assist in preparing the relevant sections of the writing—beginning, middle, end, or issue, analysis, conclusion—by presenting a view of the structure and substance from thirty thousand feet to determine whether the sections flow logically.

Outlining also provides an opportunity to evaluate the information that the audience members will need. Do they need a detailed introduction to the subject matter so that they have a solid background that supports a deep analysis, or is a higher-level overview more appropriate? Will they need less context to understand the laws at issue, or do they need additional context on particular points?

You will likely utilize two kinds of outlines: broad and detailed. Organizing broadly on the large scale, from the major sections of the paper, then from the major legal points within each section, helps you assess the scope of the work and avoid the paralysis that sometimes comes with starting a new project. In addition, organizing on the large scale with major points helps you break the paper into manageable chunks; working through one chunk at a time can help you avoid the inertia that comes from feeling overwhelmed. Creating a broad outline will require you to think about the different legal arguments the paper will need to prove your thesis. Once you have a sense of the major points needed for the argument and the general structure in which those points will fit together, you can add details.

The next step is to fill in the details by identifying topics and subtopics on a deeper level. Completing a detailed outline prior to drafting helps untangle the mass of factual information and critical analysis the research is likely to uncover. The detailed outline also helps you to then group those related ideas together in a logical order. Keep in mind that writing is a fluid process that may necessitate alterations to an early, large-scale organizational model.

6.1.A When to start outlining

For many forms of academic and professional writing, writers compile lengthy and complex analyses derived from research completed over the course of weeks or months. Corralling all of that research and those analytical ideas at once can be daunting; the better route is to outline as you go, beginning the broad outline soon after you see the major points supporting your thesis emerge. As previous chapters explain, outlining as you go is vital for a couple of primary reasons: (1) Outlining early, even during the research phase, helps connect your random thoughts

more quickly, and thus is a more productive use of your time; and (2) it helps you engage better with the material and allows you to see the pieces of the analytical puzzle and how those pieces may fit together. Seeing those pieces will alert you to problematic areas or analytical holes earlier in the process. Constructing the broad outline can begin at the earliest phase of your research.

6.1.B Constructing the broad outline

Your ultimate objective in the writing process is to move from research to a draft as efficiently as possible. Noting ideas for your broad outline (sometimes called a "large-scale outline"), even as you research, will save time. If you have systematically taken and organized your notes, you will be able to make quick work of this task.

To create the initial broad outline, first set out the major components for the type of product you are writing (e.g., note, comment, op-ed, blog post, policy paper, seminar paper) in an outline form. The various components of the work's form should provide the general framework for the paper. So, for example, if you are writing a law review note, you would include an introduction, background, analysis, and conclusion. Within each section, outline the main points the analysis needs to address. Those main points should provide the overarching framework for the legal argument.

While all major points of the paper might not be evident early on, connections and patterns in the law will become more obvious as the research continues, and this broad outline will allow you to see those connections and patterns in a semblance of order. Thus, research notes can first be grouped by major point. Within each major point, subpoints will arise. For example, you will likely recognize the ideas needed for the background section early on, so go ahead and tuck those ideas into your broad outline. The following example shows an excerpt of a broad outline for a law review article that addresses social problems with imposing quarantine measures during public health emergencies.[3]

Excerpt of a broad outline

I.   Introduction

Ebola crisis 2014

Broad thesis—Many people don't comply with quarantine measures, and therefore, viruses aren't contained. Medical workers often say they cannot afford to comply with the requirements because they do not get paid for time off work, etc. Solution: provide some type of mechanism for compensating individuals subject to quarantine.

II.   Background

    A.   History of Quarantine

    B.   Legal Authority for Quarantine

        1.   Federal and state

        2.   International? How does that fit in?

Although rudimentary, the large-scale outline gives the project direction while simultaneously giving the paper a sense of structure. Now, as the writer digs more deeply into the research, there is a place to put new information, as well as a place to note questions or ideas. As other relevant points arise during research, the writer can add to the broad outline's major points and then fill in the subpoints and details. By outlining the points and filling in the details, the writer can push the analysis, and even the whole project, forward. Most importantly, outlining from the outset lessens the time spent drafting the paper. Following the broad outline, you can transition directly into a detailed outline.

6.1.C Crafting a detailed outline

After the broad outline, the next step is to create a more useful outline by adding more detail. The detail will help you support the major points by pulling together ideas, evidence, and authority from your research.

Although the main goal of a detailed outline is to make the process of writing the draft much easier, creating a detailed outline has supplemental benefits. First, the detailed outline can help you with the paper's internal structure by allowing you to see the work as a whole while simultaneously giving you a bird's-eye view of the major and minor points of each section. Thus, outlining in detail helps you organize points and ideas into a logical sequence—one that, when contained in a written draft, a new reader can easily understand. Second, a detailed outline will enable you to identify where sections of the paper may need to be restructured—maybe more substantial arguments need to be moved to the front of a section or arguments should be switched to connect analytical points more effectively. The detailed outline will also help you see which sections of the work are robust and which need more substance.

To create the detailed outline, build upon the ideas from your broad outline. Start by listing the main points you have found when researching the ideas in your broad outline, and organize those points into a logical sequence within the sections of the paper. Once you have fleshed out the general framework of main points, you can add the details.

To begin, take one discrete major point for which you have a large amount of supporting research. Next, start compiling the important ideas from the research that you want to use in your paper to support that major point. If you have kept thorough notes organized by topic or subtopic, you may already have many details written in your own words that you can transfer into your outline. If not, think about the commonalities or distinctions among the subpoints and group them accordingly. Note the relative importance of the subpoints by whatever system works best for you—color-coding, ranking with stars, or using alphanumeric notations—any system will work if used consistently. In revisiting the quarantine example, notice how the author uses historical events to build on the single point of how quarantine laws evolved.[4]

Building the detailed outline for one major point

III. Background

A. History of Quarantine (how and when quarantine laws developed)

- From Italian term: *quaranta giorni* (when ship traders had to wait forty days to go on shore) (Rothstein, et al., *Quarantine and Isolation: Lessons Learned from SARS*, at 17).

- Some major U.S. laws that changed landscape:

  ○ Late 1700s, local governments had a system to deal with quarantines of ships bringing disease from other countries/continents. Invested with power to quarantine; also had power to treat quarantined people.

  ○ In 1796, Congress and federal government got involved, enacted a law directing federal officers to help execute quarantine law in response to yellow fever outbreak in Philadelphia. (Katherine L. Vanderhook, *A History of Federal Control of Communicable Diseases: Section 361 of the Public Health Service Act* 4 (Apr. 30, 2002)).

  ○ In 1799, "An Act Respecting Quarantine and Health Laws" bill was passed to authorize government to help states with quarantine measures. (Vanderhook).

  ○ After cholera and yellow fever epidemic in 1893, law was expanded. National system of quarantine was then created with the "National Quarantine Act." (Tyson, *Short History of Quarantine*, NOVA).

- Early history of quarantine: Bible (lepers were quarantined in *Bible NASV*, Leviticus 14:4–8); Greeks (Hippocrates: "avoid[ ] the contagious." (Markel, QUARANTINE: EAST EUROPEAN JEWISH IMMIGRANTS AND THE NYC OF EPIDEMICS OF 1892, at 2)).

- More modern times: Middle Ages, Black Death in Venice

- ○ *Question: What happened with the laws in 1400–1647 as the building of large ships spurred world exploration?*
- More recent times:
  - ○ U.S. Colonies, Mass Bay Colony in 1647—first quarantine law.
  - ○ 1663, NYC law forbidding entry to people from regions with small pox.
  - ○ 1783, NYC on Bedloe's Island (where Statue of Liberty is) quarantine station established. (Tyson, *Short History of Quarantine*, NOVA).
  - ○ *Question: How did the law change as antibiotics and anti-viral drugs were developed?*

You can see from this sample that the author is now pulling together ideas from various sources and putting them into a logical order. The author starts with major legislation, then steps back and uses a chronological organization in tracing the history of the topic, adding salient points about the law's evolution. You can also see that the author decided to use bullet points rather than the traditional Roman numeral outline—that is fine. Outlines should be flexible to allow for the writer's preferences, so do not feel constrained by formal outline structure at this stage.

Thinking through what to include in the detailed outline should help you determine whether you have the most effective and logical flow of ideas within the major and minor points. If not, changing the organization of an outline is much easier than changing the organization once the paper is in full paragraph form. The detailed outline will also allow you to see smaller holes in the research or breaks in the connection of ideas. In the previous example, such holes may include what happened with quarantine laws around the world as the shipping industry bloomed in the 1400s–1600s or how federal and state laws in the United States evolved in light of scientific and medical discoveries relating to the spread of disease. Notice how the author puts questions directly in the outline to mark the holes. By noting these questions, the author now has clear direction on what research needs to be done and what information needs to be added; this clear direction likely means focused research and a more productive use of her time. The bottom line is that, by fleshing out the major points one by one as the author did in the above excerpt, you will methodically make headway on your document. After all, fleshing out ideas about each discrete point is a much less overwhelming task than trying to write a whole section in one sitting.

Within the detailed outline, remember to include the necessary citation (including the pincite reference to the precise page on which the material can be found) wherever needed. Citing properly as you go will save you time and, even more importantly, help you to avoid plagiarism.

Once the detailed outline is complete, you are ready to move forward to the next stage of writing—getting the first draft down on paper (explained in section 6.2, below). What should you do, however, if you cannot get through the detailed outline stage? What if you cannot figure out what the logical sequence of ideas should be? What if the legal concepts are too unclear to sort or too intertwined to break apart? The next section has a strategy for overcoming organizational blocks and getting you back on track to write the first draft.

6.1.D Breaking through blocks: Using the free write and the reverse outline

Although creating a detailed outline is the reasonable next step for drafting legal scholarship, sometimes that step feels like a big one. If your research is not well organized, if you have too much unconnected research, if you are not sure how to approach the analysis, or if you simply cannot discern what to put where, you can get stuck. Getting bogged down in the research and organization phases can deplete your energy, confidence, and time. If you find yourself stuck, consider sparking the writing process by "free writing" your way to a solid draft.

Keeping in mind the inevitable imperfection of any initial writing, writers who feel stuck should consider free writing to get something on the blank page. In the free write, the writer compiles ideas and substantive notes from the research process on paper within the structure of the broad outline without regard to quality and without belaboring the precise flow of logical points. Put simply, all you need to do is write. Write to explain the information to yourself or to your ideal reader. Write about what you know so far, and maybe even insert statements about what you do not yet know. Do not worry about writing conventions during the free write; instead, just get the ideas down on paper. The next example shows the kind of work and ideas a free write can yield.[5]

Example of a free write

Healthcare workers may want to defy quarantine orders, especially when they are not showing symptoms, because of the financial hardship they pose. A financial incentive could help encourage compliance with quarantine. Some healthcare workers who had volunteered in Africa when the Ebola outbreak erupted brought lawsuits after being quarantined unnecessarily. The quarantines had caused extensive financial hardship for their families.

For example, Nurse Kaci Hickox filed a lawsuit after being sequestered in a medical tent in New Jersey for days after returning from Africa where she had been volunteering with Doctors Without Borders. First, she was quarantined in New Jersey. She complained she had not been treated well, was not showing any symptoms, and had been improperly subjected to quarantine in New Jersey. She finally returned to Maine where the governor of Maine also ordered that she remain quarantined, even though she tested negative for Ebola. While being quarantined, Hickox could not work nor be with her family. (Should I explain more about the financial hardship here?) She defied the order and this controversy gained national media attention.

A judge ruled that the quarantine measures placed upon her were too restrictive and that she was not a threat unless she was showing symptoms.

In New Jersey, a bill was proposed that would provide compensation to healthcare workers such as Hickox, but after the Ebola crisis ended, so did the momentum with the bill, and the bill was not passed.

Even in this short excerpt, you can see how the logical flow of legal points is unfolding. After free writing, the author can see what subpoints have appeared and make decisions based on the information, such as whether a topic needs to be narrowed or broadened, whether the flow of ideas makes sense, or whether that area needs to be fleshed out with more research.

Be warned, the work product derived from the free write may not end up in your final draft. Usually, the way we write to understand information ourselves is not the best way to present that information to an audience. The free write shown here is not a polished piece of work—some parts are more like rough thoughts on paper without regard to grammatical norms. But the free write may yield important results. This free-flow exercise spurs creativity and ultimately makes the writing process less painful. It also generates a semblance of order by identifying key subpoints and a possible organizational model.

After each free write, try crafting a "reverse outline"[6] from the points contained in the prose. Noticing what points you wrote about and their order will give you a sense of the work's natural structure. Effectively, you are generating a list of bullet points summarizing the main idea of each paragraph. Many authors also construct reverse outlines from free writes by extracting salient points and statistics and placing them in a logical order. You will end up with a document that allows you to see if the outline derived from the free write proves the thesis in a logical, cohesive way. The reverse outline may also draw attention to where the draft diverges from the logical path. A reverse outline for the free write featured on the prior page may look something this:

Moving from free write to outline

Example of a free write	Example of a reverse outline
Healthcare workers may want to defy quarantine orders, especially when they are not showing symptoms, because of the financial hardship they pose. A financial incentive could help encourage compliance with quarantine. Some healthcare workers who had volunteered in Africa when the Ebola outbreak erupted brought lawsuits after being quarantined unnecessarily. The quarantines had caused extensive financial hardship for their families.	Claim: Financial hardship makes healthcare workers hesitate to quarantine themselves. Providing financial incentives may encourage compliance and protect public health.
For example, Nurse Kaci Hickox filed a lawsuit after being sequestered in a medical tent in New Jersey for days after returning from Africa where she had been volunteering with Doctors Without Borders. First, she was quarantined in New Jersey. She complained she had not been treated well, was not showing any symptoms, and had been improperly subjected to quarantine in New Jersey. She finally returned to Maine where the governor of Maine also ordered that she remain quarantined, even though she tested negative for Ebola. While being quarantined, Hickox could not work nor be with her family. She defied the order, and this controversy gained national media attention.	A. Volunteers like Hickox quarantined after returning from contamination zones. B. New Jersey and Maine governors ordered quarantine even when person was not showing symptoms.
A judge ruled that the quarantine measures placed upon her were too restrictive and that she was not a threat unless she was showing symptoms.	C. Judge rules quarantine measures too restrictive.
In New Jersey, a bill was proposed that would provide compensation to healthcare workers such as Hickox, but after the Ebola crisis ended, so did the momentum with the bill, and the bill was not passed.[7]	D. Compensation model proposed in New Jersey legislature but not enacted once immediate threat of deadly illness had passed.

By reverse outlining a free write, an author can quickly locate useful pieces of information and disregard extraneous text. Performing this technique routinely can both bolster drafting efficiency and ensure organization is maintained throughout the draft. When stuck, free writing may move you beyond the mental paralysis a large writing project can bring and help you get thoughts on the page.

6.2 Using efficient drafting techniques

Once a detailed outline is attained (whether you got there through a methodical process or through multiple free write exercises), you are ready to convert that outline to a working first draft, sometimes known as a "down draft."[8] The down draft is so named because you are writing just to get the information down on paper. The idea of a down draft appears in all kinds of writing, not just legal writing, and can be called by other names like the zero draft. This draft may be a "terrible first effort,"[9] and it will likely contain many errors, but this draft serves a purpose of propelling you into the writing phase of your paper. No matter the name of the draft or the genre of writing, the end goal of producing a finished piece of work can only be reached by actually writing it.

Most likely, the more organized your research and the more detailed your outline, the easier the process of creating that first draft will be. This stage of the writing process, when transforming notes to cogent prose, can be a time of good productivity as you move toward your project milestones. The following sections will give you strategies for this all-important stage of the process.

6.2.A Pace yourself by using time management strategies

As you enter the writing stage, make sure to give yourself time to write and pace yourself. A quality law review article, academic paper, or professional paper cannot be written like an undergraduate paper in which ideas flow so freely that a decent paper can be crafted in a few days. Rather, legal scholarship, whether academic or professional, is generally layered with ideas and nuances. Thus, thoughtfully and methodically advancing through the process always surpasses attempts to rush to the end.

As discussed in Chapter 1, *Exploring Topics and Establishing a System*, time management is paramount. Many scholars find that setting aside a block of time—at least an hour or two every day—is helpful. Setting aside time every day, or every other day, rather than just picking one day per week, can be the most efficient way to work. Absent a consistent schedule, you will forget ideas and spend time you could be writing trying to figure out where you were at the last sitting—what you had researched, what you had read, and what next steps you had intended to take. Adhering to a consistent schedule helps you to avoid becoming distracted by other tasks. Many writers will tell you that when they sit down to write they feel an overwhelming need to do just about anything other than writing—cleaning the house, doing a load of laundry, and even scrubbing grout with a toothbrush often seem like more attractive options than writing. Creating a consistent schedule and honoring it is one of the best ways to be kind to yourself.

6.2.B Start with the introduction

Another piece of helpful advice is to start with the introduction section (or the corollary to that section for other writing forms such as the exposition to a creative story or the opening paragraph for an op-ed). That section usually provides a framework for writing the other sections. It also provides an excellent litmus test for the writer—if you have sufficient information for easily writing the introduction, you probably are ready to write the rest of the paper. Some writers struggle to craft the introduction but, once they get through the struggle, they are more productive when working on others sections. If you are not able to craft a cogent introduction section that encapsulates the major points of your paper, you may need to research and outline more before writing.

6.2.C Remember that the writing process is not linear

As you have heard several times in this book, and probably throughout your law school career, legal writing is not a linear process. You will continue to research as you find new information and formulate new insights. Most likely, as you write, you may continue to see holes in your analysis or discover novel arguments that require more research. This process is normal. It shows that your mind is expanding and that the writing process is helping you think about the issues in a deeper and more nuanced manner.

6.2.D Create a process for saving drafts and deleted work

When writing your drafts, think about how and where you want to save your work-in-progress. Some ideas for saving your work were presented in Chapter 1, *Exploring Topics and Establishing a System*, and with luck, you already have a good system in place. Now that you are writing actual drafts and do not want to lose any of your effort, make sure your system is practical. In particular, pay attention to two things: First, figure out a way to save your work (including old drafts) in an organized manner throughout the writing process. Second, protect your drafts—save them to a safe location that you can access even if your computer crashes, breaks, or is stolen. Never store your work-in-progress only to one location, particularly not a single laptop, hard drive, or thumb drive.

When saving drafts, use a consistent process from the outset. Different parts of the paper can be combined in one document or you can create a folder system to organize the work by its parts. For instance, you can create a folder for each component of your paper (introduction, background, analysis, conclusion) for major legal points or principles in your outline or use a combination of those two organizational schemes. Whatever your system, stick to it and stay organized.

One word of caution: Always save *previous* drafts. You can save each new version as a separate document and then create a distinct folder for old drafts. Especially with major revisions, consider saving the new draft as an entirely separate version with the current date. If one version is lost or becomes corrupted, you will have an older version to rely on. Another "best practice" is to create a place, whether at the end of the document or in a distinct document or folder, for all material that you delete from the paper. Doing so will give you a means to find information that you have cut or inadvertently omitted during a revision.

When protecting your drafts, cloud-based services or institutional networks can provide a safe haven for documents. Your school or office may have a secure drive from which files can be accessed. You might consider writing your drafts on a cloud-based platform like Google Docs, which saves automatically, allows you to see a record of changes, and allows you to collaborate with another author simultaneously. Keep in mind, however, that cloud-based platforms use different formatting features than a traditional word processing program like Microsoft Word. Accordingly, documents may not seamlessly transport from one platform to the other.

Another option is to write your paper using a platform housed on your computer—like Dropbox—but that saves any documents to a secure cloud location. These cloud storage systems provide secure storage for documents, protecting your work if your computer crashes or is stolen. The benefit of this platform type is that you can access the work from any other computer or device, and many platforms keep the formatting integrity of whatever word processing program you are using. You can even remotely share the work with someone else like a professor or co-worker. But many of these platforms, however, do not allow collaborators to work on the document simultaneously.

Numerous other cloud-based providers are available. If you do not want to use a cloud-based platform, at least make sure to email yourself a copy after every work session or save the work in two places. Remember, whatever your choice, protect your drafts so as not to lose pages of research, notes, outlines, or text.

6.3 Revising and polishing your draft

Legal writing usually does not yield first drafts that are ready for publication. The opposite is true. Effective legal writers often spend more time revising than they did researching and writing the first draft. In fact, some widely published writers may spend more than half their time on the sole task of revising. You will likely go through several drafts when revising your work for structure and content, so be prepared.

Moreover, revising must happen in rounds. An effective revision process requires the writer to read section by section and do separate checks per section. For example, checking for paragraph cohesion, sentence structure, and citation errors all at the same time is simply too much, especially with early drafts. Further, fixing one problem might affect other areas of the paper. So, after checking for problems separately, you should review your document as an integrated whole. Once the document is substantively sound, the writer must then polish, which includes "wordsmithing" and proofreading the work (discussed in detail later in this chapter).

6.3.A Revising

When revising, check that each paragraph, sentence, and word is clear, accurate, and deliberate. If the down draft is where you just get your ideas down on paper, the revisions are where you take the time to make sure the structure and content are sound. The revising process is a lot like Russian nesting dolls, in which wooden figures are nestled inside larger wooden figures. Each figure opens to another doll contained inside until one gets to the tiniest doll made from a single piece of wood. Creating these dolls takes a lot of skill, both in the shaping and cutting of the dolls and in the intricate painting that follows. The process of revising will require skill as well, and you will move from large components of the paper like overall structure, working your way inward one component at a time until the draft is solid.

This section addresses large-scale revising concepts and some basic legal writing conventions for paragraphs and sentences.[10] Although the section mentions some of the frequent issues that appear in scholarly writing, it is no substitute for a good style manual. You will find a more comprehensive discussion of grammar, punctuation, and legal writing style in other popular style guides, writing manuals, and textbooks.[11]

• Overall organization

Within each major section of the paper, the ideas should flow in logical order. General concepts should be introduced before specific concepts. Major substantive points should be presented in the order that a reader can most easily understand, not necessarily in the same way that you came to understand the concepts when researching and outlining. Those main points should be connected so that the reader can track the analysis and see how one main point flows into the next. The more complex the legal topic or underlying legal principles, the more clarity you must provide so that the reader can understand those principles.

Using thesis sentences to organize your paragraphs is a helpful way to ensure that a reader can follow the major points of your analysis. Just as headings and subheadings should flow together, thesis sentences should—when read independently of the paragraphs that follow—logically guide the reader through the major points of your analysis. One way to check the logical structure of your paper is to pull out the main and subheadings along with the first sentence of every paragraph and either highlight them or paste them onto a separate page. With just the headings and first sentences of the paragraphs, ask yourself whether the organization makes sense. Also, ask whether the progression of points would be logical and clear to a new reader. If the highlighted portions do not give the reader a clear roadmap to the major and minor points of the analysis, revise the organizational structure.

Example of highlighting thesis sentences to verify structure and main points

By the 1700s, quarantine laws gave local authorities the power to quarantine people, as well as to provide care for those quarantined. For example, in 1783, in response to smallpox and yellow fever outbreaks, New York City set up a quarantine station on Bedloe's Island—where the Statue of Liberty would later find her home—to place contagious passengers and crew arriving in the United States....

The federal government became involved in quarantine in 1796 when Congress enacted a quarantine law directing federal officers to help execute state quarantine law. In 1799, Congress passed an Act Respecting Quarantine and Health Laws that authorized the federal government to assist state officials with quarantine....

Quarantine laws and policy have changed with medical and scientific advancement. By the late 1800s, scientists learned that germs and bacteria were responsible for diseases, which resulted in quarantine policy becoming more tailored. Following the discovery of antibiotics and the use of vaccines, public health officials began to consider "large-scale quarantines a thing of the past," and the CDC reduced the number of quarantine stations from fifty-five to eight....[12]

• Paragraph cohesion

Just as the paragraphs within an article should flow in a logical order, the sentences within a single paragraph should be cohesive in two respects: The sentences should flow together, and each sentence should support the paragraph's thesis sentence. When revising each paragraph, work on thesis sentence content and also examine how the sentences within the paragraph fit together to convey a single idea.

First, verify that thesis sentences are strong so that the reader will not be taxed to figure out what the paragraph is about. The first sentence of each paragraph can be either a thesis or a topic sentence. A thesis sentence makes an assertion or takes a position that the paragraph will support, while a topic sentence identifies a topic that the paragraph will discuss in more detail. In either case, the paragraph's first sentence should accurately reflect the content of the entire paragraph that follows. If it does not, then revise it.

Second, have one main idea per paragraph. All sentences in the paragraph should be united in clarifying that one idea. If you find that some parts of a paragraph fall outside the scope of the thesis sentence for that paragraph, either revise the sentence to accurately reflect the paragraph as a whole or divide the paragraph, giving each idea its own paragraph and corresponding thesis sentence. (If the paper is a law review or law journal article or other type of work that includes substantive footnotes, you may consider adding the tangential information to a corresponding footnote).

Go through every paragraph in the paper to make sure that each paragraph has a solid internal structure with cohesive ideas. If you cannot quite formulate the thesis sentence for a paragraph, ask yourself why. Are too many ideas being forced to live together in a single paragraph? Are the ideas truly related? If not, the paragraph is probably not cohesive, and you need to revise.

• Sentence cohesion and clarity

Once each paragraph is sound, you can move to the next "nesting doll"—sentence structure. Again, revisions are best done in rounds, so you might want to revise sentence structure once the organization structure and substantive content are sound. As you work through the draft, review each sentence examining the following:

Sentence Content. Try to make one point with each sentence. If a sentence is making more than one point, consider breaking it down into two sentences, especially if the two points are only marginally related.

Sentence Length. The general rule of thumb is that if the sentence is more than twenty-five words, it may be too long. That rule is usually true, and so a sentence that spans three or more lines should catch your attention. Longer sentences, however, are not always problematic. Sometimes we simply need more words to express a single idea completely. So, do not automatically cut a sentence longer than twenty-five words. Instead, give that sentence a hard look and decide whether the length is warranted. As you are deciding, pay attention to the other sentences in the same paragraph and even in the surrounding section. Are many of the sentences three lines or more? If so, you may need to revise some of them. If not, a longer sentence peppered throughout the section may enhance the flow.

Sentence Structure. First, pay careful attention to the subjects and verbs. For subjects, nouns are usually better than pronouns. For verbs, as you have probably heard multiple times, active verbs are much better than passive ones. An active verb is one in which the subject is actually *doing* something ("*MacLean scored a goal.*"). With active voice the subject will usually appear before the verb. In contrast, with a passive verb, something is being done to the subject, but we are not sure who is doing it ("*A goal was scored.*"). Readers prefer active voice for a couple of reasons: First, active voice is more engaging for the reader, often because active verbs tend to be more vivid and passive verbs tend to be weaker. Second, active voice can result in shorter, clearer sentences because the reader knows who is doing what. Passive voice can sometimes be useful when you intentionally want to minimize the role of the actor (for example, "*mistakes were made*" or "*the skateboarder was hit*"); even so, use passive voice sparingly and strategically.

Once you have chosen a good noun and an active verb, put the subject and verb close together, near the front of the sentence if possible. Remember, subjects and verbs are buddies, and they like to be together. Truly, nouns and verbs together make a sentence, and your reader will embrace the simplicity of that notion. If you see a sentence in which the subject and verb are miles apart, especially those with prepositional phrases or restrictive and non-restrictive clauses coming between them, revise the sentence.

When you do use pronouns, be sure that the pronoun agrees with the noun it is replacing. For example, look at the following sentence: "After the **court** hears the case, **they** decide the issue." The pronoun "they" is plural and does not agree with the singular noun it is replacing. Although the plural pronoun "they" is now an acceptable replacement for a gendered pronoun in many genres, be intentional if using it in formal legal writing.[13] For example, look at this sentence: "**A writer** can quickly move from research to a written draft if **he or she** uses a detailed outline." Here, the pronouns do agree with the noun they are replacing, but gendered pronouns often make a sentence clunky and do not encompass those who are nonbinary. One fix would be to select a single gender ("he" or "she") and use it throughout the piece. Another fix would be the intentional use of a singular "they": "**A writer** can quickly move from research to a written draft

> **Some resources you may want to consult include:**
>
> Bryan A. Garner, Legal Writing in Plain English (2d ed. 2013).
>
> Richard Wydick & Amy Sloan, Plain English for Lawyers (6th ed. 2019).
>
> William Strunk, Jr. & E.B. White, The Elements of Style (4th ed. 2019).

if **they** use a detailed outline." Again, here the pronoun does not agree with the noun it replaces, but this version is becoming the standard in many kinds of writing. Another option would be to revise the sentence to eliminate the pronoun altogether: "**A writer** can quickly move from research to a written draft **by using** a detailed outline."

Sentence Punctuation. If sentences contain multiple commas or semicolons, consider what you are trying to say and whether you can say it more simply. Often, sentences with multiple parts can be broken into multiple sentences or streamlined in other ways. Legal concepts are hard to follow, but legal writing should not be.

- **"Wordsmithing" your work**

When all of the heavy lifting is done and you have revised content until you have a document with a good structure, logical arguments, and cohesive paragraphs, you can begin one of the most fun tasks — "wordsmithing" the document. First, study each sentence to determine whether every word is necessary for the reader's understanding. If unnecessary words can be eliminated, do so.

Second, examine each word and determine whether it is the most precise and simplest word you can use given the situation. Remember, scholarly and professional papers convey complex theories and ideas. The reader is more likely to understand and retain the information if the author uses the simplest form of the word. So, for example, consider using words like "prove" instead of "substantiate" or "start" instead of "commence."

Remember that simplifying word choice will not dumb down your writing. Rather, it helps the reader understand and remember your position and arguments, making it more likely that the paper will be read, published, or receive a good grade.

Last, but not least, avoid using nominalizations — in other words, using nouns that are really verbs. They make the paper less concise and harder to comprehend. So, instead of *having a discussion of* (verb disguised as a noun) techniques, we can *discuss* (verb) techniques that make it easier to get published.

- **Revising for flow**

Another step in revising your work is using techniques to help the reader glide or flow through the separate sections of the paper. Two tools you can use to help create better flow are: (1) roadmaps and (2) transitions.

Roadmaps. A roadmap is any passage that indicates the organization ahead. You should include a roadmap paragraph in your introduction to show the reader the analytical path ahead. Similarly, mini-roadmaps are useful at the beginning of sections or whenever a legal concept breaks down into more than one argument. Roadmaps and mini-roadmaps also help your reader transition more easily from one argument to the next.

Example of a roadmap:

This article briefly examines the history of quarantine, the legal authority that relates to the government's ability to order quarantine, and many of the adverse impacts related to quarantine. It explains how providing a mechanism for compensation limits the adverse impacts and furthers public health goals. The article examines and evaluates existing federal, state, and international laws, and private employer-based compensation structures that could be used to compensate individuals undergoing quarantine, and concludes that a simple and accessible state-based approach via standalone legislation provides the most workable means of providing compensation. The article asserts that bipartisan planning, dialogue, and compromise — before the next infectious disease crisis — will be essential to creating a system that is both workable and equitable.[14]

Example of a mini-roadmap:

B. State Protections

State laws vary widely on the issue of compensation for time spent in quarantine. Under state law, healthcare workers and others could obtain compensation in the event of a quarantine via state statute, workers' compensation, or under the legal theory of wrongful discharge.[15]

Paragraph discussing compensation via state statute

Paragraph discussing compensation via workers' compensation

Paragraph discussing compensation under legal theory of wrongful discharge

Transitions. A "transition" is any word or phrase that indicates to the reader the relationship between two ideas. Transitions help your reader make the leap from one developed idea or argument to the next. By explaining the relationship between two ideas, transitions create a bridge from the former idea to the next. Below are some common transitions:[16]

Example of common transitions

Introduce	First, Initially, To begin, Primarily, In general, Alternatively
Restate	That is, In other words, As noted
Add	Again, Moreover, Additionally, Similarly, Also, Likewise, Further
Sequence	First, Second, Third; Initially, Then, Finally; Before, Next, Last
Exemplify	For example, For instance, To illustrate, In particular, Specifically
Contrast	However, Although, But, Yet, Unlike, In contrast, Nevertheless, Rather, Despite, Instead, Still, On the other hand
Connect	Because, Thus, As a result, Thereby, Therefore
Conclude	Finally, Thus, In sum, As a result, Therefore, Consequently

Using transitions strategically can elevate the importance of key concepts that support the claims. Conversely, using contrasting transitions can separate ideas that the writer does not want the reader to agree with from those that support the writer's position.

6.3.B Polishing with proofreading

After revising, you will want to proofread the paper, maybe several times. Proofreading is one of the most important ways that you, as a legal scholar, can establish credibility. You do not want silly errors to distract from your important message.

At this point in your education, you probably have developed some proofreading techniques that work for you. Be sure to use those. However, many writers need to use additional techniques. We all know what the paper *should* say (or what we *intended* it to say), but many times it is quite difficult to see what the article actually *does* say. While spell check, grammar apps, and other similar programs will catch some mistakes, your own eyes are the most fail-safe tools.

Here are some recommended proofreading techniques you may want to consider:

Spell check will not be able to find some common mistakes such as:

Less versus Fewer
To, Two, Too
It's and Its
They're, Their, and There
Who's and Whose
Your and You're
Trial and Trail

- **Set your work product aside for a time (a few days or a week work best) before you proofread.** Distance from the paper will help you see your mistakes.

- **Proofread for only one kind of error at a time.** Read through your article and look for only one category of errors (such as grammar, punctuation, citation, and typographical) at a time. You will not likely see punctuation errors when you are reviewing citation errors, nor will you likely see citation errors when you are reading for paragraph cohesion. While multiple reads may seem repetitive, a single read will not reveal all of the mistakes hiding in the pages.

- **Read every word in the paper aloud.** This technique forces you to say each word and hear patterns of phrases and sentences. Reading aloud is helpful to locate missing words and misspelled or misplaced words. Silent reading enables you to speed up your pace, which in turn, promotes unconscious correction; speaking out loud will force you to slow down and thus improve your ability to see errors.

- **Print out a hard copy.** Print a copy of the paper or article to proof. Finding errors on the screen is difficult, and it tends to be much easier to see errors on the printed page. For maximum accuracy, try reading aloud from the printed page.

- **Use a blank sheet of paper to cover up the lines below the one you are reading.** This technique keeps you from skipping ahead of possible mistakes. Having a separate piece of paper will also isolate each sentence, which increases your ability to spot errors.

- **Use the search function of the computer to find mistakes you are prone to make.** For example, many people confuse "its" and "it's." A search for "it" will locate both categories. Once isolated, you can more easily see if you used the term correctly.

- **Circle every punctuation mark.** As you circle, ask yourself if the punctuation is correct. Checking punctuation marks is especially important in making sure your citations are correctly formatted and that marks that come in sets, like quotation marks or parentheses, have a proper partner.

- **Read the paper backwards, section by section.** This technique is helpful for checking spelling. Start with the last word on the last page and work your way back to the beginning, reading each word separately. Although this technique seems odd, it allows you to concentrate on the spelling of each word rather than the content of the sentence or paragraph.

- **Double space.** When you print your document to proofread it, double space the text—the extra white space on the page will allow you to focus more on each word.

- **Have someone else proof your work.** Perhaps the best strategy for proofreading is to have someone else do it. Your own familiarity with the work may obscure your view. Ask a trusted friend or colleague to proofread your paper. An objective individual is in a better situation to identify mistakes and will also be able to give you important feedback about whether the work product makes sense.

6.4 Perfecting citations

Citation, whether you love it or not, is an important part of scholarly and academic writing. Since citations can make or break the ultimate credibility of the article, you will want to pay painstaking attention to them. Not only is a work product that is properly cited more likely to be read, published, or receive a top grade, but as we discussed in the last chapter, careful citation can help you avoid unintentional plagiarism. Proper citation can also support your analysis by allowing the reader to specifically understand the weight of authority of the background sources. Creating good citations during the note-taking process can simplify your life during the final stages of the writing process when time is short and your focused attention may be at its end. The following tips eliminate some of the tedium of citing properly.

- **While you are drafting, keep track of citations, no matter what.** After drafting each sentence or paragraph, immediately put in the citations, no matter how much you want to put off the task. To repeat, any sentence derived from a source should be cited at that moment. The primary exceptions would be topic sentences, conclusions of paragraphs or sections, and passages of pure analysis that contain only your original thoughts.

- **When taking notes, include full citations with them.** While you may want to create some shortcuts and not necessarily place a full citation in proper form during the writing process, having as much information with each citation as possible saves loads of time in the end. Avoid using "*id.*" during the writing process. Because sentences, phrases, paragraphs, and sections tend to move significantly during the editing process, using "*id.*" could lead to a mass of confusing citations that do not correctly relate to the actual sources of information. You can add in appropriate short citations when you are in the final stretch of polishing.
- **Create a quick reference sheet for common citations you are using in the work.** You will save time by keeping a citation manual close by or using an official and up-to-date online citation system as you draft each citation. You may find it helpful to create a list of citations that you are using frequently. Also, tab or bookmark pages of the rules you will use frequently, especially if many of your sources are not common like cases, statutes, and law review articles. You may also want to pay attention to signals as you take notes and write the paper to ensure that you are using the authority in the most accurate way.

Some commonly used signals and their meanings[17]

Signal	Meaning
See	Authority supports the proposition even if the authority does not state the proposition explicitly; implicit support would allow the use of this signal.
See also	Additional support for the proposition with which the citation is associated. Often, this signal is used after the proposition at issue is discussed. A parenthetical explanation for each authority is useful.
E.g.	This signal, meaning "for example," is used when the cited authority is one of many that support the proposition, but additional citations to additional authorities are not particularly useful to the reader.
Accord	Means that other authorities, not explained, are in accord with or support the authority that is cited.
Cf.	Authority supports by analogy. Because this signal is a directive for the reader to compare a source to others, explanatory parentheticals briefly indicating the specific points of comparison are helpful to the reader.
Compare … with …	Comparison of authorities that supports the stated proposition.
Contra	Authority cited is contrary to the stated proposition.
But see	Authority supports the contrary of the stated proposition.
But cf.	Authority supports the contrary by analogy.
See generally	Authority presents useful background.

- **Scholarly work should be grounded in well-established authority.** In a traditional format, a reader will expect to see a citation to an authority after most sentences, and citing one or more authorities consistently will help build credibility with both the primary and secondary audiences. Make sure you are consulting and citing a variety of sources. Like with citations, the primary exceptions would be topic sentences, conclusions of paragraphs and sections, passages of pure argumentation that contain your original thoughts, or where several integrated sentences in a paragraph all relate to the same source and a single citation clearly shows support for the related assertions in each sentence.

Although the task of writing (and thinking) inherently comes with some degree of frustration, the writing process can also be a rich and rewarding one. Writing about the law may be one of the most intellectually challenging things that you do as a law student, practicing lawyer, or law professor. Do not let fear of the blank page, the thought of producing inferior scholarship, or even the enormity of the project hold you back. Just start writing. Getting something—anything—on the page is the crucial first step that allows later refinement and editing. If you embrace the process of outlining and drafting set forth above, you will have a defined pathway toward completion. You will progress through the writing process and toward a solid draft that explains your thesis.

The next several chapters will dive into various genres of legal scholarship that you may want to consider for your project: In Chapter 7, we will delve into *Law Review and Law Journal Articles*; Chapter 8 covers *Seminar Papers and Capstone Projects*; Chapter 9 reviews *Bar Journal Articles*; Chapter 10 discusses *Policy Papers (White Papers)*; Chapter 11 looks at *Op-Eds*; Chapter 12 examines *Blogging and Other Types of Social Media*; and Chapter 13 explores *Creative Works*. After learning more about the genre for your project, you may want to review some of the tips again from this and earlier chapters. While each form of scholarly and professional writing may have different norms or organizations, implementing an effective process for research, analysis, and writing will be the core of your work.

Notes

1. Anne Lamott, Bird by Bird: Some Instructions on Writing and Life 25–26 (1994).
2. *See, e.g.*, Lisa T. McElroy & Christine N. Coughlin, *The Other Side of the Story: Using Graphic Organizers to Counter the Counter-Analysis Quandary*, 39(2) Univ. of Baltimore L. Rev. 227, 237–39 (2010) (discussing how graphic organization systems can help with structure, organization, and sequence).

3. *See generally* Christine Coughlin, *Public Health Policy: Revising the Need for a Compensation System for Quarantine to Maximize Compliance*, 7 WAKE FOREST J. L. & POL'Y 415 (2017) [hereinafter "Public Health Policy'].

4. *Id.*

5. *Id.*

6. *See* Rachel Gurvich & Beth Wilensky, *Add Reverse Outlining to Your Writing Toolbox*, abaforlawstudents.com (Sept. 5, 2017).

7. *Public Health Policy, supra*, at 416–17.

8. *Id.*

9. *Id.*

10. Portions of this section were derived or adapted from these works: CHRISTINE COUGHLIN, JOAN ROCKLIN & SANDY PATRICK, A LAWYER WRITES 259–91 (3d ed. 2018) [hereinafter A LAWYER WRITES]; JOAN ROCKLIN, ROBERT ROCKLIN, CHRISTINE COUGHLIN & SANDY PATRICK, AN ADVOCATE PERSUADES 281–310 (2015); ROBIN BOYLE LAISURE, CHRISTINE COUGHLIN & SANDY PATRICK, BECOMING A LEGAL WRITER: A WORKBOOK WITH EXPLANATIONS TO DEVELOP OBJECTIVE LEGAL ANALYSIS AND WRITING SKILLS 233–45 (2019).

11. *See* A LAWYER WRITES at 259–91.

12. *Public Health Policy, supra*, at 422–24.

13. *See, e.g.,* Heidi K. Brown, *Get With the Pronoun,* forthcoming LEGAL COMM. & RHETORIC: JALWD (2020) (on file with authors); Heidi K. Brown, *We can honor good grammar and societal change together,* abajournal.com (April 1, 2018); Joseph Fawbush, *The Fun and Easy Way to Use Gender Pronouns in Legal Writing,* findlaw.com (Aug. 29, 2019).

14. *See Public Health Policy, supra*, at 420–21.

15. *Id.* at 438.

16. A LAWYER WRITES, *supra*, at 259 (citing LAUREL CURRIE OATES, ANNE ENQUIST AND KELLY KUNSCH, THE LEGAL WRITING HANDBOOK: ANALYSIS, RESEARCH AND WRITING, 613–22 (3d ed. 2002) and BRYAN A. GARNER, LEGAL WRITING IN PLAIN ENGLISH: A TEXT WITH EXERCISES 68 (2001)).

17. *See* THE BLUEBOOK: A UNIFORM SYSTEM OF CITATION R. 1.2, at 54–56 (Columbia Law Review Ass'n et al. eds. 20th ed. 2015).

Chapter 7

Law Review and
Law Journal Articles

*"A unifying focus of legal scholarship ... should be making law
better serve society."*[1]

A law journal article involves a deep and critical examination of a
legal doctrine, institution, social movement, historical event, or policy.
Within the legal academy, scholarship in the form of law review or journal
articles is part of a larger conversation or critique about law, with each
author adding a new or unique observation to the discussion.

Writing a scholarly article can both enhance your résumé and expand
your critical thinking and writing skills. Even though you may not often
be called upon to write a formal scholarly article in practice, many of the
skills you learn from writing such an article (or editing someone else's
written work if you join a law review or law journal) will transfer to the
other forms of writing that you will commonly do as a practicing lawyer.

No matter the impetus for writing a scholarly article, this kind of
legal writing teaches you many things. First, you will develop expanded
skills into researching secondary sources, gathering and synthesizing information, and using those resources to support your ideas. You will be
exposed to sophisticated writing styles and, consequently, may notice
how other writers use words and tone. You will learn to work with substantive footnotes and gain proficiency in citation skills. You will also
learn to read others' scholarly writing critically, and the critical eye that
you acquire may help you see the analytical holes in your own work.
Whether you are advocating for a change in the law or predicting the
future legal outcome for a law, reading other law review and law journal
articles may also help you create sound arguments by showing you different

kinds of structures and writing techniques. The amount of research required for a scholarly article means that you will read a lot, thus expanding the breadth and depth of your legal knowledge. Most importantly, by writing a scholarly article, you will contribute to the body of law by finding your own voice and expressing your own legal opinion on an issue. This practice can yield great benefits for your skill set and your reputation.

7.1 Differences between scholarly articles and other types of legal writing

Law review and law journal articles are not so different from other types of legal documents lawyers and law students draft. The primary difference is the audience. Rather than a limited audience of a legal writing professor, senior partner, client, or even a judge, a law journal article may be circulated to a wide variety of legal professionals—judges, academics, scholars, and lawyers—with a wide variety of expertise. While this potential exposure might seem intimidating, first-year legal writing courses generally teach the foundational concepts of legal analysis needed for legal scholarship. Many characteristics of effective memoranda or briefs are equally applicable to legal scholarship.[2] The form of the work product is tweaked to ensure that the article's analysis, organization, tone, and style appeal to the expectations of the wider audience that is focused not only on what the current state of the law *is* and *why* but also on what the law *ought to be.*

Now you may have heard the criticism that some law review and law journal articles are so focused on the theory of what the law ought to be and why that they are divorced from reality. The intense focus on theory, so the critique goes, makes journal articles inaccessible to the public, outside the realm of legal practice, and of little or no use to society. In fact, Chief Justice John Roberts once famously stated, "Pick up a copy of any law review that you see and the first article is likely to be, you know, the influence of Immanuel Kant on evidentiary approaches in 18th-century Bulgaria, or something, which I'm sure was of great interest to the academic that wrote it, but isn't of much help to the bar."[3]

Although a few theory-laden articles may deserve the criticism, many scholarly articles do benefit both society and the law. This chapter began with legal scholar and jurist Harry T. Edwards's assertion that "a unifying focus of legal scholarship … should be making law better serve society."[4] Legal scholarship serves society best when it is "all inclusive,"[5] so the reader understands how and why the problem exists and why any proposed solution helps, based on an in-depth analysis of both theory and doctrine.

As you will see in this chapter, properly written scholarly articles can, and should, be theoretical *and* make a positive impact on the bar, bench, or society as a whole.

7.2 Common elements of scholarly articles

On average, a law journal article takes approximately 150 hours to write.[6] That averages out to be approximately ten to eleven hours per week during a fourteen-week semester. Given this substantial time investment, this section dissects the component parts that will comprise the article so you can understand how the parts work together.

This chapter focuses on the typical forms of scholarly articles that law students are most likely to write: (1) Notes and (2) Comments. Like the ubiquitous "it depends" answer in law school, while legal scholars universally recognize these categories, no uniform definition describes what constitutes either a Note or a Comment. Because many law schools (and even law professors) define Notes and Comments inconsistently, the components and requirements of each depend on the institution, journal, or professor overseeing the project. So, if an article needs to be categorized as either a Note or Comment—as it may for publication requirements or for citation purposes under the rules of *The Bluebook*[7]— use the definition provided by your institution. For this book, focus not on the characterization but on the *purpose* of the article, which should always be an in-depth critique of a narrow legal doctrine, issue, theory, or policy. While the sky is the limit for your topic, you may consider addressing the topic in one of the following common ways:[8]

- A legal doctrine, decision, legislation, regulation, or order that:
  - is now irrelevant or antiquated because of new facts or circumstances.
  - needs to be modified due to a new type of societal harm.
  - creates inconsistency or unpredictability in the law.
  - ignores logic, historical or social policies, legislative history, or common sense.
  - should properly be considered under a new legal regime.
  - is one of first impression.
  - creates a new legal, social, philosophical, or political concern.
  - fails a rhetorical analysis.
  - has an unintended consequence on a part of society, such as the economy, business, consumers, vulnerable populations, employment, or education.

- Developments in legal doctrine derived from a case or series of cases, a statute or statutory scheme, a legal trend, other law journal articles, administrative rulings, or executive orders.
- The origins, history, and shortcomings of a legal doctrine, a legal institution, or legal education.
- A comparison of a legal doctrine to a legal doctrine from another jurisdiction, a doctrine in a different area of law, or a doctrine in another academic discipline.
- An empirical study concerning a legal doctrine, area of law, or social issue.

While the range of potential topics and critiques are limitless, generally the underlying organization of the scholarly article is consistent and usually includes four essential structural components: the introduction, background, analysis, and conclusion sections.

Four essential structural components of a scholarly article

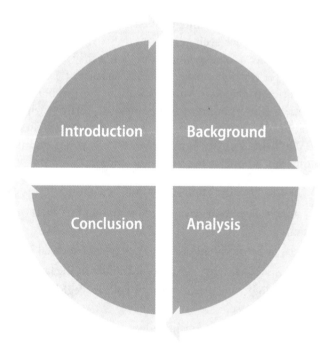

Some of these individual components may be divided into sections or subsections depending on the topic. A few article styles may contain additional components, such as the Statement of the Case (as defined below), when the focus of the article concerns the effect of a new decision or recently enacted statute, or a "methods" section for an article related to an empirical study. But, as the circle reflects, each component is related to and dependent upon each other to create the entire article.

So, now comes the all-time favorite question: "How long should each section be?" The answer is (again): "It depends." Each section's length will depend on the article's topic and focus. For the sole purpose of providing a thirty-thousand-foot view of the typical law journal article, the table below sets forth a loose approximation[9] of each component's length:

Length approximation by section

Substantive section of your paper:	Approximate portion of the paper:
Introduction and thesis statement	5–10%
Background section	30–40%
Analysis and recommendations	40–50%
Conclusion	5% or less

In the following sections, each component is examined in detail.

7.2.A The introduction: Creating your research space

The introduction creates the research space for your article.[10] Your "research space" is the area in your article where you demonstrate why you—as the legal researcher and scholar—care about the topic and why readers should invest their time in this paper. In other words, the introduction should pique readers' interest and entice them to continue reading the article. The introduction also explains your original contribution to the research and scholarly conversation. Put differently, it shows where the legal or social gap may exist, why prior attempts to address or fix the issue have been inadequate, or what new twist you are adding to the scholarly discussion. In sum, the introduction provides a compelling opening, conveys the general topic, the original point and the writer's thesis, and gives the reader a roadmap to the main points of the article.

• **The opening**

The first part of the introduction component is the opening, and its job is to capture the reader's attention. There is a famous saying, "If you can dream it, you can do it."[11] So, dream big and let your creativity soar in the opening by using techniques that both entice the reader and provide the reader with context. Commonly used techniques for the opening include: (1) a fictional, autobiographical, or biographical story; (2) a powerful quote; (3) a rhetorical question; (4) a comparison of how two different jurisdictions or disciplines treat a certain issue; (5) a summary of why the issue is important; or (6) an explanation of the history or effect of a certain legal doctrine or institution.[12]

The following two pages contain examples of effective openings along with an explanation of the technique authors use to pique the reader's interest.

Examples of introductory techniques for an opening

Author(s) and Title	Example	Technique
Andrew Jay McClurg, *Preying on the Graying: A Statutory Presumption to Prosecute Elder Financial Abuse*, 65 Hastings L.J. 1099, 1100–01 (2014).	A ninety-three-year-old man takes a walk in his South Florida neighborhood, using a cane for assistance. A year earlier he lost his wife of thirty-five years to cancer. He lives alone. His children live out of state. A thirty-eight-year-old woman approaches him near his house and strikes up a conversation, asking for directions to the nearest hospital. She suggests they meet sometime for coffee. A week later, she calls him although the man does not recall giving the woman his phone number. She begins visiting him at his house, showing him attention and affection. During one of these visits, she tells the man she has cancer and needs surgery but that the hospital will not treat her unless it is paid up front and in full. She states that the surgery will cost approximately $15,000. The man begins loaning her money. She continues asking for more money, saying it is needed for more medical treatment. He gives it to her. The woman tells the man she owns an apartment building in New York that she is selling and will be able to pay him back when that transaction occurs but refuses to provide the building address. As time passes she tells the man she is free of cancer but now needs money for her sick grandmother and son. She assures him she is a single woman and that the man she lives with is her brother, but official records show that he is her husband. The course of dealing between the young woman and the old man continues until, during a ten-month period, the man, who lives on Social Security, transfers $60,000 to her. The above story is common, but in this case, the man was our father, Donald McClurg.	The author uses narrative to tell the story, depersonalizing the protagonist. At the end of the introduction, the writer provides an autobiographical revelation that personalizes the legal issue.
Kenji Yoshino, *A New Birth of Freedom?*: Obergefell v. Hodges, 129 Harv. L. Rev. 147, 147 (2015).	The decision in *Obergefell v. Hodges* achieved canonical status even as Justice Kennedy read the result from the bench. A bare majority held that the Fourteenth Amendment required every state to perform and to recognize marriages between individuals of the same sex. The majority opinion ended with these ringing words about the plaintiffs: "Their hope is not to be condemned to live in loneliness, excluded from one of civilization's oldest institutions. They ask for equal dignity in the eyes of the law. The Constitution grants them that right."	Strong, descriptive words to summarize why the issue is important, along with a powerful quote from the case.
Nancy Levit & Douglas O. Linder, *Happy Law Students, Happy Lawyers*, 58 Syracuse L. Rev. 351, 351 (2008).	"The logic of the rebel is to want to serve justice so as not to add to the injustice of the human condition, to insist on plain language so as not to increase the universal falsehood, and to wager, in spite of human misery, for happiness." — Albert Camus[13]	A powerful quote.

| Russell M. Gold, *Compensation's Role in Deterrence*, 91 NOTRE DAME L. REV. 1997, 1998–99 (2016). | In 2014, Pepsi settled a labeling class action regarding Naked Juice for $9 million. Of that $9 million settlement fund, $5.5 million was allocated to compensate customers. A few years ago, Facebook settled a privacy class action for $9.5 million; in contrast to the Naked Juice settlement, none of the money went to victims. It went instead to charity and class counsel as attorneys' fees. There are, of course, noneconomic reasons to care whether victims are compensated in class actions: class counsel's professional responsibility or agency obligations to the class, philosophical commitments to compensating victims, or the Rules Enabling Act. From an economic perspective, however, scholars have argued that for purposes of tort law's primary objective—deterring wrongdoing—it does not matter whether victims are compensated in class actions. Rather, they argue, only the aggregate amount and likelihood of payment matter when considering the settlement's deterrent effect. Whether class actions typically follow the Naked Juice approach of giving much of the judgment to victims or the Facebook approach of giving nothing to victims—the thinking goes—does not affect deterrence. This article challenges that notion. | A comparison of two cases to show that with respect to damages in class actions, compensating victims likely deters more wrongdoing than other forms of relief. |
| Meghan Boone, *Lactation Law*, 106 CALIF. L. REV. 1827, 1829 (2018). | In 2010, Amy Anderson, a substitute teacher in Maine, gave birth to a stillborn baby. Within days, her body began automatically producing breast milk. Unsure what to do, Ms. Anderson sought advice online, where she discovered that her breast milk could help other babies, particularly those with health problems or born prematurely. Despite her grief, Ms. Anderson was inspired by the idea that she could help other babies, so she began to pump and donate her breast milk to nonprofit milk banks. The school administrators where Ms. Anderson worked, however, informed her that she was not entitled to unpaid breaks or a private place to express breast milk during the workday. Even though other recently pregnant teachers in her school were entitled to these benefits, the school maintained that Ms. Anderson was not—because her baby was dead. Maine law specified that an employee was entitled to breaks only "to express breast milk for her nursing child." The law did not protect Ms. Anderson because she was expressing breast milk to process her grief, help other needy infants, and honor her stillborn baby—not to directly benefit her own nursing infant.

    Ms. Anderson's story is not an anomaly. In fact, most state and federal laws that address the rights of lactating women often explicitly exclude women like Ms. Anderson and other women who are lactating in a "non-traditional" manner. Despite the sustained government interest in increasing breastfeeding rates as a matter of public health over the last several decades, most state and federal laws aimed at doing so protect only certain breastfeeding women and only certain types of lactation. Why might this be? | Discusses the publicly available facts from an actual case in the form of a story. |

- Importance of topic and thesis

Following the opening, the introduction should demonstrate why the topic of the article is important to the reader or why the author's framing of the information in the article contributes an original point to the body of existing scholarship. In addition, this explanation should link the opening to the thesis. (See Chapter 3, *Crafting Your Thesis*.) The excerpt below, from *Preying on the Graying*,[14] examines this link:

Explaining the importance of the topic and connecting the thesis

Despite substantial evidence that elder abuse and exploitation of all types is widespread and increasing, and research showing that many elders are susceptible to exploitation for reasons associated with aging, too little is being done to address the problem. While states and the federal government have passed hundreds of laws protecting children based on the assumption that they are vulnerable and unable to protect themselves, **older at-risk adults have been comparatively ignored even though they are vulnerable for some of the same reasons.**

....

By their nature, elder exploitation cases do not involve situations in which perpetrators conk their victims on the head and steal their wallets. Many victims are tricked or deceived into "voluntarily" parting with their assets. **To outsiders, the transfers may look like gifts or loans, when in fact they occur because of undue influence, psychological manipulation, and misrepresentation.** Even when property is taken by stealth, the incapacity or death of the victim often prevents prosecutors from being able to prove that the transfers were the result of theft or exploitation.

Researchers and commentators agree that this is one of the primary hindrances to prosecution: **the inability of prosecutors to prove that the financial transfers at issue were the fruits of exploitation rather than gifts, loans, or other legitimate transactions.** Speaking in the context of sweetheart scams, one fraud investigator identified the problem as "the dirty word called CONSENT." Proving exploitation in any type of elder fraud case is complicated because the transactions usually occur in secret and victims may make poor witnesses due to cognitive or other impairments, or because they refuse to cooperate with authorities.

This Article proposes the adoption of state criminal statutes that create a permissive presumption of exploitation with regard to certain financial conveyances from elders to non-relatives. It sets forth a detailed statute intended as a conceptual framework for states to use in fashioning a permissive presumption statute that fits within their existing elder protection legislative schemes.

Here, the author discusses a broad range of social science research regarding aging and the lack of legislation to show social prevalence of the problem and to demonstrate the need for a legislative solution.

Here, the author explains up front one of the primary barriers to prosecution in this area. By doing so in the introduction, he predisposes the reader to understanding the need for his statutory presumption, which takes this obstacle into account.

- **Roadmap paragraph**

The final portion of the introduction is the roadmap paragraph that provides the reader with an outline of the article's structure. Because scholarly articles tend to be lengthy, having a detailed roadmap allows the reader to understand where the author is heading with the analysis; it may also help the reader locate the relevant portion of the article if the reader does not have sufficient time to review the entire paper. The roadmap also provides a structural overview that helps the reader understand and retain the information discussed in the article. An example of a roadmap from *Preying on the Graying*[15] is below:

Example of a roadmap paragraph

Part I explores the scope of elder financial exploitation and examines practical, cognitive, and psychological explanations for why older adults are unusually susceptible to exploitation, focusing on emerging research showing that even elders who lack obvious physical or cognitive impairments can be at risk. **Part II explains** why elder financial crimes are grossly underreported and under-prosecuted. **Part III sets forth** the proposal for the permissive presumption statute mentioned above, prefaced by a discussion of the need and justification for a presumption approach and an analysis showing the proposed presumption is constitutionally sound under Supreme Court authority. **The Conclusion offers** brief closing remarks.

7.2.B The background: Putting in your oar

When thinking about the background, consider Kenneth Burke's metaphor from *Unending Conversation*:[16]

> Imagine that you enter a parlor. You come late. When you arrive, others have long preceded you, and they are engaged in a heated discussion, a discussion too heated for them to pause and tell you exactly what it is about. In fact, the discussion had already begun long before any of them got there, so that no one present is qualified to retrace for you all the steps that had gone before. You listen for a while, until you decide that you have caught the tenor of the argument; then you put in your oar.

Likewise, a journal's background section is where you show what others have done or said, synthesize it, and then indicate what you hope to contribute—in other words, why you finally "put in your oar."[17] This section also highlights the depth of your research. In the following diagram are some techniques to consider when drafting the background:[18]

Describe the law sufficiently to identify gaps in the law.	Synthesize relevant sources rather than reporting on them.	Describe relevant trends or patterns in the law.
Write for an audience with legal training.	Provide sufficient detail for a legally trained reader who may not have specific knowledge of the legal doctrine involved.	Recognize and cite the work of scholars to establish your credibility.
	Consider relevant legal and non-legal sources that may be important in your analysis.	

A direct correlation exists between the level of background research and the level of confidence the reader will have when approaching the analysis. When the writer fully explains the background of the law and supports that explanation with extensive research, the writer's credibility and the reader's goodwill are established, making the reader more likely to accept the writer's assertions. To ensure that the background section adequately explains the problem, many scholars first write the background section in more detail with ample supporting authorities, paring down the section during the revision stage and cutting any information that is not relevant or does not support the analysis that follows.

While the background is one overall component of a scholarly article, depending on the topic and its complexity, there may be multiple subsections within the background. If using multiple subsections, consider using informative point headings that clearly establish the point or topic each subsection addresses. In fact, you *should* come up with a descriptive point heading to use in lieu of the term "Background" because providing sufficient detail in the point headings will enable the reader to see how that section relates to the overall thesis.

If you decide to use a theoretical frame for your scholarly piece or connect your analysis between law and another discipline, such as bioethics and the law, make sure to include contextual information about the framing you are using, as well as how it may apply to your analysis. As a writer, you want to make sure your reader has *all* the necessary background information to understand the lens through which you plan to focus your analysis (for a theoretical framing) or to compare and integrate different disciplines (for an interdisciplinary analysis). Your reader will appreciate it. As one scholar explained, "I would hate to read an interesting background section only to find out in the analysis section that the author is using a law and economics frame to resolve the problem."[19]

> **Theoretical Framing Preview:**
>
> A theoretical frame is when you use another established school of thought (such as a law and economics frame or a feminist frame) to structure the legal issue and your legal analysis. The frame you use will affect the kinds of arguments you will make and the type of supporting data you may use. We discuss theoretical frames in further detail below.

Brief excerpt of background section[20]

B. THE CONSTITUTIONALITY AND PARAMETERS OF PERMISSIVE PRESUMPTIONS IN CRIMINAL CASES

Several authoritative commentators have thoroughly explored the historical development of the constitutional requirements regarding burdens of proof and presumptions in criminal cases. No useful purpose would be served by retracing those developments in great detail here. The discussion below focuses on the doctrinal points most relevant to the thesis articulated in this Article.

....

In *County Court of Ulster County, New York v. Allen*, the leading relevant case, the **Supreme Court addressed the constitutionality of a New York statutory presumption** that a firearm found in a vehicle is jointly possessed by all of the occupants, subject to certain exceptions enumerated in the statute....

Note the use of **point headings** to specifically describe the contents of this subsection of the background. The author then starts this subsection with a mini-roadmap that provides some context about the area of law generally. The author then becomes more specific about what is and what is not going to be discussed in the subsection.

7.2.C The analysis: The heart of the matter

In the analysis section, the writer connects the material discussed in the background section with the thesis to show *why* and *how* the thesis is correct. You should revisit Chapter 4, *Developing Critical Legal Analysis*, to review how to construct a sophisticated analysis. This section reviews two more tools that can be used to enhance your thesis: theoretical framing and substantive footnotes.

As discussed in Chapter 3, *Crafting Your Thesis*, some articles use an entirely normative analysis, meaning that the analysis critiques the problem identified and shows how the problem reverses, extends, or deviates from prior law or how the thesis impacts policy, society, or applicable legal theory. For other articles, the writer may also want to offer a solution or a recommendation for change. Because legal scholarship is often normative, however, scholars routinely critique the law using social science theories derived from disciplines such as economics, science, psychology, and history. (For a fuller discussion of these theories, review

An article with a solution-oriented focus is Professor McClurg's article, *Preying on the Graying* (that we have used as an example throughout this chapter). The article proposes a permissive presumption statute to help combat elder financial abuse. In fact, this proposal was so compelling that the Florida legislature unanimously voted to create a permissive presumption of elder exploitation under specified circumstances. *See* Fla. Stat. §825.103(2)).

Chapter 4, *Developing Critical Legal Analysis.*) Scholars also use different perspectives such as feminist theory or critical legal studies to help explain what the law *is* and what the law *ought to be*.[21] These approaches are consistent with the shift in legal education away from the perspective of law as an autonomous discipline to the perspective that law is one of many components that make up the fabric of our society.[22]

A theoretical frame is a way of saying: "With this theoretical orientation in mind, here are the things we look for." It governs the kinds of arguments you will make and the kinds of data you would use to make them. Another way you may want to think of a theoretical framework is like a standard of review. A standard of review is the lens through which a court will look at the law and facts to decide the legal issue; likewise, a theoretical framework is the lens through which the author analyzes a particular issue.[23] When effectively used, a theoretical framing provides significant depth to the analysis.

For instance, if you use a "Law and Economics" frame (discussed below), you are adopting the normative framework of that theory that will dictate the types of arguments you may make within the frame. As a result, you would discuss the economic impact of a law or regulation rather than how the law may impact one's sense of autonomy or identity (issues that may be more appropriate for an ethical frame).[24]

Theoretical frames also provide further depth by enabling the writer to use the underlying scholarship that already exists within a theoretical school of thought. These frames (e.g., Critical Legal Theory or Feminist Legal Theory) add a unique flair to the work product by allowing the writer to make creative connections using the body of scholarship that has already been developed with the other perspective. In the chart below, some of the more common theoretical frames used by legal scholars are listed and defined:[25]

Chart of common theoretical frames

- **Comparative Jurisprudence**—An approach focused on the similarities and differences between legal doctrines or the legal systems of different jurisdictions.

- **Critical Legal Theory**—An approach focused on a critical examination that law is at odds with individual freedom because law maintains the status quo of societal power structures. Many scholars consider this theory an umbrella encompassing many other theories.

- **Critical Race Theory**—An approach focused on a critical examination of society and culture and the intersection of race, law, and power.

- **Feminist Theory**—An approach focused on the relationship between women and law and the extent to which the legal system subordinates women.

- **Law and Economics**—An approach focused on an economic analysis of the law or legal institutions.

- **Law and Literature**— An approach focused on applying literary theory to legal texts, centering especially on rhetoric, logic, and style, as well as legal syntax and semantics.

- **Legal Realism**— An approach focused not only on abstract rules but also on social interests, public policy, and other factors that influence the law.

- **Psychological Jurisprudence**— An approach focused on the effect of the law on the mind.

- **Sociological Jurisprudence**— An approach focused on the social effects of legal institutions, doctrines, and practices; a precursor to legal realism.[26]

When using theory, one mistake many students (and scholars) make is attempting to create originality by pulling disparate subjects together without the necessary fundamental understanding of how two disciplinary concepts interact. A second mistake occurs when the writer does not understand one (or both) of the subjects well enough to make a meaningful argument. To avoid these problems and ensure a strong doctrinal and theoretical foundation, conduct significant research to understand the vocabulary, tools, methodologies,

Helpful Resources:

In addition to the specific law review and law journal writing sources highlighted later in this chapter, when considering an interdisciplinary frame, you may want to consult:

ALLEN F. REPKO & RICK SZOSTAK, INTERDISCIPLINARY RESEARCH: PROCESS & THEORY (4th ed. 2021).

and viewpoints that may be relevant to the theoretical (which may be interdisciplinary) perspective the writer is integrating in the analysis.[27] Walking through the following steps at the outset of the project may give you the foundation needed for a cogent, meaningful article:[28]

Steps for integrating a theoretical approach into the analysis

Step One: Consider the issue and what motivates you to explore it.

Step Two: Ask yourself: "What type of theory would help explain or assess the problem?" For example, would a feminist perspective provide a strong frame for an issue of gender pay inequity in employment law?

Step Three: Read more about the theoretical approach to see what types of arguments are made and what type of data are used. Ask yourself: "Will this approach enhance my legal analysis?"[29]

Step Four: Conduct further research on both the legal issue and the theoretical approach.

Step Five: Identify intersecting arguments, conclusions, solutions, and insights. Identify any relevant distinctions.

Step Six: Refine your thesis to include the theoretical approach in understanding the problem and proposing any potential solutions.

Step Seven: Write. Research further as needed. Write some more. Revise, polish, and proofread.

Let's look at some examples. In *"Clientless" Lawyers*,[30] Professor Russell Gold uses a comparative approach to analyze the disconnect between lawyers and clients in both class actions and criminal matters and recommends adopting the accountability theory taken from criminal law in class action litigation.

Example of using a comparative theoretical approach[31]

Both complex litigation literature and criminal law literature separately recognize that vesting self-interested lawyers with the power to control litigation without the opportunity for meaningful client monitoring creates substantial accountability concerns. **Class counsel and prosecutors both** have entity-clients whose members, by and large, are apathetic about the litigation. **Class action scholars have widely recognized this apathy, and there is no reason to think that most members of the prosecutor's client—the public as a whole—care** (or even know) much about outcomes of individual criminal cases (save for victims and defendants about their own cases or the occasional high-profile case).

Because of this disconnect between lawyer and client and the inability of a diffuse entity-client to monitor the lawyer in any traditional sense, **both systems seek to restrain the lawyer's authority in some fashion to ensure faithfulness to her client's interests.** These two bodies of scholarship and doctrine have, however, largely marched along without pausing to notice how the other system deals with a similar problem. **That comparative analysis begins in earnest here, focusing on what complex litigation doctrine can learn from accountability scholarship in criminal law.**

For another example, in *Law's Enterprise: Argumentation Schemes and Legal Analogy*,[32] Professor Brian Larson integrates legal and rhetorical theory in the analysis. Professor Larson examines analogical legal arguments and asserts that legal arguments can be strengthened by considering theory from the rhetorical field of informal logic.

Example of using an interdisciplinary approach

The solution I propose is to increase our confidence in arguments by legal analogy by providing a formal model for creating and criticizing them. **Part II begins** by introducing a different standard for creating and assessing legal arguments, **drawn from the field of informal logic, and it explains the general formal model of the argumentation scheme. Part III then presents** the argumentation scheme(s) for legal (dis)analogy, including a means for assessing relevant (dis)similarity. That section concludes with some examples from real legal arguments.

II. A NEW TACK: INFORMAL LOGIC AND ARGUMENTATION SCHEMES

This section proposes a pivot from deductive logic to standards that are still rational and, though not formally valid, reasonable given the circumstances in

Notice how the author is explicit about the similarities between the various practice areas. The author then identifies a common underlying policy better defined in criminal law scholarship that may be applicable to complex litigation doctrine.

To ensure the reader has sufficient context to understand the interdisciplinary analysis, the author explicitly introduces rhetorical theory, provides a specific roadmap for the analysis, and explains how informal logic schemes apply to legal argumentation schemes.

which we use them. I contend here that by "reasonable" arguments we always mean to imply "dialogical" arguments. That is, any standard of reasonableness for legal arguments must anticipate that all legal arguments withstand critical scrutiny: every argument has a proponent and an opponent. Even when lawyers predict the outcome of legal disputes for clients, they are anticipating the counterarguments that other parties will make. **Subsection A introduces informal logic** and its conception of arguments that proponents assert are rational and reasonable but which are defeasible — subject to the critical questions of their opponents. **Subsection B explains how argumentation schemes formalize such dialogic arguments.**[33]

As a final example, in *Lactation Law*,[34] Professor Meghan Boone uses both critical legal theory and feminist theory to explore and critique legislation regarding breastfeeding and lactation.

Example of using dual theories to explore and critique legislation

Laws that explicitly discriminate on the basis of sex or rely on outdated ideas regarding the supposedly fundamental nature of sex differences are comparatively rare today. The dearth of laws that contain explicitly gendered standards, however, does not mean that the law is free of deeply engrained, traditional ideas surrounding gender. Law still can, and does, create "more subtle" reaffirmations of the gendered ways that society values women and promotes their adherence to traditional social roles. Laws that incorporate gendered norms perpetuate those norms, and those norms are strengthened, in turn, by the presence of laws, which rely on them.

This Article explores one example of subtly gendered law: lactation law. State and federal laws protect breastfeeding and lactation in a number of different contexts, including the workplace, the jury box, and the public square. The passage of lactation laws has been applauded by many feminist organizations as unquestionable progress in the fight for women's equality. This Article explores the idea that **although laws that seek to support breastfeeding are a positive step for women, both the conceptual framework of these laws, as well as the text of the legislation, are deeply problematic from a feminist perspective. Modern lactation laws are not designed to protect, and in fact do not protect, all lactating women or all lactation.** Instead, they protect only lactation that comports with our societal expectation of appropriate motherhood — an idealized motherhood that is inextricably intertwined with race, class, and gender expectations and norms. **They thus harm**, first, an **identifiable group of nonconforming women** and, more generally, **all women**, by further entrenching deeply held stereotypes.

Notice how the author integrates the protectionist doctrine underlying current breastfeeding and lactation laws but then uses critical legal theory and feminist theory to show that laws originally designed to protect women may, in fact, protect only a group of lactating women and may ultimately harm women by "further entrenching deeply held stereotypes."

Familiarizing oneself with the major scholars and their written works in each intersecting area is essential to using a theoretical frame and producing a quality article. Having either prior educational or professional experience can help, but if you do not have that experience, plan on conducting significant research to gain familiarity with vocabulary, concepts, theories, and leaders in the field.

Using a theoretical frame can be energizing and creative. It may increase your ability to make relevant connections between problems and solutions—valuable characteristics for an aspiring lawyer. If done properly, it can be an effective vehicle to show how "insights from another field … can enable the law to deal better with some recurring problem."[35] While integrating a theoretical approach may seem difficult at first, study and practice will help you learn to integrate theory intentionally and strategically, which will ultimately provide you with a more sophisticated and scholarly analysis.

Substantive footnotes usually start with citation "signals," which are specific terms or phrases used to clarify the weight of authority of a legal citation as it relates to the writer's proposition. Chapter 6, *Writing, Revising, and Proofreading*, provides further explanation about using signals in legal scholarship.

Another way to enhance your analysis and illustrate the depth of your research is by adding substantive footnotes. Footnotes are citations to sources that provide proper attribution to the original source and show the reader where the precise point may be found. (See Chapter 5, *Avoiding Plagiarism*: *Taking Notes Properly and Attributing Carefully*.) Footnotes also support your analysis by showing how your ideas are grounded in the law and built on the work of other scholars. In an article, you will use traditional footnotes to cite sources and authorities. But you can also use substantive footnotes, which go a step further.[36] Substantive footnotes provide a fuller discussion of additional issues mentioned in the body of the paper. They can show the reader the depth of your research and supplement your primary text with further explanation that is relevant to the analysis but that is not so important to need discussion in the body of the article. Substantive footnotes can also provide readers with citations to other sources of information.

On the other hand, substantive footnotes can also be used to inform the reader that an issue or concept is outside the scope of the paper.[37] You may have been given exam-taking advice that if you spot an issue that does not merit a full analysis, you should identify the issue and briefly explain why you are not analyzing it. The same advice can be used here. Substantive footnotes that enable the reader to understand what you are not analyzing provides your reader with the confidence that you have thoroughly evaluated all the possible consequences and secondary issues raised in your paper and that you have intentionally limited the scope of your analysis. Footnotes that explain what your article is not focusing on can aid the reader even more if you include some sources where an interested reader can obtain further information.

Examples of substantive footnotes

Text of footnote	Technique
[7] My use of the words "woman" and "women" throughout this piece are intended to include transgender women, who may wish to induce lactation for a variety of reasons, and transgender men who choose to breastfeed (or "chestfeed" as some members of the transgender community prefer). Although not the focus of this Article, the unique challenges of the transgender population with regards to legal protection for breastfeeding should not be overlooked. Due to the relative rarity of transgender men breastfeeding and the stigmas associated with transgender people and breastfeeding, transgender men face unique challenges when deciding to breastfeed, including a lack of scientific knowledge and medical support, community support and acceptance, and legal protection, plus a possibility of personal confusion in terms of gender identity. *See* Trevor MacDonald et al., *Transmasculine Individuals' Experiences with Lactation, Chestfeeding, and Gender Identity: A Qualitative Study*, BMC PREGNANCY & CHILDBIRTH, May 16, 2016, at 15–16; Emily Wolfe-Roubatis & Diane L. Spatz, *Transgender Men and Lactation: What Nurses Need to Know*, 40 ACM AM. J. MATERNAL/CHILD NURSING, January/February 2015, at 32. Trans-women face unique problems as well. Typically, they must induce lactation through the use of medications. Very little scientific research has been done, however, to investigate the interaction between hormone treatment and the medications needed to induce lactation, so often this may be done at a risk. *See* Lindsey Bever, *How a Transgender Woman Breast-fed Her Baby*, WASH. POST (Feb. 15, 2018), https://www.washingtonpost.com/news/to-yourhealth/wp/2018/02/14/how-a-transgender-woman-breast-fed-her-baby/?utm_term=.3da2c431cd73 [https://perma.cc/DJ9Q-SHGY]. Also, trans-women often lack support from the medical community and the media, and as a result have a much harder time finding medical personnel willing to help. This works along with the common prejudice against trans-women, which can be exacerbated by breastfeeding efforts. *See* Trevor MacDonald, *Transgender Parents and Chest/Breastfeeding*, KELLYMOM.COM (Dec. 19, 2016).[38]	This footnote explains the author's inclusive use of the term "woman" and "women" as related to the discussion of lactation within the article. It goes on to discuss an important secondary consideration—some of the unique challenges that members of the transgender community face. The writer provides the caveat, however, that this issue is not the focus of the article. However, the writer's treatment of the importance of the issue enables the reader who may want to find out more about this issue the ability to locate additional sources relevant to this issue.
[11] There is a distinction to be made between breastfeeding, which is the physical act of feeding a child directly from the breast, and lactation, which is the formation and secretion of milk by the breast and is (most often) a physiological response to a recent pregnancy and/or birth. The laws discussed in this Article address both breastfeeding and lactation in different contexts, but for ease of description I am referring to the laws generally as "lactation laws." Although not the focus of this project, there are interesting arguments regarding the desirability of laws which encourage or enable the use of breast pumps to express breast milk at the expense of laws which directly support or enable breastfeeding. *See* Judith Galtry, *Extending the "Bright Line": Feminism, Breastfeeding, and the Workplace in the United States*, 14 GENDER & SOC'Y 295, 304 (2000) (discussing the potential drawbacks of focusing on breast milk expression as part of breastfeeding policy).	This footnote provides the reader with an important distinction between breastfeeding and lactation. It identifies a tangential issue but clarifies what the article does not do—i.e., the article will not go into a deeper discussion of laws that encourage the use of breast pumps at the expense of those that support breastfeeding. Lastly, in the event that the reader may be interested in that issue, the writer identifies an additional resource for the reader to consult.

Examples of substantive footnotes continued

Text of footnote	Technique
[15] *See* Marcia L. McCormick, *Gender, Family, and Work*, 30 HOFSTRA LAB. & EMP. L.J. 309, 331 (2013) ("Women and men are not necessarily similarly situated physically or socially when it comes to issues surrounding pregnancy, birth, or caring for a newborn. Thus, it is probably not a surprise that the laws that prohibit sex discrimination have not necessarily been considered to address discrimination against breastfeeding mothers or to require accommodation of breastfeeding."); L. Camille Hébert, *The Causal Relationship of Sex, Pregnancy, Lactation, and Breastfeeding and the Meaning of "Because of … Sex" Under Title VII*, 12 GEO J. GENDER & L. 119, 119 (2011) ("[T]here has been active resistance by some members [of the legal community] to the notion that action taken against women because of lactation, breastfeeding, or expressing milk, particularly in the context of the workplace, violates prohibitions against discrimination on the basis of sex or gender."); Derungs v. Wal-Mart Stores, Inc., 374 F.3d 428, 430 (6th Cir. 2004) (finding that "under the … Ohio Public Accommodation statute, restrictions on breast-feeding do not amount to discrimination based on sex….").[39]	This substantive footnote provides the reader with additional authorities that support the proposition. The explanatory parenthetical with relevant quotes provides the reader with specific examples of, and precise information about, the laws prohibiting sex discrimination that have been unavailing to women claiming legal protection for breastfeeding and lactation.
[21] Pregnancy Discrimination Act, 42 U.S.C.A. § 2000e(k) (2018) (stating that "[t]he terms 'because of sex' or 'on the basis of sex' include, but are not limited to, because of or on the basis of pregnancy, childbirth, or related medical conditions; and women affected by pregnancy, childbirth, or related medical conditions shall be treated the same for all employment-related purposes, including receipt of benefits under fringe benefit programs, as other persons not so affected but similar in their ability or inability to work.").[40]	The footnote expounds on the textual reference that most courts do not consider lactation "a related medical condition" under the Pregnancy Discrimination Act. The footnote enables the writer to add the relevant statutory language without having to use a block quote in the text, which some readers may skip over.
[35] *See* CTRS. FOR DISEASE CONTROL & PREVENTION, NATIONAL BREASTFEEDING REPORT CARD (2016). The report tracks five indicators: (1) never breastfed, (2) breastfeeding at six months, (3) breastfeeding at twelve months, (4) exclusive breastfeeding at three months, and (5) exclusive breastfeeding at six months.[41]	This footnote provides the reader with knowledge that the author's proposition about the resurgence of interest in breast-feeding is supported by data from a credible, governmental source. It further clarifies which indicators were considered in developing the data.

7.2.D The conclusion: Ending on a high note

One old adage for effective communication is, "First, tell the audience what you are going to tell them. Then tell them. Lastly, tell them what you told them."[42] The reason for this long-standing advice is that an audience needs a preview and a conclusion in addition to the main portion of the message. A clear conclusion helps the audience understand and retain the writer's message. This adage is especially true for scholarly writing because the audience may need to see complex legal ideas and any proposed solutions wrapped up clearly. While the conclusion should be short, it should summarize the writer's primary position and reiterate how the thesis has been proved, as well as why the ideas and any proposed solutions explored in the article are worth remembering.

Excerpt of a conclusion[43]

This Article has concentrated on facilitating the prosecution of offenders after they are identified. Absent a meaningful threat of criminal prosecution, inadequate deterrence to the crime exists. Also, allowing elder predators to escape prosecution enables them to more easily commit similar crimes against others.

As explained, a principal obstacle to both initiating and successfully completing criminal prosecutions is the difficulty of proving that asset transfers from an elder to an exploiter were the result of exploitation rather than consensual loans or gifts, even in circumstances that raise a strong inference of exploitation. The permissive statutory presumption proposal in this Article would provide a tool to assist prosecutors in scaling that hurdle. As detailed in Part III, such a presumption would be workable and constitutional.

Society is failing to protect one of our most precious and vulnerable resources from exploitation: the elders who nurtured, clothed, fed, taught, and raised us all. We cannot ignore them as "used up" or unneeded. We owe them all that we are. Not abandoning our elders to financial or other predators is a moral imperative. While much needs to be done, the statutory presumption proposal herein constitutes a feasible, economical, constitutional, available, and concrete step toward both providing justice for individual victims and deterring exploitation before it happens.

Notice how the author reminds the reader of the legal issues; summarizes his primary points, critiques, and proposals; and then ends the article with a compelling policy reason that leaves a lasting impression on the reader.

7.3 Crafting a memorable title

A memorable title can often make the difference in an article being read or passed over by a discerning reader. A memorable title will not only pique the reader's interest, but it may also affect whether a journal editor is interested enough to publish the article. One common technique is to start the title with an impact phrase, followed by a colon and details about the paper's thesis and solution. However, using short, descriptive titles as shown below tends to be the current trend.

Titles can be chosen in other ways as well. Titles can originate from pop culture, current events, literary allusions, plays on words, original puns, or even a clever use of contradictory statutes. On the following page are some examples of some memorable titles.

Examples of Memorable Titles

Type	Title	Technique
Short, descriptive title	Akhil Reed Amar, *Intratextualism*, 112 HARV. L. REV. 747 (1999).	Identifies a technique for constitutional interpretation.
Pop culture	Rebecca L. Scharf, *Game of Drones: Rolling the Dice with Unmanned Aerial Vehicles and Privacy*, 2018 UTAH L. REV. 457 (2018).	Play on words taken from a pop-culture television show, *Game of Thrones*.
Play on words	James L. Huffman, *Chicken Law in An Eggshell: Part III-A Dissenting Note*, 16 ENVTL. L. 761 (1986).	Play on words that gives a clue to content.
Clever	David A. Hoffman, *The Best Puffery Article Ever*, 91 IOWA L. REV. 1395 (2006).	Play on words and exaggeration.
Pun coupled with a substantive title	Brian Morris, *You've Got to Be Kidneying Me: The Fatal Problem of Severing Rights and Remedies from the Body of Organ Donation Law*, 74 BROOK. L. REV. 543 (2008).[44]	Uses humor but also identifies the legal problem succinctly.
Short, pointed title	Leti Volpp, *The Citizen and the Terrorist*, 49 UCLA L. REV. 1575 (2002).	The title uses irony to identify issues of racial and cultural profiling and citizen, nation, and identity.
Literary allusion coupled with substantive description	Robert Klonoff, *Application of the New Discovery Rules in Class Actions: Much Ado About Nothing*, 71 VAND. L. REV. 1949 (2018).	The title juxtaposes a civil procedure topic with reference to a Shakespearean play.

When possible, the title should also be sufficiently detailed so that the reader knows the crux of the legal issue being analyzed. Thus, you may consider adding information about the proposed solution in the title. For example, compare the titles set forth below:

- *Analyzing Prosecutorial Accountability*

    While this title tells the reader that the article will concern prosecutorial accountability, it does not provide enough specific information to tell the reader why he or she may be interested in reading the article.

- *Reporting for Duty: The Universal Prosecutorial Accountability Puzzle and an Experimental Transparency Alternative*[45]

    This title is more effective than the first because it explains the specific issue being analyzed along with a possible solution to the problem. While this title uses both a pun and a colon to spark interest, the description following the colon also makes it an effective title.

Often, finding the perfect title may be the hardest part of writing the article. You may want to consider a working title first and continue to review and revise it during the writing process. Indeed, writers become so punchy at times during the writing process that they come up with some truly creative or humorous titles.[46]

When deciding on a title, also consider how the title will look when shortened for a footnote. So, in reexamining the titles above, Scharf's *Game of Drones: Rolling the Dice with Unmanned Aerial Vehicles and Privacy* could be shortened to "Scharf, *Game of Drones*," which sounds timely and interesting. On the other hand, a student author needed to take special care when choosing the title of her article, *From Frisbees to Flatulence: Regulating Greenhouse Gases from Concentrated Animal Feeding Operations Under the Clean Air Act.*[47] If she had chosen a different arrangement of words such as, "From Flatulence to Frisbees," to catch the reader's attention, the shortened version, "[name], *Flatulence,*" would be far less sound.

7.4 Law review and journal membership and write-on competitions

After acceptance into law school, rumors abound about the importance of being selected to join the law review or a law journal.[48] The rumors are true. Being selected for law review membership is a boon with personal and professional benefits because becoming a member of a law review or law journal can enhance your reputation and your critical thinking and writing skills.

Legal education is unique in many ways, one of which is the operation of law schools' law journals, which are student-led publications. Most other social science disciplines, such as sociology or history, do not have student-run journals with the same professional prestige. So, unlike other social science students, law students frequently have an opportunity to critique and edit professors' submissions as well as write and publish their own work.[49]

Editing other scholars' work permits a student to learn about new legal topics, to see effective writing techniques in action, and to create scholarship that positively contributes to the development of the law.[50] Membership may also open doors to opportunities for summer clerkships or permanent employment with law firms, judges, nonprofit organizations, government entities, or even with the academy as a future law professor.[51]

Most law schools allow students the opportunity to join a law journal through grades or a combination of grades and performance on a student writing competition. In these competitions, generally termed as "writing on" to a law journal, students may not be required to select the topic or complete the background research for an article. Rather, similar to a closed-universe memo that students may draft in first-year legal research and writing classes, writing competition participants will likely receive a packet of information with a closed universe of materials that limit what they can use to write the article. Be sure to take the time to read and consider *all* of the materials provided.

Likewise, students should take heed of any specific formatting instructions provided. Because the competition will require writing the article, or a portion of an article, in a week or two, and because student editors will be evaluating the articles for the purpose of extending invitations to new journal members, there may be strict requirements for page limits, page numbering, font, and other basic formatting matters. Because competitors are often evaluated in part on the ability to follow directions, editors will likely penalize students who exceed the page requirement, use an incorrect font, or otherwise submit an article that is inconsistent with the instructions and formatting requirements.

In addition to analytic and writing abilities and the ability to follow directions, competitors are also evaluated on their attention to detail. Why? Law journal staff members will be expected to participate in cite checking and verifying source materials (sometimes called "spading" or "cite checking") for articles selected for publication. Editors are seeking individuals who can reliably complete these detail-oriented tasks. Thus, prospective law review members need to set aside time to properly proofread the submission and precisely and correctly use citations.

Where the assignment's focus is the impact of a newly decided case or recently enacted statute (both frequently used for "write-on" competitions), the organizational structure should be adapted to accommodate another section that will detail the particular case or statute (or other type of law) on which the author is focusing. This section may come either before or after the background, again depending on the topic and issue being critiqued. Below are two possible organizations for such an article:

Possible organizations for law review writing competition assignments

Organization 1	Organization 2
I. Introduction	I. Introduction
II. Background	II. Description of Case or Statute
III. Description of Case or Statute	III. Background
IV. Analysis	IV. Analysis
V. Conclusion	V. Conclusion

In the discussion of the case or statute (also referred to by some scholars as the "Statement of the Case"),[52] the following considerations should be included:

Considerations for drafting the analysis of a case or statute

For a case	For a statute or regulation
• The procedural history • The facts • The social or political history • The issues presented by the court, as well as the court's holding and reasoning • Any concurring or dissenting opinions • How the case affects the area of law generally, such as the position the case holds in the legal literature	• The relevant portion or portions of the text • The text and context of the statute or regulation, including the overall framework of the statutory or regulatory title or chapter • The purpose of the statute or regulation, along with any relevant legislative history or societal, policy, or political factors • Any landmark cases that have interpreted the statute or may have triggered the statute's creation (i.e., a controversial case that the legislature intends to remedy by enacting a statute) • How the statute or regulation affects the area of law generally

Within each component of the article, you can break down that component into sections or subsections. Each section or subsection should be identified through descriptive point headings. Notice how the descriptive point headings in the following example give the reader context and break up what would be a long section.

Excerpt of a Statement of the Case

The Case: *Kentucky v. King*[53]

A. The Facts

... **King was charged with trafficking a controlled substance, possession of marijuana, and being a persistent felony offender.** The trial court denied his motion to suppress the evidence found during the warrantless search on the basis that exigent circumstances justified the warrantless entry. King appealed the denial of his motion to suppress.... The state intermediate appellate court affirmed the ruling of the trial court.

Here, the author clearly breaks down the components of the case at issue. The author starts first with the facts of the case.

B. The Kentucky Supreme Court Decision

The Kentucky Supreme Court reversed, finding that the police created the exigent circumstances on which they relied to justify the search. In reaching this conclusion, the court determined that it was reasonably foreseeable that "knocking on the apartment door and announcing 'police' after having smelled marijuana emanating from the apartment, would create the exigent circumstance relied upon, i.e. destruction of evidence.".…

The author discusses in detail the procedural history of the case through litigation and appeal.

C. The United States Supreme Court Decision

1. The Majority Opinion

The Supreme Court granted the Commonwealth's petition for certiorari and reversed the decision of the Kentucky Supreme Court. The Court held that "the

The author discusses all the relevant parts of the case, including concurring and dissenting opinions.

exigent circumstances rule applies when the police do not gain entry to [the] premises by means of an actual or threatened violation of the Fourth Amendment."....

2. The Dissenting Opinion

Justice Ginsburg, the lone dissenter, opposed the majority's adoption of such a lenient standard. She called the decision a "reduction of the Fourth Amendment's force" and believed that the decision would provide officers with a way to routinely dishonor the warrant requirement in drug cases....

A good place to start in the analysis for this type of article is to critically ask the following questions:

- *Who* or *what* is affected by this decision and legislation;
- *How* the decision or legislation affects certain individuals or institutions; and
- *Why* the decision or legislation affects certain individuals or institutions.[54]

The answers to these questions may help you understand a deeper basis for the critique. Then focus on whether historical, social science, scientific, or other reasons are at play. The most interesting part of this type of article is typically the process of uncovering any outside influences that might have played a role in the court's decision or attempting to connect the decision to a larger motive.

In conclusion, learning to write is a lifelong process, and the genre of scholarly writing can enhance and refine the skills you already have. Just as when learning any other kind of writing, for each new genre, you will need to learn the relevant norms, vocabulary, and style. As discussed in Chapter 4, *Developing Critical Legal Analysis*, one of the most effective paths to learning how to write effectively in a new genre is to read that genre. So, read as many law review and law journal articles as you can. Read these works critically, using the suggestions recommended in Chapter 4. If you do so, you will begin to recognize differences in quality and to integrate the relevant norms, vocabulary, and style. Developing these skills, in turn, will help you to produce the type of scholarship that can better serve society.

For additional information on writing law review and law journal articles, consider consulting these resources:

JESSICA L. CLARK & KRISTEN E. MURRAY, SCHOLARLY WRITING: IDEAS, EXAMPLES, AND EXECUTION (3d ed. 2019).

ELIZABETH FAJANS & MARY R. FALK, SCHOLARLY WRITING FOR LAW STUDENTS: SEMINAR PAPERS, LAW REVIEW NOTES AND LAW COMPETITION PAPERS (5th ed. 2017).

WES HENRICKSEN, MAKING LAW REVIEW: A GUIDE TO THE WRITE-ON COMPETITION (2d ed. 2017).

EUGENE VOLOKH, ACADEMIC LEGAL WRITING: LAW REVIEW ARTICLES, STUDENT NOTES, SEMINAR PAPERS AND GETTING ON LAW REVIEW (5th ed. 2016).

Richard Delgado, *How to Write a Law Review Article*, 20 U.S.F. L. REV. 445, 448 (1986).

Notes

1. Harry T. Edwards, *Another Look at Professor Rodell's Goodbye to Law Reviews*, 100 Va. L. Rev. 1483, 1499 (2014). We would like to thank Professors Laura Graham and Russell Gold, Wake Forest University School of Law, and Professor Brian Larson, Texas A&M School of Law, for their excellent insights and helpful comments on this chapter.

2. *See generally* Angela J. Campbell, *Teaching Advanced Legal Writing in a Law School Clinic*, 24 Seton Hall L. Rev 653 (1993) (relying on Richard K. Neumann, Jr., Legal Reasoning and Legal Writing 48 (1990)).

3. *See* Orin S. Kerr, *The Influence of Immanuel Kant on Evidentiary Approaches in 18th Century Bulgaria*, 18 Green Bag 2D 251, 251 (2015) (citing Interview with Chief Justice of the United States John G. Roberts, Jr., at Fourth Circuit Court of Appeals Annual Conference (June 25, 2011)).

4. Edwards, *supra*, at 1499.

5. *Id.*

6. *See* Richard Delgado, *How to Write a Law Review Article*, 20 U.S.F. L. Rev. 445, 448 (1986); Kevin Hopkins, *Cultivating our Emerging Voices: The Road to Scholarship*, 20 B.C. Third World L. J. 77, 83 (2000); Andrew Yaphe, *Taking Note of Notes: Student Legal Scholarship in Theory and Practice*, 62 J.L. Educ. 259, 296–97 (2012).

7. The Bluebook: A Uniform System of Citation R. 16.7.1, at 165 (Columbia Law Review Ass'n et al. eds., 20th ed. 2015).

8. Adapted from Delgado, *supra*, at 446–48.

9. Adapted from Patrick Eoghan Murray, *Write On! A Guide to Getting on Law Review* (Apr. 12, 2014) (unpublished comment).

10. *See* J.M. Swales, Genre Analysis: English in Academic and Research Settings (Cambridge University Press 1990); J.M. Swales, Research Genres: Exploration and Applications (Cambridge University Press 2004).

11. This quote is attributed to Walt Disney but was reportedly crafted by Disney employee Tom Fitzgerald.

12. UW Madison Writing Center, *Introductions*, writing.wisc.edu (last visited Apr. 10, 2019).

13. Albert Camus, The Rebel: An Essay on Man in Revolt 285 (Anthony Bower trans., 1956).

14. Andrew Jay McClurg, *Preying on the Graying: A Statutory Presumption to Prosecute Elder Financial Abuse*, 65 Hastings L. J. 1099, 1103–05 (2014).

15. *Id.*

16. *See* Unending Conversation, Kairos.technorhetoric.net (last visited December 18, 2019).

17. Interview with Brian Larson, Associate Professor of Law, Texas A&M Law School (July 15, 2019) [hereinafter "Larson Interview"].

18. *See* Student Writing, *The Writing Process*, NYU Law, law.nyu.edu; *see also* Eugene Volokh, Academic Legal Writing: Law Review Articles, Student Notes, Seminar Papers and Getting on Law Review 217 (3d ed. 2007); Jonathan Burns, *How to Write a Law Review Note Worthy of Publication: Writing the Note*, Girl's Guide to L. Sch. (July 11, 2014).

19. Larson Interview, *supra.*

20. *See* McClurg, *supra*, at 1122–24.

21. *See* Richard A. Posner, *The Decline of Law as an Autonomous Discipline: 1962– 1987*, 100 Harv. L. Rev. 761, 766–77 (1987); Bailey Kuklin & Jeffrey W. Stempel, Foundations of the Law: An Interdisciplinary and Jurisprudential Primer

139 (1994) (quoting Anthony Sebok, Introduction to Philosophy of Law: Jurisprudence at ix (Jules L. Coleman ed., 1994)).

22. Posner, *supra*, at 766–77.

23. Larson Interview, *supra*.

24. As Professor Brian Larson told us: "Of course, it is possible to criticize the frame from the perspective of another frame, but this is usually a more advanced technique. Critical folks have certainly done that to the law and economics frame. You really need to know two theories [] very well to pit them against each other." Larson Interview, *supra*.

25. *Id.*

26. *Sociological Jurisprudence*, Black's Law Dictionary (10th ed. 2014).

27. Allen F. Repko, Interdisciplinary Research: Theory and Process 142 (2008).

28. Adapted from *id.*

29. *See generally* Stephen E. Toulmin, The Uses of Argument (Cambridge Univ. Press 2003).

30. Russell M. Gold, *"Clientless" Lawyers*, 92 Wash. L. Rev. 87 (2017).

31. *Id.* at 89–90.

32. Brian N. Larson, *Law's Enterprise: Argumentation Schemes and Legal Analogy*, 87 U. of Cinn. L. Rev. 663, 692 (2019).

33. *Id.*

34. Meghan Boone, *Lactation Law*, 106 Calif. L. Rev. 1827, 1830–31 (2018).

35. Delgado, *supra*, at 447.

36. While substantive footnotes are widely used in law review and law journal articles, this practice has also been criticized. *See, e.g.*, Joan Ames Magat, *Bottomheavy: Legal Footnotes*, 60 J. Leg. Ed. 65–105 (2010).

37. For an excellent discussion of footnotes in scholarly writing, see Jessica L. Clark & Kristen E. Murray, Scholarly Writing: Ideas, Examples, and Execution 90–94 (2d ed. 2012).

38. Boone, *supra*, at 1829–30 n.7.

39. *Id.* at 1832 n.15.

40. *Id.* at 1833 n.21.

41. *Id.* at 1835 n.35.

42. *See* Burns, *supra*.

43. McClurg, *supra*, at 1143.

44. Adapted from Kevin Underhill, *Law Review Article Titles: Stop the Madness*, Lowering the Bar (July 27, 2009).

45. Marc L. Miller & Ron F. Wright, *Reporting for Duty: The Universal Prosecutorial Accountability Puzzle and an Experimental Transparency Alternative, in* The Prosecutor in Transnational Perspective, 392–407 (Erik Luna and Marianne Wade eds., 2012).

46. According to Professor Andrew McClurg's site, Lawhaha.com, the winner for the best name for a law review article is Erik S. Jaffe, *"She's Got Bette Davis['s] Eyes": Assessing the Nonconsensual Removal of Cadaver Organs Under the Takings and Due Process Clauses*, 90 Colum. L. Rev. 528 (1990). *See* Andrew Jay McClurg, *Best Law Review Article Title*, Lawhaha.com (Nov. 25, 2011).

47. C. Steven Bradford, *As I Lay Writing: How to Write Law Review Articles for Fun and Profit: A Law-and-Economics, Critical, Hermeneutical, Policy Approach and Lots of Other Stuff that Thousands of Readers Will Find Really Interesting and Therefore You Ought to Publish in Your Prestigious, Top-Ten, Totally Excellent Law Review*, 44 J. Legal Edu. 13 (1994).

48. Law schools generally have one official law review and, perhaps, additional specialty law journals that focus on certain topics such as health law, animal law, or intellectual property. For ease of reference and inclusion, the entire group of publications are referred to as "law journals."

49. Andrew Yaphe, *Taking Note of Notes: Student Legal Scholarship in Theory and Practice*, 62 J. Legal Educ. 259 (2012).

50. Remember, the rewards of engaging in legal scholarship are not limited to law journal work—any law student can engage in and reap the benefits of the scholarly writing experience. Students can write a law journal article and submit it for publication regardless of whether they are a member of the journal. Students also can participate in seminar courses, capstone courses, and independent studies that have law journal or similar types of papers that serve as a final work product for academic credit. *See* Chapter 8, *Seminar Papers and Capstone Projects*, for more details.

51. Wes Henricksen, Making Law Review: A Guide to the Write-On Competition 3 (2d ed. 2017).

52. Elizabeth Fajans & Mary R. Falk, Scholarly Writing for Law Students: Seminar Papers, Law Review Notes and Law Competition Papers 72 (4th ed. 2011).

53. Elizabeth Sargeant, Note, Kentucky v. King: *The One Where the Supreme Court Dishonors the Warrant Requirement in Drug Cases*, 47 Wake Forest L. Rev. 1269, 1270–72 (2012).

54. Fajans & Falk, *supra*, at 9–11; Volokh, *supra*, at 25–26.

Chapter 8

Seminar Papers and Capstone Projects

8.1   Seminar papers generally

8.2   Capstones generally

8.3   Audience expectations

8.4   Traditional seminar papers and capstones

8.5   Less traditional forms of seminar papers and capstones

When taking a seminar class or participating in a capstone project, you may be assigned to write one or more academic papers. These academic papers can be interesting (and even fun) to write because they allow students to explore and expound on a legal topic, sometimes in a non-traditional form. As an added bonus, for many of these classes, the paper becomes the final work product in lieu of a comprehensive exam. Sometimes, though, these papers can be challenging to write because their substance and form can vary widely from course to course. Because the expectations for these papers can vary, make sure you understand both the parameters of the assignment and the professor's requirements. This chapter explains the basic format for traditional and non-traditional seminar papers and capstone projects, examines the typical components of each type of paper, and provides strategies for constructing an effective paper.[1]

8.1 Seminar papers generally

Seminar classes are often very different from standard doctrinal classes. They may cover broad topics, like rhetoric, or take a deep look into a narrower topic, like renewable energy law. Seminars may be more relaxed, and the format may focus on conversation, rather than the Socratic method, as the primary mode of discussion. Likewise, a seminar paper may also differ from traditional scholarly writing in both substance and structure. A seminar paper might be a shorter version of a scholarly article, or it might be an analytical paper more akin to the term or research papers assigned in undergraduate courses. No matter the class's style or the paper's format, the seminar paper will still require the same analysis of legal concepts present in other kinds of legal scholarship.

The goal of a seminar paper, at its core, is to find and analyze some area of conflict in the law and present that conflict in a concise, thoughtful way that showcases the writer's own ideas and conclusions about the topic. The paper should consider possible ways to resolve the legal conflict and select the best potential resolution.

8.2 Capstones generally

Many law schools require students to complete an upper-division writing requirement[2] called a capstone paper or capstone project, commonly referred to as simply a "capstone." A capstone is usually meant to be a crowning research and writing experience, often completed during the final year of law school. A capstone can stem from a course, or it might be a freestanding independent study. Sometimes, these types of projects are also called "thesis" projects. While the names and requirements of capstones vary among educational institutions, the hallmark features of most capstones are the requirements of extensive research, sophisticated critical thinking, and clear written analysis.

Capstones come in many formats. In some schools, only a formal paper styled as a scholarly article will satisfy the requirement. Other schools may be more flexible, expanding the options to include other types of writings like legal handbooks, annotated briefs, or compilations (such as a series of essays) on related topics. No matter the vehicle for a capstone, the work should demonstrate that the writer has thoroughly researched the topic and drawn out the complexities and nuances of the analysis.

The timelines for capstones may also vary. A project may span one or two semesters, again depending on a particular law school's requirements and the supervising professor's preferences. Because capstones usually require several months of intensive work, the topic should captivate your attention and, when possible, use a format that works with your skills, strengths, and interests.

8.3 Audience expectations

The first step for any seminar paper or capstone (and actually, for any writing) is to understand the audience's expectations. Identifying that audience and its needs will help focus the research, analysis, and discussion.[3] As with other kinds of law school assignments, the paper will have a primary audience (the professor or advisor and reading committee) and possibly a secondary audience (the person or groups to whom the writer is directing the substantive content).

First, understand the assigning professor's goals for the substantive content and parameters of the assignment, including the structure, length, and format of that content.[4] Clarify whether the professor will focus on substantive content, technical writing skills, or both. Further, clarify whether the professor wants a scholarly analysis, a practical document such as a brief or a pleading, or an instructive document like a handbook that surveys the law or a legal process. For example, one professor may want an extensive discussion in the format of a law review article. Another professor may want a detailed substantive discussion of elder law but allow the student to choose which form is used to convey that discussion. Understanding the project's goals and parameters can help you ensure that your work is on target with your professor's expectations.

As with any academic or professional scholarship, a paper may flow more easily if you focus on the secondary audience to whom the substantive content is directed.[5] For example, a seminar paper explaining the legal problems with non-unanimous juries will be directed primarily to the professor but may also be directed to practitioners, judges, or state representatives as a secondary audience. Consider what that audience needs to know and how the audience can best understand the analysis in the paper.

8.4 Traditional seminar papers and capstones

As with other scholarly formats, a traditional seminar or capstone requires an in-depth examination, analysis, and critique of a particular legal topic. While these types of papers are often akin to the types of scholarly articles discussed in Chapter 7, *Law Review and Law Journal Articles*, they may provide a little more room for creative flair.

The general structure of a traditional seminar or capstone paper can vary from a basic paper with only an introduction, body, and conclusion to a paper that mirrors the style of a formal law review article with distinct sections like a table of contents, introduction, background, analysis, and conclusion. The professor's guidelines will determine the specific sections a seminar paper should include. For instance, while seminar and capstone papers typically range from twenty-five to fifty pages of polished work, some professors may want more or less analysis depending upon their own curricular objectives or the academic credits the paper needs to satisfy.

Like a law review article, the goal of a traditional seminar paper or capstone is to highlight the writer's own thinking regarding a particular problem. Thus, you will strive either to say something new or to cast a fresh perspective on a longstanding topic. Most of the time, a paper that is merely descriptive, that is, one that merely describes a legal problem without analyzing the consequences or proposing solutions, will not satisfy the project's requirements. (You may want to review the discussion explaining the difference between description and analysis, as well as which to use when, in Chapter 4, *Developing Critical Legal Analysis*.) As you read the following sections of this chapter, keep in mind that bringing your own thoughts and ideas to the paper may be a critical part of your grade.

8.4.A Components of a traditional seminar paper or capstone

When tackling a traditional seminar paper or capstone, a good structural formula (often dictated by a professor's required structure or components) is vital to getting started. The example below illustrates the components of the two primary formats of traditional seminar papers or capstones: the "scholarly article" format and the "typical essay" format.

The basic components of a traditional seminar paper or capstone

Scholarly Article Format	Typical Essay Format
I. Introduction II. Background and development III. Analysis and recommendations IV. Conclusion	I. Introduction II. Analysis of topic III. Conclusion

8.4.B Introduction

The introduction for a traditional seminar paper or capstone equates to the introduction section of other forms of scholarly legal papers in many ways. First, the introduction should grab the reader's attention, convincing the reader that the paper is worth reading. Usually, good topics involve conflict — conflict among laws, the people to whom those laws apply, or even groups of people who want diametrically opposed laws. (For strategies on how to find a suitable topic, review Chapter 1, *Exploring Topics and Establishing Goals.*)

What is a précis?

Some professors may ask you to complete a précis — that is, a summary or abstract of your article. The précis is more than just an outline of your work; instead it should be a synopsis of your thesis and the main points supporting your arguments. Make sure to understand what your supervising professor expects in the précis. Your introduction section may fulfill those requirements or may at least be adapted to meet the expectations. You might also review the guidelines for creating an abstract, explained in Chapter 14, *Submitting and Publishing Your Work.*

An effective introduction will quickly plunge the reader into the heart of the conflict and convince the reader to care about the topic. One good guiding principle is that the introduction should be "compelling enough to draw us in, [and] make us want to know more."[6] Accordingly, consider different techniques that will pull the reader in quickly. For example, consider linking the topic to current events, using a real or hypothetical example of the problem created by the topic, or posing the paper's question directly to the reader at the outset. When catching the reader's attention, also think about how to make the topic resonate with a reader who might not initially understand the topic's importance. (Chapter 7, *Law Review and Law Journal Articles,* also provides a more detailed explanation and examples of introductory techniques.) If the topic resonates with the reader, the reader will likely care enough to keep reading. In the table below, notice how the writers use varying narrative techniques to draw out the conflict while pulling the reader into the work.

Examples of an introduction's opening paragraph

Topic, Title, and Type	Introduction: Opening Paragraph	Technique
Topic: Effective use of classical rhetorical techniques **Title:** *John Roberts's Use of a Dog in a Plane and a Canary in a Mineshaft to Evince Intelligence and Establish Ethos in Alaska v. EPA*[7] **Type:** Traditional Seminar Essay	When John Roberts was a brief-writing lawyer, at least one United States Supreme Court Justice described John Roberts's brief representing the State of Alaska Department of Environmental Conservation as probably the "best brief" the judges on the Supreme Court had seen. In legal writing, credibility is the currency of the writer. As defined in classical rhetoric, the writer's ability to establish credibility, or ethos, in the eyes of the audience is a key component of persuasion. This credibility, this ethos, lays the foundation to other persuasive techniques and thus plays an essential part in the effectiveness of the writer's work. Professor Michael R. Smith has identified eleven "traits of intelligence" that evince credibility. Although writers often try to evince credibility in their work, including all eleven traits of intelligence is not easy. With his brief, Chief Justice Roberts evinces credibility in his work by demonstrating mastery of all eleven traits.[8]	The writer also catches the reader's attention with an interesting and relevant anecdote about the Chief Justice of the Supreme Court.
Topic: Aid in dying legislation **Title:** *Right to Die in California and Beyond: Constructing a Model for the Future*[9] **Type:** Traditional Seminar Scholarly Article	Death, be not proud, though some have called thee Mighty and dreadful, for thou art not so; For those whom thou think'st thou dost overthrow Die not, poor Death, nor yet canst thou kill me. From rest and sleep, which but thy pictures be, Much pleasure; then from thee much more must flow; And soonest our best men with thee do go, Rest of their bones, and soul's delivery. Thou art slave to Fate, chance, kings, and desperate men, And dost with poison, war, and sickness dwell, And poppy or charms can make us sleep as well And better than thy stroke; why swell'st thou then? One short sleep past, we wake eternally And death shall be no more; Death, thou shalt die. — John Donne In one of his most famous sonnets, John Donne wrestled with the surety of facing death and rejected the notion that it is something to fear, for his soul's eternal life would in fact bring death to its own fateful end. This resounding theme of facing death has reverberated throughout history, as every human will come to meet this imminent end.… As the causes of death have changed, society's view on the matter—particularly the way in which one should die—have followed a similar trajectory.	The author begins the paper with a creative flair by using a poetic viewpoint to frame the underlying legal question.

Examples of an introduction's opening paragraph continued

Topic: Creating a cause of action for revenge porn **Title:** *Eradicating Revenge Porn: Intimate Images as Personal Identifying Information*[10] **Type:** Traditional Capstone Paper	When Annmarie Chiarini's possessive boyfriend accused her of sleeping with other men, she tried to reason with him. Instead of believing her assurances of fidelity, he threatened her; if she would not reveal how many men she was sleeping with, he would auction online the naked images he had of her and send links to her family and friends. She had finally let him take the pictures after months of pressure. He followed through on his threat, sending the images to her ex-husband, her babysitter, and her work colleagues. He posted the material on Facebook pages associated with the college where Annmarie taught. At first, she was able to remove the auction and Facebook content, but more than a year later her pictures appeared on a porn site alongside her name and place of work. Due to the perpetrator's chosen method of dissemination, the Internet, Annmarie feared that the "torture was never going to end." Revenge porn, also known as nonconsensual pornography, refers to the display and dissemination of an individual's sexually explicit images without her consent. Efforts to eradicate the crime have met with limited success due to the serious shortcomings of existing remedies.[11]	Here, the author introduces the problem with an interesting and true story.
Topic: Constructing a framework to consider how remains of the dead can be legally and ethically used in medical research. **Title:** *The Law and Ethics of Using the Dead in Research*[12] **Type:** Thesis for joint JD/MA degree	85.8. That is my life expectancy. As of today, I am expected to die when I am 85.8 years old. 100%. That is my death expectancy. As of today, I am expected to die. Indeed, my chance of dying is 100%, and 100% of us have this same death expectancy. Of course, my life expectancy is an estimate. Further, it is continuously affected by a myriad of factors, some within my control and some beyond it. Furthermore, as I age, my life expectancy will correspondingly increase — from 88 by age 62 to 89.5 by age 70. But my death expectancy never changes. Studies say that I have an estimated 0.89% chance of dying in a car accident, 3.4% chance of dying from a chronic lower respiratory disease, and a little more than 14% chance of dying from heart disease or cancer. Still, I have a 100% chance of dying. We all do. But what will happen when I die? Beyond the philosophical questions is an indisputable fact: some part of me — my body or the parts or even information therefrom — will remain. But the questions persist. To whom do my remains belong? What rights do I have today in my future remains? Will I have any interest in my own remains after I have died?[13]	The writer uses statistics contrasting life and death expectancy to highlight that the issue of what happens with bodily remains is an issue for all of us to face.

Another goal of the introduction is to concretely identify the crux of the conflict being explored and why that argument is important. In identifying the problem, include enough contextual description so that a reader — even one who is unfamiliar with the topic — can understand the thesis and the main analytical points supporting that thesis. Contextual information in the introduction may include defining key terms and concepts, providing examples that illustrate the issue or problem, and explaining the legal significance of the topic. In the excerpts below, the writers identify the conflict and provide sufficient contextual information so that the reader can see the crux of the problem and how the writers believe it should be solved.

Ways to establish the thesis within the introduction

The thesis paragraph	What it does
Paper: *Right to Die in California and Beyond: Constructing a Model for the Future*[14] Extended life expectancies have given rise to not only more extensive end of life medical intervention but also a growing movement empowering individuals to choose when and how their lives should end. European nations, particularly the Netherlands and Switzerland, have been at the forefront of legalizing assisted suicide.... Such cross-cultural analysis supports the proposition that the California's new assisted suicide law (the End of Life Option Act) should serve as a model for other U.S. jurisdictions seeking to adopt similar legislation because the ELOA's safeguards mitigate the concerns raised by critics of physician-assisted suicide, while also approbating an individual's autonomy and fundamental right to determine his or her own destiny.	This paragraph sets out the author's points and general thesis, specifically, that the California's End of Life Option Act legislation should be a model for other states.
Paper: *Eradicating Revenge Porn: Intimate Images as Personal Identifying Information*[15] Although the Supreme Court has greatly limited the privacy rights of victims of sexual abuse, information privacy laws show promise for revenge porn victims. Under the umbrella of information privacy, personal identifying information is afforded strong privacy protection—without running afoul of the First Amendment. This Paper advocates the treatment of intimate images as personal identifying information. .... Amid a surge in revenge porn, victims, advocates, and legislators are attempting to find the best remedy, or combination of remedies, to protect victims and redress the harms they suffer. To adequately address revenge porn, legislators must consider the Internet's ability to magnify the dissemination of the images and create a permanent record of the betrayal, thus intensifying the psychological and reputational harm suffered. This may require "that old doctrines be modified to account for this new harm," as occurred in the context of information privacy law. Because the Internet can amplify the audience and create an enduring record of the injury, legislatures, advocates, and courts should treat the sharing of intimate images no differently than the sharing of personal identifying information, which is afforded increasingly robust protection in the face of technological innovation.	The writer directly explains the crux of the legal problem and shows why, given the rapid advances in technology, this "new harm" will require that legal doctrines be modified to protect victims of revenge porn.

Finally, similar to a law journal article, the introduction section should also act like a roadmap of the paper, detailing the parts of the paper, the main points of the paper, and the order in which those points will be presented. Generally, the roadmap paragraph is found in the final paragraphs of the introduction section. In the table below, the writers create a roadmap for the reader, establishing the organization of the paper and the order of the general points in the paper.

Roadmaps

Roadmap for a seminar paper[16]	
In the brief, Roberts demonstrates his intelligence through a variety of different methods. First, Roberts demonstrates through his structural decisions that he is organized, informed, and deliberate. Second, Roberts demonstrates through the substance of his arguments that he is analytical, practical, and empathetic to the reader. Third, Roberts demonstrates through his stylistic choices that he is eloquent and innovative. Finally, Roberts demonstrates through his subtle highlighting techniques that he is detail-oriented and adept at legal research. Through each of these purposeful choices, Roberts positions himself as a capable and authoritative source of information for the reader, which in turn makes his brief much more persuasive. Thus, in his brief in *Alaska v. EPA*, John Roberts adeptly illustrates how to use Smith's eleven traits to establish ethos.	In this section, the author establishes a roadmap showing the main points and sub-points and the order in which those ideas will be presented. The author briefly indicates how the writer demonstrates the eleven traits of intelligence and previews how those traits will be grouped and explained.
Roadmap for a capstone paper[17]	
Part II of this Paper discusses remedies available through copyright, tort, and criminal law as well as the benefits and shortcomings of each. Part III considers the limitations the First Amendment imposes on the remedies discussed in Part II. Part IV analyzes the Supreme Court case of *Florida Star*, which greatly limited privacy torts in the face of First Amendment concerns. Part V argues that the rationale underlying information privacy laws—to protect privacy in the face of technological innovation to foster a society in which all members may participate—applies equally to intimate images.	This paragraph follows the traditional format typically seen in a law journal article. The paragraph again acts as a roadmap, alerting the reader to the main ideas each part of the paper will explore.
Roadmap for a capstone thesis project[18]	
Chapter I, Death and the Dead, provides a brief introduction to death itself. Specifically, it (a) analyzes the biological, social, and psychological functions of death, (b) assesses the definitions of death throughout human history, with an emphasis on the modern re-definition of death, and (c) explores the posthumous treatment of the dead, with an emphasis on the American way of death. Chapter II, Using the Dead and Their Remains in Research, assesses the use of the dead and their remains in research. Specifically, it (a) explores historical uses and controversies, with an emphasis on Judeo-Christian concepts of a literal resurrection and the dreaded "Resurrection Men," and assesses modern uses and controversies such as (b) practicing medical procedures on the dead, (c) using the dead in educational exhibitions such as the infamous BODY WORLDS, and (d) using the dead in researching and developing products such as cars, firearms, and body armor. Finally, it (e) analyzes alternatives to cadavers for use in research. Chapter III, The Law of the Dead, discusses the current legal framework (or lack thereof) in the United States with an emphasis on the problematic quasi-property status of the dead and their remains, the potential for alternative legal rights in and of the dead and their remains, and the issue of to whom such property and rights belong. Specifically, Chapter III assesses (a) the living's present rights in their own future remains, (b) the living's present rights in another's current remains, and (c) even the possibility of the dead's rights in their own "present" remains. Chapter IV, A Call for Change in the Law of Using the Dead in Research, calls for clarification of the law, regulation, and policy surrounding the use of the dead and their remains in medical research, as well as a change in perspective within the medical and ethics communities and our death-denying culture as a whole.	Because this project is a lengthy capstone project in the form a master's thesis, the writer sets forth the roadmap in multiple paragraphs, each of which correspond to a different chapter of the paper. Note that the author sets forth the name of the chapter in the reference.

8.4.C Background

Interesting topics typically involve a conflict. Thus, the next section, the background, will explain the conflict at the heart of the seminar paper, noting what caused the conflict, how that conflict developed over time, and how the conflict is relevant. An effective background section helps a reader understand how the specific topic fits into the broader legal field, as well as how the specific conflict at the heart of the issue arose.

The background should give the reader, even someone who is not trained in the law, enough information to understand the origin of the legal issue. In addition, the background should also give the reader any information that will be needed to understand the writer's thesis and main arguments in the analysis section that follows. In determining how much background information to include, the writer must discern what information is truly necessary for a reader to understand the analysis. Attempting to explain the background of the entire legal field surrounding the topic will confuse the reader and needlessly lengthen the paper. For example, in the excerpt below, the writer strives to condense the most salient information into a concise and accurate description.

A background section for a traditional seminar paper[19]

B. The American approach to the Right to Die

Even though our European sister nations have been at the forefront of legalizing assisted suicide practices since the mid and late twentieth century, discussion of right to die laws have been part of the conversation in the United States since the early 1900s. Two bills, called the "chloroform bills," were introduced in the legislatures of Iowa and Ohio in 1906 and proposed the idea that "physicians should be able to 'painlessly part incurable from this world' by administering to them a lethal dose of chloroform."

....

One fundamental case that served as a cornerstone for many of these right to die challenges was *Cruzan v. Director, Missouri Department of Health*. In *Cruzan*, the parents of Nancy Cruzan, a woman who was in a persistent vegetative state following injuries sustained in a severe car accident, wished to terminate their daughter's life-sustaining medical treatment, but the hospital employees refused to carry out this request because it would result in Cruzan's death. The U.S. Supreme Court held that the Fourteenth Amendment's Due Process Clause protects a competent individual's "liberty interest in refusing unwanted medical treatment."

....

Several years following the Cruzan case, the U.S. Supreme Court granted certiorari to two companion cases, *Washington v. Glucksberg* and *Vacco v. Quill*, and faced the right to die issue directly, thereby defining the Court's view on the matter. "[A]s illustrated in *Vacco* and *Glucksberg*, the states, by way of the Tenth Amendment, also have a right to legalize such practices through legislation. Hence, assisted suicide advocates then turned their efforts to state legislative bodies to implement

The author uses a descriptive phrase for the background rather than labelling the section "Background." This wording provides the reader further context.

In this seminar paper, the author establishes current approaches to the right-to-die legislation used in other jurisdictions.

Although an essay-style seminar paper might not include a full literature review or as in-depth of a background section as discussed in Chapter 7, *Law Review and Law Journal Articles*, writers should include whatever background the reader will need to understand the analysis of the legal problem or topic.

change." In 1997 Oregon became the first state to enact an assisted suicide statute, the Death with Dignity Act ("DDA"). Since Oregon's trailblazing legislation was enacted, Washington, Montana, and Vermont have also adopted similar statutes. California is the most recent state to legalize physician-assisted suicide.

The length of the background section will vary depending on the topic and the depth and breadth of material the reader needs to understand before the analysis begins. The background section may even be broken into multiple subsections. Typically, the background section should not be more than one-third of the paper's overall length. One way to keep the background section manageable is to focus only on the most pertinent background pieces the reader will need to understand the thesis. For example, in the next excerpt taken from a traditional capstone paper on the use of the "reasonable person" standard in federal jury trials of Native American people, the author needed to include background information on several areas of law before she could analyze how those laws should change. Accordingly, notice both the multiple parts of the background and how the descriptive sub-headings alone can help the reader gain context:

Tip:

Remember to always consult the guidelines or instructions for your specific project because those parameters may vary from the more general guidelines set forth here.

> II. BACKGROUND
>   A. American Indian Statistics
>   B. Historical Trauma
>   1. American Indian genocide
>   2. Colonization and boarding schools
>   C. Trauma Affects Cognition, Emotional Control, and Reasoning
>   D. Acculturation and Effects on American Indian Health[20]

Although the background section should give the reader enough information to understand the crux of the problem and how the problem originated, take care that it does not overwhelm the reader with too much detail or unnecessary length.

If the parameters of the assignment do not require a background section, you will still need to include some general background or context about the conflict in either the introduction or the analysis section.

8.4.D Analysis

The analysis showcases *the writer's* thinking and opinion on what complexities, tensions, connections, nuances, or obstacles exist and how those problems should be resolved. It should include the specific analytical arguments that support the thesis along with any opposing arguments that contradict the thesis. The analysis section should also identify any solutions that would solve the problem.

While the analysis section in a seminar or capstone paper might have a more conversational tone than that of a scholarly article, it should be written in an objective voice, with the goal of persuading the reader that the thesis is correct. (As with any academic paper, however, let the assigning professor's instructions and preferences guide the tone, always adjusting the formality of the tone to suit both your primary and secondary audience.) In the following two samples, the authors include their own critical thinking about the topics. The differences in tone and mechanical style are evident, so notice the first paper's conversational tone and essay-type structure compared to the more traditional, formal tone and structure of the second paper.

Differences in tone and style

Less formal essay structure and tone	Throughout his brief, Roberts makes deliberate stylistic choices that effectively present Roberts as a much more authoritative source on technical jargon than he might otherwise have been perceived to be. The first stylistic technique that jumps out at the reader is his use of italics to shape the readers' understanding of quoted material.	Notice the conversational tone, including the use of colloquial language like "jumps out at the reader."
More formal article structure and tone	One fundamental case that served as a cornerstone for many of these right to die challenges was *Cruzan v. Director, Missouri Department of Health*. In *Cruzan*, the parents of Nancy Cruzan, a woman who was in a persistent vegetative state following injuries sustained in a severe car accident, wished to terminate their daughter's life-sustaining medical treatment, but the hospital employees refused to carry out this request because it would result in Cruzan's death. The U.S. Supreme Court held that the Fourteenth Amendment's Due Process Clause protects a competent individual's "liberty interest in refusing unwanted medical treatment."	In this example, the language is less conversational, has a more formal tone, and focuses on direct legal issues and outcomes.

The analysis section will likely comprise the majority of the paper. As in the background section, the analysis may also be divided into multiple parts. If the analysis contains multiple subsections, those subsections should reflect a logical progression of thought and build on each other to support the thesis.

The analysis for a traditional seminar paper is similar to that of a law journal or law review article, so you will want to review some of the common types of analytical critiques discussed in Chapter 4, *Developing*

Critical Legal Analysis, and in Chapter 7, *Law Review and Law Journal Articles*. Most professors want to see an analytical critique—not a descriptive paper that reads like a book report. Professors usually want to see deep and sophisticated analysis of a topic and, perhaps, see the student make a new or novel point about the underlying law. The following techniques will help you create deeper analysis in either a seminar or capstone paper.

Techniques	Explanation
Rather than just describing, take a stand	Most professors prefer that students take a stand on the legal question at issue and advocate for the change or outcome that the student believes is most appropriate. Rarely should papers merely describe a problem without providing a solution or suggestion. If the analysis takes a fresh look at how the underlying thesis extends from or limits prior law or if the paper hypothesizes on how the thesis would affect current policy, you may write a descriptive paper that does not advocate for a particular path. If you want to write a descriptive paper, however, make sure to discuss that approach with the professor and confirm that it will meet the professor's expectations.
Write a sophisticated, not superficial, analysis	Whether you are taking a stand or describing an issue, ensure that the analysis is sophisticated, not superficial. Go beyond the obvious to explore the nuances of the law, and if possible, look at different facets of the law holistically, rather than looking at one doctrine in a silo. Just as in a brief to a court or a memorandum to another attorney, illustrate and support the paper's points with specific examples from cases, statutes, or other sources of law.
Synthesize the law	Professors usually want to see students synthesize the body of law, rather than to see just a case report that summarizes individual cases sequentially without tying them together.
Show both sides of the issue	Tackle the weaknesses of your arguments as well as explaining your argument's strengths. Confront opposing arguments but take care not to give those arguments more airtime than your own argument. Instead, present *your* argument first, and rebut the opposing argument within the framework of your assertions.
Suggest possible solutions	The analysis should tell the reader what the next step is—how the law should change or what the individuals or groups behind the conflict should do. If the paper proposes a solution or recommends a course of action, explain that choice and the authority that supports that choice along with any potential consequences.

Review the excerpt below (taken from *Right to Die in California and Beyond: Constructing a Model for the Future*)[21] to see how the author uses the techniques above to create a sophisticated and nuanced analysis.

In the last legislative cycle, twenty-six states as well as the District of Columbia contemplated similar assisted suicide laws and regulations. Given the exponential growth in the visibility of this critical issue, jurisdictions considering enacting similar statutes legalizing physician-assisted suicide should rely on California's ELOA as a model because the statute has integrated safeguards that mitigate some issues that have surfaced under similar statutory schemes of other countries, like the Netherlands and Switzerland. For instance, unlike the Netherlands' statute, which listed "unbearable pain" as a prerequisite to taking advantage of these services, the ELOA requires a terminal illness diagnosis. While this distinction may seem purely a matter of semantics, it has a profound effect. The requirement of "unbearable pain" sets a malleable standard and is heavily determined by the subjective belief of each individual patient; conversely, requiring a definitive diagnosis that is tethered to life expectancy rather than a subjective pain threshold establishes a much more objective standard.

Notice how the author boldly asserts her position.

Additionally, the ELOA does not offer the option of physician-assisted suicide to individuals suffering from psychological conditions, unlike its international counterparts. In the Netherlands, the broadly worded 2002 Act offers assisted suicide practices to individuals suffering from autism, depression, schizophrenia, and other psychological conditions. Recent statistical evidence from the Netherlands indicates that individuals who are electing physician-assisted suicide are increasingly citing physiological conditions rather than terminal illness as the cause for their decision. For example, thirteen patients cited unbearable mental illness in 2012, and this figure increased to forty-four in 2013 — indicating nearly a fourfold increase. Again, such a concern is moot under California's statutory scheme because the statute requires the patient to suffer from a terminal illness with only six months left to live.

The author provides analysis on not only what the law does but also explicitly analyzes what it does not do and why that is important. This level of detail provides a more sophisticated analysis.

. . . .

Further buttressing this argument in support of the California model is the mounting evidence of successful implementation of physician-assisted suicide laws in states like Oregon. Oregon's Death with Dignity Act ("DDA") served as the foundation to California's new law. The DDA has been in effect for nearly 20 years and has proved to be successful; the fears of abuses frequently discussed by critics never manifested. A ten-year statistical study of the DDA published in 2008 revealed that vulnerable groups, like the elderly, disabled, and the poor, were not disproportionately affected by the law but rather that the majority of individuals electing the procedure were well-educated, insured, and diagnosed with cancer. Others have also tried to suggest that the increasing number of individuals choosing assisted suicide with each subsequent year would give rise to an assisted suicide epidemic. This concern is undermined by the fact that physician-assisted suicide accounts for very small fraction of deaths in states like Oregon — in 2010 only 65 individuals died from consuming the prescribed medication. By coalescing the statutory skeleton of such successful legislation like the DDA with its own statutory provisions, California has built upon a law that has been thoroughly tested though years of successful implementation. Moreover, adding its own additional precautions such as the written attestation requirement makes the ELOA a sound, well-drafted statute that minimizes risks of abuse while maximizing benefit to the public.

Here, the author synthesizes the law by examining the results of Oregon's Death with Dignity Act. This explanation allows the reader to understand the spectrum of law and how fears that the law may be abused have not panned out.

The author creates a
sophisticated analysis
by examining policy
arguments and remind-
ing the reader of Justice
Rehnquist's somewhat
prophetic comments in
a landmark case on
this topic.

Furthermore, numerous policy arguments support the adoption of California's ELOA as a statutory model for other U.S. jurisdictions. Promoting a similar legislative model would establish uniformity among the states with regard to regulating assisted suicide. Such uniformity, in turn, would allow for more effective and efficient regulation, diminish confusion often spurred by inconsistent laws, and would help somewhat normalize the practice among society. Arguably, the resulting increase in public acceptance due to this normalization may then serve to influence the U.S. Supreme Court to find a constitutionally protected right to die at a future juncture. **Foreshadowing such a possibility in the *Glucksberg* opinion, Chief Justice Rehnquist opined, "Americans are engaged in an earnest and profound debate about the morality, legality, and practicality of physician-assisted suicide. Our holding permits this debate to continue, as it should in a democratic society."** Just as changing societal consensus on controversial issues such as gay marriage had an effect on the Court's stance on these issues, a similar change may come to America's perception on the right to die.

By discussing the law's
shortcomings, the author
shows both sides of the
issue and provides a bal-
anced approach that will
be more credible to the
reader.

Despite the numerous protections previously discussed, the California statute is not without its shortcomings. Increasing pressures on the healthcare system due to staggering costs may make physician-assisted suicide more attractive for economic reasons, thereby leading to abuse. Anecdotal accounts have surfaced that suggest additional safeguards may be necessary to address this concern. For example, as of January 2016 it will be easier to qualify for physician-assisted suicide under Medicare than for hospice. Similarly, in 2008 an Oregon couple was outraged when the state Medicaid program denied funding treatment for the husband's prostate cancer and the wife's lung cancer but informed the couple that the state was willing to cover the costs of assisted suicide.... In addition, more measures should be set in place to prevent patients from doctor shopping to obtain a lethal prescription, and the statute should provide more guidance as to who qualifies as a consulting physician.... Of even greater concern is the possible flood of discrimination lawsuits that may follow the adoption of such laws brought by patients who suffer from various illnesses but do not meet the statutory requirements, thereby seeking to challenge the constitutionality of these statutes. While these issues should certainly be addressed, the risks associated with these concerns do not outweigh the benefits of enacting this legislation. Most of these issues can be resolved through legislative means or by enacting regulations to help administer this law, and evidence of success in states like Oregon underscores that these concerns are possible but not necessarily probable.[22]

As we discussed in Chapter 7, *Law Review and Law Journal Articles*, substantive footnotes, also known as textual footnotes, can also contribute to deeper analysis in your paper. Substantive footnotes include citations to the sources and authorities supporting your analytical ideas in the body of the paper; they also expand the discussion by explaining any additional points raised by or relevant to those sources that are not quite important enough to be included in analysis itself. Traditional scholarly articles tend to have a plethora of footnotes, a practice that has been criticized consistently over the years.[23]

For any seminar or capstone paper, you will, of course, cite all of the sources you have relied on in writing the article, but the extent to which you expand those footnotes depends on the parameters of the project and your professor's instructions. First, determine whether your professor wants footnotes or in-text citation.

For example, one professor may want citations like those in a law review article, accompanied by substantive footnotes that greatly expand on ideas or information brought up in the text. Another professor may not want substantive footnotes at all but may instead want citations contained within the text as they would be in a document submitted to a court. Second, if your professor is expecting substantive footnotes, ascertain the professor's expectations for the number of footnotes and the depth of each.

Whether the professor wants substantive footnotes or in-text footnotes, be sure to properly format every citation according to your chosen citation manual.

8.4.E Conclusion

Finally, the conclusion is a place in which you may summarize the analysis, wrap up the proven thesis, and highlight the best option identified for solving the conflict. The conclusion section typically does not include any new substantive information or arguments, nor does it make a proposal or recommendation for the first time. To write the conclusion section, first explain how the thesis or main point has been established, including how the key points of the analysis supported the thesis. When analyzing a conflict of law that needs resolution, identify any next steps that should be taken. In either situation, you will want to identify any legal concepts that are yet to be resolved.

Examples of the conclusion section

Type and Topic	Conclusion	Technique
Seminar Paper on Aid in Dying Legislation[24]	The new California statute offers a model for other states that wish to introduce assisted suicide laws in a limited and regulated manner, thereby preserving the autonomous right of terminally ill individuals to determine their own futures. This option may serve as a comfort for the aggrieved as they face imminent death and allow them, too, to proclaim boldly, *"Mighty and dreadful, for thou art not so."*[25]	Notice how the author concludes this paper with the poetic framework used in the introduction. The author does not introduce new information but instead sums up the major points of the paper. This parallel use of the material provides an excellent structure for the reader to follow.

Examples of the conclusion section continued

Type and Topic	Conclusion	Technique
Seminar Essay on Classic Rhetoric[26]	Roberts establishes the substance, style, organization, and high-lighting of his brief through thoughtful, thorough displays of the different intelligences. By drawing on all forms of intelligence he establishes ethos with the reader. With strong ethos, Roberts's brief has a formidable persuasive effect on readers, predisposing them for his legal arguments and conclusions. In addition, he increases readers' receptiveness to his pathos and logos.	The conclusion for this paper is not long or cumbersome; it succinctly sums up the main points of the paper and restates the author's thesis.
Capstone Project on Revenge Porn[27]	Information privacy laws widely recognize that consent in one context does not equal consent in other contexts. The juxtaposition of the acceptance of this principle when applied to the privacy invasion of a high-powered man in the form of disclosure of what movies he likes to watch, with the rejection of such a principle when applied to a woman sharing her intimate images with her sexual partner, hints at why revenge porn laws have not been treated like information privacy laws: gender. We as a society are generally willing to recognize that privacy is context-specific, but we refuse to do so when sexual practices are involved, *particularly* the sexual practices of women. However, the sharing of intimate images with a partner should subject revenge porn victims to no more blame than when an agent of a bank commits identity theft using a customer's personal identifying information and disclosing that information incident to a transaction. Refusal to protect privacy in the context of revenge porn not only condones such invasions, but also denies women control over their sexual identities, their digital legacies, and their lives.	This conclusion recaps the main points of the argument and reiterates the writer's assertion of the harm that will result if laws are not changed.
Capstone or Thesis on Using Bodily Remains for Medical Research[28]	This thesis has explored how the dead are treated (from a research perspective) and how the dead may be treated (from a legal perspective), but it is now up to us—bioethicists, lawyers, and the public—to give the question of how the dead should be treated the careful consideration it merits. Until the existing law of the dead is amended to accurately reflect the rights that people (living or dead) do have in dead bodies—or until new laws and regulations are created to establish the rights that people (living or dead) should have in dead bodies—the dead, the living, and the research enterprise as a whole are at grave risk of harm.	Following a lengthier description of some of the philosophical questions the thesis addressed, the author re-emphasizes the paper's bottom-line assertion.

8.4.F Title

As with other types of scholarly writing, another fundamental component of the traditional seminar or capstone paper is the title. The title is a great way to capture the reader's attention and to distinguish the paper from others on the professor's desk.

The title can be used to pique the reader's curiosity. Using irony, a play on words, or an unusual pun can work well. For example, a title like, "Why Blackstone was a Broad" is intriguing for several reasons.[29]

William Blackstone was a famous English jurist whose writings in the eighteenth century formed the basis of current legal education in Great Britain. The term "broad," while likely a derogatory term in today's vernacular, originated around the 1930s as a slang term for an assertive woman. The juxtaposition of the slang term with the historical figure creates interest—the reader will immediately wonder how this jurist is like a pre-World War II assertive woman. Was he an advocate for women? Was he pro-

Sir William Blackstone

gressive in his views? Was he assertive in ways evocative of the English suffragette movement in the 1920s and 1930s? Is the writer using the term "broad" in a derogatory or respectful way? The reader will want to know more.

Further, a *fresh* pun or play on words can make a title sing. For example, one student used a popular TV show as the basis for his seminar paper's title: "*Orange is the New Trash: Assessing the Ethical Conundrums Behind the National School Lunch Program.*"[30] Of course, a short, punchy title, such as *The Most Dangerous Degree in the World*,[31] will also work well.

Although clever styling of a phrase can yield a catchy title, a writer must always choose words carefully. Using tired puns, common clichés, or derogatory terms can be offensive and alienate a potential audience. If you have any qualms about the propriety of a title, err on the side of not using it. Chapter 7, *Law Review and Law Journal Articles*, provides further details and examples on crafting a memorable title.

8.5 Less traditional forms of seminar papers and capstones

Depending on a school's requirements and the assigning professor's preferences, a wide array of formats may be used for non-traditional seminar and capstone papers, provided that the paper reflects thorough research and deep analysis that goes beyond superficial legal concepts. For example, constructing an annotated brief or a handbook on a discrete topic may provide a creative way to convey deep analysis. Just as with any academic or professional writing project, try to combine the seminar or capstone with an area of research in which you are particularly interested or with a legal topic arising from a project at your job or clerkship. If your professor's requirements are flexible, consider doing something out of the ordinary for a seminar or capstone paper.

Depending on the type of project, non-traditional papers may not have a traditional thesis. Such less traditional projects will, however, need a guiding principle for the project. For example, in a brief, the writer will anchor claims to controlling rules of law. With a handbook, the writer will undoubtedly have a unifying purpose for the piece and an idea of the audience to whom the piece is directed. Examples of less traditional styles are illustrated below.

8.5.A An annotated brief

A professor might allow a brief or other document that requires in-depth research and analysis to satisfy the course requirement. If crafting such a document is not enough to satisfy the writing requirements, the writer might propose supplementing the brief writing process by using scholarly works to inform either the substance of the paper or the analytical process of brief writing and then annotating the brief to show how those works shaped the paper.[32] This option requires research and complex analysis just as with any brief, but it may also require review of outside works, such as books or scholarly articles that address advanced skills in persuasion, rhetoric, or brief writing. Footnotes can detail the choices the writer made in drafting and revising the brief and how outside works informed those choices. For instance, the writer could read scholarly works relating to rhetoric and persuasion then use those ideas to enhance the brief.

In the example below, the writer of a less traditional seminar paper had the following two goals: First, she wanted to improve her foundational writing skills by revising a brief on complex issues of federal law that she had written in her first year of law school; next, she wanted to implement the concepts of persuasion and rhetoric she was learning in an upper-division seminar class. To achieve these goals, the writer read textbook chapters along with various articles on effective persuasion strategies then revised the brief to incorporate those strategies. She used annotations to show how the readings informed her choices and changed her original work. Although the footnotes do contain citations, they primarily reflect the writer's thinking and are not styled as the formal footnotes of a scholarly paper. The following excerpt shows how the writer accomplished her goals while meeting the requirements for a non-traditional seminar paper.

An annotated brief as a seminar paper[33]

I. Summary judgment should be reversed because Princeville denied Colton equal access to educational benefits in contravention of Title IX.[1]

The district court erred as a matter of law in granting summary judgment in favor of Princeville because the record supports an actionable Title IX claim. Title IX of the Education Amendments of 1972 provides, in relevant part, that "no person in the United States shall, on the basis of sex, be excluded from participation in, be denied the benefits of, or be subjected to discrimination under any education program or activity receiving financial assistance." 20 U.S.C. § 1681(a).

The Supreme Court has held that schools subject their students to discrimination in violation of Title IX when they respond inappropriately to known incidents of peer sexual harassment. *Davis v. Monroe County Bd. of Educ.*, 526 U.S. 629, 649 (1999).[2] To hold schools liable for peer sexual harassment, victims must establish three elements:

(1) The harassment must have been severe, pervasive, and objectively offensive;

(2) The harassment must have deprived the victim of access to the educational opportunities and benefits provided by the school; and

(3) The school must have responded to the harassment with deliberate indifference.[4]

Id. at 650. The district court erred when it dismissed Colton's claim against Princeville because the harassment that Colton suffered at school meets each of the *Davis* elements for actionable peer harassment.[5] Accordingly, the judgment of the lower court should be reversed.

A. The unwelcome sexual advances and touching that Colton suffered at school constitute severe, pervasive, and objectively offensive sexual harassment.

The unwelcome sexual advances and touching that Colton suffered during school hours by his classmates at Princeville School constitute severe, pervasive, and objectively offensive sexual harassment. To fall within the ambit of Title IX, the offending conduct must constitute "sexual harassment."[6] *See Gabrielle M. v. Park Forest-Chicago Heights IL. School Dist. 163*, 315 F.3d 817, 822 (7th Cir. 2003). Additionally, the sexual harassment must be severe, pervasive, and objectively offensive. Whether harassment meets that standard is a fact-specific inquiry that depends on the surrounding circumstances. *Davis*, 526 U.S. at 651. In making this determination, courts consider the type of harassment along with its frequency and duration. *See id.*

Footnotes:

1. Many of the following footnotes reflect lessons learned from our textbook, Michael R. Smith's *Advanced Legal Writing* (3d ed. 2013). I changed wording of this heading to eliminate use of the passive voice. Eliminating passive voice was suggested in several class presentations on improving writing, and the tactic is favored because it clarifies who has done what to whom. Now my main point is clear and free from distractions.

2. Rather than leading with the text of the statute, I revised the thesis sentence to explain better the point of the paragraph.

3. I also removed conclusory language (i.e. "sexual harassment") from this heading and throughout my brief, and this change will increase the persuasive power of my brief by evincing good moral character. **Character** is one of the three fundamental aspects of ethos, and it is of upmost importance in legal writing. *See id.* at 123–44. The use of conclusory language is likely to lead a reader to believe that the writer is of questionable moral character—and if the reader thinks the writer is prone to lying, deceiving, or misleading, the reader will approach the writer's arguments with skepticism and doubt.

....

7. Talking about the requirement that the conduct be "sexual in nature" as a "threshold question" was confusing. I changed the way I discussed this factor throughout the brief, and I did this by boiling it down to its essence: even though the Seventh Circuit talks about a "threshold question" that the conduct be "sexual in nature," the court is really just emphasizing what we already know: Title IX applies to sexual harassment and not bullying. I looked back at the cases to ensure that I would not misstate the requirement by simply calling it "sexual harassment," and I do not think it does. Now the reader can quickly and easily understand the real issue without being bogged down by the unnecessary and confusing language in the first draft. Using the standard precisely boosts the pathos, ethos, and the logos of my argument. The change boosts the pathos through **medium mood control**—understanding my argument no longer requires the reader to wrestle with confusing language, so the reader will be more receptive to my arguments. It boosts the ethos because it demonstrates that I am **empathetic** (clear, concise explanation) and **analytical** (effective synthesis of the legal rule).

This type of seminar paper gave the writer a chance to hone the basic skills of brief writing while employing new theoretical concepts of persuasion and rhetoric. In revising the brief, her tasks required thorough and accurate research, concise analysis, and good communication of that analysis through strong writing. Moreover, talking about the concepts of persuasion and rhetoric and incorporating corresponding strategies into her paper allowed the student to internalize those strategies. Thus, this non-traditional seminar paper gave the writer a chance to enhance the skills she would need in everyday law practice while at the same time allowing her to engage in and use more sophisticated, theoretical ideas on a practical level.

8.5.B Creating a legal guide or handbook

Creating a legal guide, such as handbook or Continuing Legal Education (CLE) materials, can also be the basis of a seminar paper or capstone that integrates sophisticated analysis and theoretical concepts into a document with a practical application. The options for a paper of this style are broad—guides, handbooks, or CLE materials are just a few options. This type of paper may have more practical appeal to a student than a scholarly paper, and it can sharpen those writing skills a student will use daily as a practicing lawyer.

One student chose to create a handbook for law enforcement officers, district attorneys, social workers, and others, that explained state and federal law regarding sex trafficking crimes against juveniles.[34] The handbook also set out guidelines and best practices in identifying victims of sex trafficking, thereby allowing law enforcement agents to employ re-habilitative options rather than criminal prosecution for those victims. The handbook required the same depth and breadth of research and analysis as a traditional capstone paper, but the handbook also included powerful graphics and a visually inviting layout. Thus, the student was able to combine typical legal analysis with artistic elements to create a practical and creative document. Not only could the student educate the target audience, but she had the option to use the handbook as a piece of advocacy in effecting policy changes that protected sex trafficking victims rather than running them back through the criminal justice system.

A legal handbook that combines text and visual elements[35]

HUMAN TRAFFICKING
Where the Juvenile System Fails Youth

BY ANJANA KUMAR

Introduction

Across the nation, at both the federal level and state level, legislatures are enacting laws to address the growing concern of domestic sex trafficking of youth. These laws mandate local agencies to provide services and assistance to youth who have been trafficked. However, while these services and assistance are of the utmost importance, these laws fail to address the first step in providing such services and assistance: proper identification.

Seventy-five percent of young people who experience commercial sexual exploitation endure multiple years of abuse before anyone intervenes.[1] Despite the growing understanding that youth are, in fact, not "prostitutes," but rather victims of sex trafficking, many states currently have no articulated or standardized identification method to identify potential survivors and victims of human trafficking. Without a standard identification process, agencies that interface with the most vulnerable  youth lack the tools necessary to identify these victims, thereby failing these youth. Agencies and officials also fail to do other key things: connect youth with trauma-specific services, prevent the re-traumatization of the youth, and prevent further exploitation.

The juvenile justice system is one of the largest agencies to interact with youth on a daily basis. The population of youth who are vulnerable to exploitation overlaps considerably with the population of youth who are vulnerable to incarceration. Thus, it is vital for juvenile facilities to implement a specific screening tool aimed at identifying youth who may be victims of sex trafficking. If appropriate identification tools are not developed and implemented, victims of sex trafficking will continue to fall through the cracks; they will continue to be traumatized, abused, and thrust back into the system.

While Oregon has made considerable headway in enacting anti-trafficking legislation and developing a systematic response to victims of trafficking, only a small fraction of trafficking victims have been identified. System stakeholders and policymakers can capitalize on current identification pilot programs enacted across the nation to help guide their development of their own identification process and tools within Oregon juvenile facilities. To facilitate the discussion of the importance of implementing a screening tool in juvenile facilities, this report will:

1. Explore the crossover between victims of human trafficking and incarcerated youth;
2. Address the current procedures of identifying victims; and
3. Detail recommendations for new identification procedures.

What Is Human Trafficking?

Human trafficking is the action of illegally transporting a person from one place to another, typically for the use of labor or sex. The Trafficking Victims Protection Act, 22 U.S.C. § 7102, enacted by Congress in 2000, defines "severe forms of tracking" as:

> (A) Sex trafficking in which a commercial sex act is induced by force, fraud, or coercion, or the person induced to perform such act has not attained 18 years of age; or
> (B) The recruitment, harboring, transportation, provision, or obtaining of a person for labor or services, through the use of force, fraud, or coercion for the purpose of subjection to involuntary servitude, peonage, debt bondage, or slavery.

The statute defines sex trafficking as:

> (a) Whoever knowingly—
> (1) In or affecting interstate or foreign commerce, or within the special maritime and territorial jurisdiction of the United States, recruits, entices, harbors, transports, provides, obtains, or maintains by any means a person; or
> (2) Benefits, financially or by receiving anything of value, from participation in a venture which has engaged in an act described in violation of paragraph (1), knowing, or in reckless disregard of the fact, that means of force, threats of force, fraud, coercion described in subsection

(e)(2), or any combination of such means will be used to cause the person to engage in a commercial sex act, or that the person has not attained the age of eighteen years and will be caused to engage in a commercial sex act, shall be punished as provided in subsection (b).[2]

18 U.S.C. § 1591, Sex Trafficking of Children or by Force, Fraud, or Coercion. Oregon's human trafficking statute, O.R.S. § 163.266 (2018), defines human trafficking using much of the language from the federal statute.

In 2016, Oregon enacted an additional statute, O.R.S. § 147.480, *Establishment of Funds to End Commercial Sexual Exploitation of Children*, to further address the issue of child sex trafficking within Oregon. The fund grants the Department of Justice to allocate money earmarked for the fund to provide financial assistance for various efforts such as: (a) services, interventions and treatment for children who have or may experience sexual exploitation, (b) outreach to educate the public about the exploitation of children, (c) preventing and reducing the sexual exploitation of children, (d) training for investigators and service providers regarding the identification and treatment of sexually exploited children, and (e) advocacy.

Notes

1. Basson, Danna, *Validation of the Commercial Sexual Exploitation-Identification Tool (CSE-IT). Technical Report*. WestCoast Children's Clinic, westcoastcc.org/wp-content/uploads/2015/04/WCC-CSE-IT-PilotReport-FINAL.pdf (last accessed Jan. 4, 2019).

2. Sex Trafficking of Children or by Force, Fraud, or Coercion, 18 U.S.C. § 1591 (2018).

Another example is a student-created office handbook addressing an area of law frequently litigated in her employer's office. In this example, a student who was working for a local district attorney's office wrote a handbook evaluating a set of laws that presented an obstacle in proving child abuse charges.[36] The student set out the line of appellate court decisions, explaining how the obstacle originated through the appellate courts' interpretation of two statutes. Specifically, the student traced the courts' narrow interpretation of "physical injury" as it related to child abuse cases. The narrowly interpreted definition of physical injury required victims to articulate that they had experienced substantial pain. That rule, however, posed significant challenges for prosecutors in child abuse cases because young victims—particularly toddlers and infants—do not always have the cognitive or verbal ability to articulate experiences of substantial pain.

The student identified the problems with the existing law, traced the evolution of the case law, and included a policy discussion of why and how the law should be changed to comply with the legislature's original intent. The topic was interesting to the student, and the project became a helpful handbook for practicing attorneys in her office. Moreover, the district attorney's office was able to use the paper when lobbying the legislature to change the law.

By choosing this type of project, the student was able to explore an area of law that was interesting to her and helpful in her work. In addition, the student provided other attorneys in her workplace with a valuable resource that they could use in briefs and arguments before both state court judges and the legislature when arguing that the law should be interpreted differently or changed. This type of practical capstone was useful and interesting to the student because it was a topic the student was passionate about and the resulting work product had positive, real-world implications.

An example of a legal handbook containing textual analysis[37]

II. Current problem with the statutory definition of physical injury and explanation of current proposed changes.

Because the judicial development of the definition of physical injury has been inadequate, a legislative remedy should be implemented. The statutory definition of physical injury should be amended to include bruises because the Court of Appeals' interpretation of the definition of physical injury is inconsistent with the legislature's intent because it does not protect children from harm. Senate Bill 526 is the current proposed legislation to amend the definition of physical injury. The proposed statute reads:

> (7) "Physical injury" means physical trauma, impairment of a physical condition or substantial pain.
> (8) "Physical trauma" includes but is not limited to fractures, cuts, punctures, bruises, burns or other wounds.

Advocates of the bill argue that the amended definition prevents the Court of Appeals from coming up with more decisions like *Wright* and *Lewis*. Advocates also argue that the amended definition does a better job of protecting domestic violence and child abuse victims. The proposed statute does offer a solution to the problems created by *Wright* and *Lewis*. However, although the proposed statute includes bruises, the proposed definition is too broad because fractures, cuts, punctures, and burns are covered by the "impairment of a physical condition" element of physical injury. Thus, the statute should be amended to include bruises and nothing more.*

* Internal citations have been omitted.

Less traditional seminar papers and capstones can indeed be a crowning achievement in law school that enhances the writer's educational experience while simultaneously expanding the writer's analytical and writing skills. Although traditional scholarly articles meet most capstone objectives, other forms of a capstone may be equally interesting and may more aptly achieve the curricular goals.

Notes

1. Thank you to Hadley Van Vactor, Assistant Professor of Lawyering, Lewis & Clark Law School, for her contribution to parts of this chapter.

2. This project might also be referred to by other names, such as an Upper Level Writing Requirement ("ULWR"), an A or B paper, or even a Thesis paper, depending on the law school. Most capstones or ULWRs stem from the American Bar Association's upper-level rigorous writing requirement. *See 2019–2020 ABA Standards and Rules of Procedure for Approval of Law Schools*, A.B.A. Sec. Legal Educ. and Admissions to the Bar 15 (2019).

3. If you are writing a seminar or a capstone paper in an academic setting, your professor or advisor may even have their own materials describing those requirements, general tips on research and writing, and possibly a rubric used for assessment. Thank you to Lewis & Clark Professors who shared their guidelines. *See, e.g.,* Professor Mike Blumm, *Blumm's 18 Commandments of Paper Writing* (Aug. 2012) (on file with authors); Professor Bill Chin, *Some Scholarly Writing Guidelines* (on file with authors); Professor Susan Mandiberg, *Term Papers* (on file with authors); Professor Janet Steverson, *Suggestions and Criteria for Term Papers* (on file with authors); Professor Chris Wold, *Writing a Law School Paper* (Nov. 7, 2001) (on file with authors).

4. *See generally* Phillip C. Kissam, *Seminar Papers*, 40 J. Legal Educ. 339 (1990).

5. *Id.* at 345–46.

6. Anne Lamott, Bird by Bird: Some Instructions on Writing and Life 62 (1994).

7. The examples on the topic of "revenge porn" used throughout this chapter were adapted from a capstone paper written by Kelsey Benedick, student at Lewis & Clark Law School (2017) (on file with authors).

8. Seminar paper examples here and throughout chapter are adapted from works of former students Jessie Schuh and Kate Acosta, Lewis & Clark Law School (2015) (on file with authors).

9. Some examples used throughout this chapter were adapted from a seminar paper written by Anna Baitchenko, student at Wake Forest University School of Law (2015) (on file with authors).

10. *See* Benedick, *supra.*

11. *See id.*

12. Catherine Hammack, The Law and Ethics of Using the Dead in Research (2014) (M.A. Thesis, Wake Forest University) (on file with authors).

13. *Id.* at vi.

14. Baitchenko, *supra.*

15. Benedick, *supra.*

16. Schuh & Acosta, *supra.*

17. Benedick, *supra.*

18. Hammack, *supra,* at ix–x.

19. Baitchenko, *supra.* We have eliminated most internal citations in the examples for purposes of this book. However, because much of the content of the background will be factual or legal, most, if not all, sentences in the background should include a citation to the source of the information.

20. Example adapted from capstone paper written by Genevieve Steel, student at Lewis & Clark Law School (2019) (on file with authors).

21. Baitchenko, *supra*.

22. *Id.*

23. *See, e.g.*, Joan Ames Magat, *Bottomheavy: Legal Footnotes*, 60 J. Leg. Ed. 65–105 (2010).

24. *Id.* (internal citations omitted).

25. *Id.* (internal citations omitted).

26. Benedick, *supra*.

27. *Id.*

28. Hammack, *supra*, at 83.

29. Thank you to Professor Steve Johansen at Lewis & Clark Law School for sharing this example (student author unknown).

30. Adapted from a seminar paper written by Mark Huffman, student at Wake Forest University School of Law (2017) (on file with authors).

31. Adapted from a capstone paper written by Brandon Chirco, student at Lewis & Clark Law School (2017) (on file with authors).

32. The annotated paper is based upon assignments developed by Professor Ruth Anne Robbins (Rutgers University School of Law) and adapted by Professors Daryl Wilson and Steve Johansen (Lewis & Clark School of Law).

33. This non-traditional capstone example adapted from former students Jessie Schuh and Kate Acosta, students at Lewis & Clark Law School (2015) (on file with authors).

34. Non-traditional capstone example created by Anjana L. Kumar, student at Lewis & Clark Law School (2019) (on file with authors) (citations omitted).

35. *Id.* The first image is by MoreISO via iStockphoto. The second image is courtesy of Maria Charitou, via Flickr (https://creativecommons.org/licenses/by-nd/2.0/legalcode).

36. Adapted from a non-traditional capstone paper written by Lanee Danforth, student at Lewis & Clark Law School (2015) (on file with authors).

37. Danforth, *supra*.

Chapter 9

Bar Journal Articles

9.1 Choosing a topic
9.2 Drafting the bar journal article
9.3 Publishing the bar journal article

As a practicing attorney, and sometimes even as a law student, preparing a CLE presentation or publishing an article in a general law journal, magazine, or bulletin can be a way to expand your own knowledge base and build your professional reputation among colleagues and potential clients. Professional articles are typically short, focused pieces of writing concentrated on a narrow point of law or law-related topic—most often a point or topic on which the author has some element of expertise. The goal of these articles is to convey useful information to other busy professionals in a succinct but informative format. As busy professionals, attorneys often lack the opportunity to devote significant amounts of time to reading scholarly articles. Journal or magazine articles frequently help bridge the literary "gap" between scholarly articles, often too detailed for quick learning, and blog posts, typically too short to provide much analysis.

Similarly, while this chapter focuses generally on drafting and preparing writings for distribution through professional journals or other similar publications, many of the principles, particularly those concerning topic selection, are equally applicable to preparation and publication of CLE materials. Frequently, CLE presentations require discussion of a predetermined practice for a predetermined audience, but the specific topics and the methods of presentation are usually left to the individual presenter or panel. As you might expect, the goal of attorneys attending these CLE presentations is twofold: (1) to meet a state bar organization's annual continuing education requirements and (2) to learn about a particular field of law, issues of interest to lawyers, or issues affecting lawyers (e.g., ethics and substance abuse topics).

Whether you are drafting an article for a bar association journal (or other similar publication) or preparing CLE materials, the process of drafting documents tailored to practicing professionals can help sharpen your expertise in a particular field of law while also helping to build your reputation and "brand" among peers or future peers. Professional publications might also help shape your own views concerning one or more practice areas.

9.1 Choosing a topic

When selecting a topic for a professional publication, consider the following questions:

- Do you know enough about the topic to provide new or informative insight to others?
- Is the topic currently relevant to practicing attorneys or other professional readers?
- Is the topic one that will hold the interest of professional readers, either broadly or for a specific group?

9.1.A Knowledge of a topic

Consider the article *Talking to the Judge (or Maybe Not)* by the Honorable Michael Robinson of the North Carolina Business Court and Professor Ellen Murphy of Wake Forest University School of Law. In this piece, the authors explain lawyers' ethical obligations regarding *ex parte* communications to help practitioners remain in compliance. The authors' professional experiences (one a Business Court Judge who specializes in complex business cases and the other a law professor who teaches professional responsibility) inform the piece's recommendations and bolster their credibility as individuals with substantial expertise who are well situated to address the topic.

Teaching others about a topic in which you have little to no knowledge or background is difficult. As a result, most authors gravitate toward topics with which they have significant experience or at least a working knowledge. For example, when practicing attorneys draft articles, the articles often relate to the attorneys' particular practice area—bankruptcy discussions for bankruptcy attorneys; civil procedure, discovery, or litigation topics for litigators; and tax, real estate, or mergers and acquisitions for transactional attorneys. Of course, these are broad generalizations, but they reflect that authors are best able to prepare informative articles when they have familiarity with the topic. Similarly, law students, while lacking experience in a particular practice area, may nonetheless elect to focus their publications on topics with which they are most familiar—those examined in courses or through work experience, such as clerkships or jobs.

Selecting a topic in which you have a substantial working knowledge—or where you intend to develop competency—assists in establishing your expertise regarding that particular field and potentially an entire area of law. When readers see an individual author's name on an article that they find particularly informative, they may possibly associate the author with the topic and practice area going forward. As a result, if you are able to maintain an ongoing publication schedule concerning related topics, you may develop a reputation as someone who can provide valuable expertise on a given topic.

9.1.B Relevance of the topic

After determining that you, as the author, have sufficient knowledge of a topic to thoroughly discuss it and to provide helpful insights, consider whether the topic you have in mind is relevant to practicing attorneys. Assessing the relevance of a topic requires a practical analysis, including a hard look at the timeliness of the topic.

As an initial matter, professional publications such as journal articles are frequently intended to address recent legal issues or those of particular legal importance. As with scholarly articles, some of the best article topics are often those that either explain conflicts in the law and identify potential solutions, or that identify potential issues of importance that do not yet have solutions. Other articles identify inconsistencies in the law or its application or recent decisions that change or advance the law in some way. These topics might include recent court opinions, regulatory rulings, statutes and regulations, and related matters. New laws or regulations, changes in the law, and shifts in policy also provide rich areas from which to choose topics. For example, writing about a recent regulatory commission ruling might mean analyzing and addressing the future impact of the decision rather than simply providing a summary of the decision itself. In any case, the topic should be tailored to help the legal audience understand the resulting implications.

Generally, the more recently an event occurred, the more relevant it will be to a broad range of potential readers. Consider whether the topic is one that has recently been in the news or trending on various social media outlets. In each case, the existing discussion indicates the topic is already of interest to a large group of people. Beware, though, the topic may have already been exhausted. If a topic has been newsworthy for days or weeks, it might mean that other articles, blog posts, or publications have already addressed the issue. If not, you might be the first person to address the topic as a whole or to address particular points within the topic.

Topics discussing obscure cases from decades ago or topics that have little practical impact on a practicing attorney's daily activities are unlikely to have much relevance to a modern reader of bar or professional publications. If, however, new law has recently overturned those decades-old cases or superseded old law, the topics may be ripe for writing. In each such situation, the new case or law should likely be the focus of the article.

Other articles achieve relevance by touching on non-doctrinal issues that nonetheless affect the legal workplace environment. For example, topics related to professionalism and legal ethics are always important, and practice management suggestions or problem solving might also be particularly relevant. The article, *Talking to the Judge (or Maybe Not)*,[1] previously mentioned in the sidebar, explains an overlooked legal ethics situation. When to engage in *ex parte* communications is a problem often unnoticed until an attorney is confronted with a pressure-filled situation. This article's suggestions help attorneys recognize potential problems and offer a concrete way forward before high-stakes situations arise.[2]

9.1.C Interest in the topic

Once you determine that you have sufficient knowledge of a topic and that the topic is relevant, consider whether the topic is one that actually would be of interest to your audience—specifically, practicing attorneys and others reading professional legal journals—and also whether the topic is of interest to you. Because practicing attorneys rarely have extra time to spare for reading non-essential articles or for other pleasure reading, remember that your article will need to grab their attention by focusing on issues that are both interesting and applicable to them.

As an initial matter, consider your audience. You may want to ask yourself questions such as the following:

- Are you writing to a large audience or to lawyers in a particular practice area?
- What are the journal's requirements with respect to length and scope?
- Will the article be published in a specialty publication, such as one that focuses on issues relevant to lawyers who practice healthcare in Georgia, or will it be published in a broadly distributed publication, such as the *ABA Journal*, which may distributed to attorneys in all areas of practice all over the country?

Choosing a specialty publication limits the range of potential topics but also increases the likelihood that your topic will be of interest to its readers. If you want the article to be distributed to a broader population of practitioners in a general publication, the article should address a topic of common interest to practitioners from different practice areas.

In further evaluating a topic, consider whether the topic really interests you. Just as drafting an article or presentation about a topic on which you have no knowledge is difficult, devoting the necessary time and resources to preparing an article or presentation concerning a topic in which you have little interest is similarly difficult. In general, when an author is not substantially invested in the subject matter of an article, that lack of investment is reflected in the end product and readers notice. In much the same way that publishing in professional journals can help build your reputation as a knowledgeable attorney or student in a given practice area, a half-hearted effort can also lessen any goodwill you might have developed and can lead to a lackluster reputation.

9.2 Drafting the bar journal article

Once you have selected a topic with which you are adequately familiar, that is relevant, and that is of interest to your potential audience and yourself, you will be ready for the next step: drafting the article. The drafting process, as with any other type of writing, always involves the basics. These include ensuring that the article is clear, flows well, and is free of typographical errors. Below is a sample bar journal article—one written for legal practitioners on the mechanics of writing.

Excerpt from a bar journal article

Three Writing Rules That Are "More What You'd Call 'Guidelines'"[3]
By Professor Laura Graham

In Disney's first "Pirates of the Caribbean" movie, there is a classic moment when the heroine, Elizabeth Swann, invokes the Pirate's Code to save herself from the villainous Barbossa. Barbossa replies that because Ms. Swann is not a pirate, the Code does not apply to her. He then adds, with a sardonic grin, that "the Code is more what you'd call 'guidelines' than actual rules."

The same can be said about some of the rules of proper writing that have been taught and observed slavishly for centuries. I realize that I am entering dangerous waters here; many lawyers are sticklers for proper grammar, and some of you may disagree with what I'm about to say. Nonetheless, after consulting a wealth of resources, I feel safe in asserting that the three "rules" below have become "more what you'd call 'guidelines'" for good legal writing.

1. **Never begin a sentence with a conjunction.**
    Put simply, a conjunction is a word that functions as a connector between two sentences, clauses, phrases, or words. The mnemonic FANBOYS is often used to remember the most common conjunctions: *for, and, nor, but, or, yet,* and *so.*

    The "never begin a sentence with a conjunction" rule perhaps originated from the common-sense notion that because conjunctions connect two smaller structures into a single larger structure, they should appear only between those two smaller structures. But experts in modern writing style agree that it is acceptable to begin a sentence with a conjunction. The *Chicago Manual of Style* calls the "never start a sentence with a conjunction" rule a "monstrous doctrine" that has "no historical or grammatical foundation."[4] Legal writing expert Joseph Williams calls the rule "folklore." Professor Joseph Kimble, a leading proponent of the Plain English movement, writes, "Listen to how you talk. 'But' is far more common and more deft than 'however' to show contrast at the beginning of a sentence."

    If you choose to start a sentence with a conjunction, don't put a comma after it. "The purpose of these punchy conjunctions is to force the reader into the rest of the sentence. A comma does nothing but stop the flow." And be sure that what follows the conjunction is a complete sentence; the "never use a sentence fragment in formal writing" rule is still very much a rule, not a guideline!

    If you take the time to count, you will see that in this column, I chose to begin a sentence with a conjunction *five times*! The key is that I *chose* to break the rule

Notice how the writer starts by catching the reader's attention with an interesting story. Also, notice the conversational and less formal tone the author uses to engage the audience. The author is writing about a topic she knows well—the mechanics of legal writing.

Creating a list of numbered points can be an effective organizational tool for the reader in many forms of professional writing. The bolded headings also help the reader "chunk" the information into memorable bites. These concepts will be discussed in this chapter.

in those few sentences, to make my writing more powerful. If you break the "never start a sentence with a conjunction" rule too many times in the same piece of writing, your writing will seem choppy and unnatural to the reader.

2. Never end a sentence with a preposition.

Sir Winston Churchill is widely credited as responding to an overzealous editor by saying that the rule against ending sentences with prepositions "is the type of arrant pedantry up with which I shall not put." Churchill's statement is a perfect illustration of the convoluted writing that sometimes results from our efforts to avoid sentence-ending prepositions, a rule that likely was pounded into our heads as elementary school students.

I recently saw the following sentence in a student memo: "It was clear from the look on the defendant's face that he had no idea what the prosecutor was talking about." To avoid ending this sentence with a preposition, the student could have written, "It was clear from the look on the defendant's face that he had no idea about what the prosecutor was talking." But this version of the sentence would have been unnatural, and I probably would have stumbled over it.

Keep in mind that one of your chief goals as a legal writer is to make your writing as precise, clear, and concise as possible. You want your writing to be highly readable; you want your words to flow smoothly across your reader's mind. Thus, if putting a preposition at the end of a sentence results in smoother, more natural writing, then you should break the rule prohibiting it. It bears repeating, though, that you should not break the rule too often within the same piece of writing.

....

A final note: Deborah Bouchoux, author of the *Aspen Handbook for Legal Writers*, aptly points out that "legal readers are notorious perfectionists," many of whom would find a split infinitive or a dangling preposition jarring. If you know your reader is a "grammar curmudgeon," you should err on the side of caution and treat these three "guidelines" as hard and fast rules. But I think that most legal readers value clarity highly enough that they, too, will be willing to see these rules as "more like guidelines" that can, and occasionally should, be broken.

Every article should have a conclusion paragraph, and articles for practitioners give the legal writer a bit more license to end creatively.

9.2.A General drafting considerations

Professional articles must be concise. In general, the length of a professional article will be governed by two limitations:

- Any word limits imposed by the publisher, and
- The attention spans and time constraints of professional readers.

Many journals or CLE publishers will have an express word or time limitation for articles, providing a finite amount of space and number of words within which to convey the message of your article. These publishers also typically provide explanations of word count, citation, and formatting requirements on their websites. Because of the busy nature of law practice for attorneys and other legal professionals, many simply cannot take the time from their work to read an article unless they can do so quickly. This tendency means that the article must be sufficiently concise (*and* sufficiently interesting) to convince practitioners to read the article. To ensure conciseness, sentences should be short and pertinent, without extraneous language.

To increase readership, a successful article must also make it easy for readers to get all of the information they need to obtain the full benefit of the article. For example, if an article references a recent opinion, regulation, or other information that is readily available online, provide a hyperlink (if published online) or a URL (for hardcopy documents). Providing citations where applicable directs readers to locations where they might obtain additional information or a more thorough discussion of a particular area of law.

In addition, avoid jargon unless necessary to the topic at hand. While practice-area-specific vocabulary may be necessary for some specialized practice areas such as bankruptcy, tax, and intellectual property, more well-known practices areas, such as general litigation and real estate, are often more conducive to using plain vocabulary. Avoiding unnecessary jargon helps broaden an article's appeal to individuals who might not otherwise have familiarity with a given topic, whether they are interested in the article due to its relation to an ongoing case they might have or simply for their own edification.

To make an article easier to read and more appealing to practicing professionals, many authors use "chunking,"[5] which is conveying information in small groups or sections informally known as "chunks." These sections can vary widely based on the content to be conveyed, but they often take the form of bullet points, enumerated lists, linear graphs, bolded words and sentences, or other methods to place emphasis on concise bits of information. Chunking helps draw readers' attention to the particularly important aspects of an article. It also allows busy readers to skim the article for key points that apply to their practices. In the following example, notice how Professor Suzanne E. Rowe uses this method to make the information easy to read, understand, and retain.

Excerpt of an article that "chunks" information to make it easier to read

Perfect Proofing: 10 steps towards error-free documents[6]
By Professor Suzanne E. Rowe

Even after a legal document is written, revised and edited, it's still not finished. A final document must be subjected to perfect proofing before it can be filed with a court, mailed to a client, or handed to a supervisor. This final step is mechanical and sometimes tedious, but it's crucial to producing a professional document. The following proofreading tips take just a little time, and only some make you look silly.

Click on "print"

First, you must print the document. Proofing is almost always more effective when looking at a piece of paper than when staring at a computer screen.

....

Use spell check

Your word processor is a free editor, but many attorneys ignore its proofing capabilities. First, use spell check. Be sure to run every document through spell check one last time before printing the final version.

When using spell check, add to your computer's dictionary any legal terms or client names that it does not recognize. This keeps the computer from repeatedly identifying these terms or names as mistakes. If the computer doesn't know the spelling of Ms. Smythe's name, it will underline every appearance of the name in the document as a mistake. You're likely to ignore the underlining, even when you've misspelled her name. If you enter "Smythe" into the computer's dictionary, when you misspell Ms. Smythe's name as "Smyhte," the computer will identify only the mistake.

....

Go for coffee

If possible, allow enough time in the writing process to rest between edits. Two short edits separated by a break are often more effective than one longer session. Just tell your colleagues that the trip to Starbucks will make you a better writer.

If your workload doesn't allow for a coffee break, at least turn to another matter for a few minutes. When you shift gears back to the proofing project, you'll read it with more distance and see more mistakes.

....

Find a friend

Even the best proofreader is more likely to miss mistakes on her own work than on a colleague's work. If possible, find a co-worker who can review your document for you. Some firms have a proofreading department. Some secretaries have made reputations for finding tiny, but embarrassing errors. If time allows, and a willing helper is available, pass your document to a new set of eyes.

Perfection!

After a few weeks, these proofreading techniques can become second nature. They'll take less time, and they'll help produce perfect documents.

Notice how the author uses the chunking concept with short headings and active verbs to introduce each section. The headings are bolded, visually breaking up the chunks without slowing reading time.

The author conveys a lot of information in a short amount of space — exactly what a busy reader wants to see. This approach allows readers to quickly identify each recommendation.

9.2.B Professional drafting considerations

While many aspects of drafting are intended to ensure that readers are interested and that articles are clear and easy to read, other considerations are more practical and require professional consideration. For example, you should consider whether your article is one that your employer will approve, one that your clients or future clients will not find problematic, one that is consistent with your workplace's values, one that does not give rise to conflicts within your workplace (or, for students, future workplaces), or even one that does not jeopardize any political ambitions you might have.

To address these concerns, many employers—law firms in particular—maintain formal internal guidelines for their attorneys to follow when drafting articles or similar publications. These guidelines can range from restrictions on naming or identifying clients to those limiting publications through which articles may be distributed. Many firms, for instance, refuse to allow attorneys to disclose the names of firm clients, even where the attorney-client relationship is heavily publicized in the news. Other firms decline to allow attorneys to publish any article discussing cases or transactions relating to firm clients, even where the article is not directly connected to the firm's representation of that particular client. Often, firms require that *all* articles published in third-party journals or publications be peer reviewed by a partner-level attorney and that the articles receive the firm's final, formal approval prior to publication. Accordingly, even if your employer does not have specific policies, absent permission from the client, the best practice is to avoid situations where the article identifies or discusses a client, publicizes any aspects of a client's case, or discusses a situation in which a client was involved.

> **Practice Tip:**
>
> In addition to law firm guidance, be mindful of your jurisdiction's rules of ethics and professionalism, particularly as they relate to maintaining attorney-client confidentiality. The ABA's Model Rules of Professional Conduct, Rule 1.6, provides that "A lawyer shall not reveal information relating to the representation of a client unless the client gives informed consent, the disclosure is impliedly authorized in order to carry out the representation or the disclosure is permitted." Some jurisdictions broadly interpret this rule to even apply to client identity. In addition, the ABA's Ethics Committee recently issued Formal Opinion 480, which concludes that "Lawyers who blog or engage in other public commentary may not reveal information relating to a representation that is protected by Rule 1.6(a), including information contained in a public record, unless disclosure is authorized under the Model Rules." This opinion is broad in scope and it includes situations where a lawyer describes a client's "hypothetical" situation "if there is a reasonable likelihood that a third party may ascertain the client's identity or legal situation."

For law students and attorneys writing about practice areas in which they are not currently practicing, consider whether the manner in which you address an issue will present *future* conflicts. Anticipate whether the article relates to an area in which you are likely to practice in the future or are likely to have clients at some point in your career. Many potential clients heavily research their attorneys prior to hiring them, and a history of publications concerning decisions adverse to the potential client or maintaining stances adverse to the client's viewpoints are unlikely to garner goodwill or business.

Finally, consider whether the analysis contained within an article conflicts with your own personal beliefs as the author, and also consider how your beliefs could result in bias. The legal profession is rife with examples of attorneys who take positions contrary to their own personal beliefs when representing clients, with many criminal defense attorneys and commercial litigators providing prime examples. While an inherent conflict exists in drafting an article that reaches analytical conclusions contrary to your own personal convictions, that conflict should not prevent you from drafting such an article or undertaking an objective analysis. Rather, provided you are conscious of your personal beliefs and how those beliefs affect your review, such a conflict can benefit the overall article by providing an outlet for both viewpoints. Nonetheless, a professional article should not become a forum for dogmatic views or offensive ideas. Instead, the goal is to be interesting, useful, and thought provoking while appealing to a widespread professional audience. That audience might include attorneys in your own office, those in other offices, judges, or current and future clients. The article should maintain a professional tone and a reasonable position as you present reasoned analysis, whether that analysis upholds or contradicts your own beliefs.

To help ensure ongoing compliance with all professional and ethical responsibilities, make sure that you maintain a list of your published articles in an easily accessible place. Reread these articles periodically (every couple of years) to ensure all ethical obligations are still being met and that no previously expressed viewpoints need clarification in light of new facts. This caution is particularly important if an author plans to seek elected office or government employment. Past writings—even if the author no longer holds those views—can be used to paint an unflattering picture. Therefore, make sure any writing you place in the public domain is well grounded in both law and fact and supported by credible sources.

9.3 Publishing the bar journal article

The final aspect of publishing a professional article is to shepherd it through the publication process. Depending on the topic of the article and the end goal of publication, you may already have a publisher in mind before drafting the article. For example, someone from a local bar association might reach out to specifically request that you draft an article for the association's publication, or one of your colleagues might request that you co-author a journal article for which a publisher has already been obtained.

In instances where you have identified a publisher before drafting your article, consider what the publisher needs with respect to both form and content, and draft the article as closely as possible to meet those needs. As mentioned earlier in this chapter, make your publisher's job easy— adhere to the requirements for publication with respect to font, line spacing, formatting, and above all, length. For print publications particularly, the length of your article often will be dictated by the amount of space left in the publication after advertisements and regular monthly columns are inserted. The publisher or editor will almost certainly specify the maximum and, if applicable, minimum word counts. When such requirements are specified, follow those with exacting care to ensure that your article will fit in the journal. Otherwise, the publisher is likely to return the article for additional editing, or the editor might unilaterally edit the article without your input. Furthermore, make sure to obtain permissions for any material that may have a copyright, a particularly important concern if you incorporate any visual images. Adhering to requirements makes the publisher's task easier, and it also demonstrates your professionalism and ability to conform your articles to various requirements.

In other instances, you may need to shop your completed article to find a publisher who is willing to publish it. Usually the content of the article will dictate, in large part, the publishers' willingness to consider it. If so, the goal should be to identify a publication in which your article would be an appropriate fit. For instance, if your article concerns a recent decision concerning civil procedure, a publication marketed to litigators might be an appropriate forum. If your article is intended to be broadly applicable to all attorneys or a large subset of attorneys, a widely distributed bar association journal, such as a state or national bar association journal, might be a more appropriate option for publication. In either instance, shop your article to the best fitting publication.

Current law students might ask professors and practicing attorneys about bar association sections in which they are involved and that have section-specific publications. Law students also have some publication locations uniquely available to them. The ABA publishes *Student Lawyer Magazine*,[7] a quarterly publication featuring stories written for law students by their peers. With such journal publication opportunities, students get a voice in the legal discourse surrounding the evolution of law even before they start practicing!

Regardless of the publication you choose—or the publication that chooses you—keep all of these guidelines in place to ensure that your article is published promptly and reaches the broadest possible audience. So, consider writing a bar journal or other professional article, and help your professional reputation soar.

Notes

1. Michael Robinson & Ellen Murphy, *Talking to the Judge (or Maybe Not)*, N.C. St. B. J., Winter 2018, at 34–35.

2. *Id.*

3. Laura P. Graham, 23 N.C.L. Mag. 30, 30 (2013) (internal citations omitted).

4. Univ. of Chicago, The Chicago Manual of Style § 5.206 (16th ed. 2010).

5. John DiMarco, Communications Writing and Design: The Integrated Manual for Marketing, Advertising and Public Relations 27 (2017).

6. Suzanne E. Rowe, *Perfect Proofing: 10 Steps Towards Error-Free Documents*, Or. St. B. Bull., Dec. 2006, at 33, 33.

7. *See* A.B.A., *Student Lawyer Magazine*, abaforlawstudents.com (last visited Aug. 4, 2019).

Chapter 10

Policy Papers (White Papers)

10.1 Focusing on a topic

10.2 Experience with the topic

10.3 Research on the topic

10.4 Different types of policy papers

10.5 Drafting a positional policy paper

10.6 Drafting an analytical policy paper

The process of drafting white papers and policy papers, grouped together in this chapter as "policy papers," often presents an opportunity for practicing attorneys, law students, and others to assist clients with establishing formal positions on particular topics.[1] White papers originated as official government publications beginning around the 1920s, setting forth official government positions on given issues.[2] The term "white paper" was coined because government papers were color-coded for distribution purposes and white was assigned for public access.

More modern policy papers are generally detailed, analytical pieces of writing that address a specific topic, often either providing a particular institution's formal positions or policies on that topic or analyzing the appropriate positions or policies to implement. Because requirements for policy papers vary widely, so do their goals.

For many employers and clients, policy papers might be used to articulate and advocate for a particular governmental policy—such as the passage of certain statutes or regulations—and are distributed to third parties to publicize that position. Others are merely intended for internal distribution or policymaking and are not intended for distribution to third parties; in fact, a client might request that the analysis be shared only among senior decision-makers on its team. Policy papers might also be used to describe best practices for a given issue. In other instances, policy papers are intended to be an internal analysis that helps determine an official position to be publicized in the future. In short, a policy paper might be considered an infomercial for people who like to read. The purpose of a policy paper is to persuade through education—to persuade outsiders that a client's position is correct or to persuade the client about the appropriate course of action.

Policy papers, unlike law review articles or professional journal articles, will often be prepared for clients or employers. Nonetheless, preparing a policy paper presents the opportunity to practice analytical drafting skills. In addition, to the extent a policy paper is for a client or employer, the paper will provide the opportunity to analyze those entities' official positions and to ensure that the analysis is in tune with current and potential clients' views. In the process of drafting a policy paper, writers might also further develop their own views concerning the particular topic of the paper.

This chapter addresses the particular elements of focusing the topic for a policy paper, drafting the policy paper to achieve the client's final goals, and preparing the policy paper for distribution to employers, clients, or other parties.

10.1 Focusing on a topic

When focusing on a topic for a policy paper, there are often two principal considerations:

- Has an employer or a client requested that the policy paper address a specific topic?
- Is there a problem to be solved or an issue for which the employer or client needs a particular analysis?

10.1.A Employer's or client's requested topic

By their very nature, policy papers are most often intended to formalize a particular position on a very specific issue, rather than to broadly address a topic. While a professional article might be a "mile wide and an inch deep," a policy paper is the opposite, with a very in-depth analysis of an issue structured in a way that is similar to a memorandum drafted on behalf of a client.

In many instances, clients or employers will actively seek out an attorney to draft a policy paper on a given topic. In these instances, the topic-selection aspect of drafting a policy paper becomes much easier, since the topic is already dictated by the client's or employer's needs. Still, it is important to understand *why* a policy paper might be appropriate on such a topic. Because policy papers are often intended to represent a party's official position on a given issue, a request for a policy paper is likely to arise most frequently in one of the following situations:

When a party has
not yet taken an official
position on an issue

When changes
in the law or other
circumstances require
the party to take a
new position

When a party
wishes to change its
position on an issue

Although the need for a policy paper can arise at other times, these three situations most often precipitate the creation of a policy paper.

A common example of such a situation is when Congress begins the legislative process for a new statute or when a regulatory commission initiates the rulemaking process for a new rule affecting a client. Often, the client potentially affected by the statute or rule is likely to reach out for advice regarding the manner in which the proposed statute or rule is likely to impact its business interests. For example, a statute or regulation affecting minimum wage or workers' compensation requirements for employers is likely to garner significant interest from various chambers of commerce, employers, and other entities with a vested interest in business operations, spending, and other economics. Here, the client might need assistance in evaluating the practical impact on its business or its constituents' business interests.

Because the topic selection process for a policy paper is likely to be driven by client or employer needs, a writer might have little discretion in selecting a topic. Indeed, rather than *selecting* a topic, the writer's job will likely be to *narrow* or *focus* a topic to meet the client's or employer's requests. Consider the example above of a new minimum wage statute, in this case passed by a state-level legislative branch. If a client is a local or state-level chamber of commerce whose business objective is to increase economic activity, typically on the business or employer side of transactions, the chamber of commerce would most likely oppose increases in statutory minimum wages, particularly on a federal level. However, the chamber might have a less developed position on state-level statutes.

As a result, the client might ask for assistance in preparing a policy paper to analyze such state-level minimum wage statutes and to help develop its own position on the matter. In doing so, the topic should be focused:

- on the client requesting assistance;
- on the particular proposed statute at issue; and
- on the statute's effect on that particular client.

10.1.B Focusing on a topic without a client request

One aspect of attorney-client relationships and brand building is to anticipate clients' needs, which, on rare occasions, might involve drafting a policy paper that would be beneficial to a client. For instance, after learning of an impending regulatory decision or a statute that a client might not know is coming, you might draft a policy paper without the client's prompting.

In such a case, proactive anticipation and evaluation of a client's possible needs will help narrow the topic in large part and determine the final product that might be presented to the client. The goal of a self-generated policy paper should be to provide a reasonable analysis of a given issue in a way that the client might be able to use the analysis to develop and present its own official position on that issue in the future.

10.2 Experience with the topic

As with most professional publications, another principal consideration when drafting policy papers is quite basic: Do you have sufficient experience in and knowledge of the topic to adequately inform the client or other readers about the topic in an authoritative way? Because policy papers are intended to be authoritative analyses of a topic or of a client's position on a topic, a thorough and well-developed knowledge of a topic is needed to prepare a policy paper. Also, because policy papers are often meant to address a very specific aspect of the law, they might require expert analysis that falls outside the purview of your own practice or experience.

In light of these issues, consider whether you have sufficient knowledge and experience to write a policy paper on the specific issue that a client wants addressed. Some clients might demand that the person preparing a policy paper be an expert on the topic or otherwise have substantial experience in that field of law. Even where a client does not demand that an expert be the main drafter for a policy paper, it is often wise to consult an experienced colleague in the practice area at issue. This measure ensures that the client is best advised concerning not only the implications of a particular statute or regulation but also concerning the potential ramifications on the client generally.

10.3 Research on the topic

As practitioners or law students, most authors are able to evaluate facts, draft summaries of those facts, and present them in an articulate manner. A recitation of facts, while important to a policy paper's overall structure, will not be the main focus of the policy paper. The real substance of a policy paper is its analysis.

To prepare analysis for a policy paper, one vital question is: How much research is enough? The answer depends in large part on how familiar you are with the topic. If you are an expert in the field and are well versed on the topic of the policy paper, the research might be limited to confirming that nothing has changed in the state of the law to affect your current understanding. If you are not yet an expert in the field or do not at least have a substantial background in it, more substantial research will likely be necessary.

In general, research for a policy paper should permit at least three things:

- The research must allow you to concisely explain the issue to be resolved.
- The research must allow you to propose at least one viable solution to that issue.
- The research should implicitly assure the audience of your credibility based on the degree and thoroughness of your process.

10.4 Different types of policy papers

Because the topic for a policy paper is often predetermined by a client or employer, and because experience with a particular practice area will often be the impetus for the client's request to prepare the policy paper, the most important aspect of the policy paper process for practitioners and law students is the drafting process itself. Although policy papers come in various forms and formats, they most commonly take one of three forms: positional, analytical, and marketing.

Different types of policy papers

Type	Purpose
Positional	Takes a formal position on an issue of relative importance.
Analytical	Thoroughly analyzes an issue and helps determine whether a party should take a position, and if so, what that position should entail.
Marketing	Most often introduces new products or services to a specific consumer group.

Both positional and analytical policy papers may effectively serve as a memorandum to or for a client concerning the legal issue at hand. The remainder of this chapter will focus on positional and analytical policy papers because lawyers more frequently draft those types of papers for their clients.

10.4.A Consider the audience

Prior to beginning the drafting process for a policy paper, you must first consider the audience. The policy paper should be tailored to the needs of the audience because without an engaged audience, a policy paper is of little benefit to a client. The audience will dictate the approach to a policy paper, the lines of reasoning to use, and the overall presentation. Consider which form the policy paper will take:

- Will it be positional and intended for third parties on behalf of a client; or
- Will it be analytical and directed mainly to the client?

Without a complete understanding of the audience, the policy paper is likely to frustrate readers, deviate from their expectations, and fail to provide the information that they need.

In examining the audience, develop a basic profile of common characteristics. Where a single client is the entire audience, the analysis is likely to differ significantly from instances where an entire group of individuals is the intended audience. Some common considerations in thinking about the audience across the spectrum might, however, include the following non-exclusive considerations:[3]

Pro writing tips when considering the audience:

1. Present the analysis of the issue or problem objectively, even if it is intended to persuade the reader;
2. Write the paper in such a way that a reader without prior knowledge of the issues would be able to follow;
3. Provide sufficient detail so that the reader understands all the aspects of the issue; and
4. Avoid unnecessary legal jargon.

Considerations in thinking about your audience

Considerations	Options
What sophistication does the audience have, generally?	Consider changing the tone and language in response to the audience's sophistication level. For example, include more conversational and straightforward language for audience members who are not trained in the law or who may not have extensive education on the topic, and use more technical language or formal tone for audience members who have greater knowledge or legal sophistication.

Considerations in thinking about your audience continued

Considerations	Options
How much experience does the audience have in this particular area?	More experience often means less explanation. Where the audience lacks experience, it might be helpful to define technical terms or avoid industry specific jargon. If you are writing to practitioners in that field, you may find the added detail unnecessary.
Is the audience familiar with the backstory or context of the problem you are describing?	Consider a short explanation of historical context, explaining how and why the policy paper is relevant and necessary.

In some instances, multiple policy papers are more appropriate than a single policy paper. To illustrate, if a client requests a policy paper to address a contentious issue, the approach, tone, and reasoning might vary for different parties with different interests in the same issue. As a result, it might be appropriate to "repackage" the analysis depending on the third parties to whom a policy paper will be submitted, ensuring that the client's position is maintained but that it is presented in a way that is least likely to create conflict or raise objections.

10.4.B General drafting considerations

Before discussing the various types of policy papers and considerations for drafting those, remember that the basic rules of drafting continue to apply when drafting policy papers:

- **Use short paragraphs.** Shorter paragraphs help ensure that each paragraph remains on point; without too many sentences, the paragraph will be less likely to stray from its thesis. Also, short paragraphs will allow readers to get through the paper more easily, lessening the likelihood that readers will either become bogged down by overly long passages or skip important paragraphs entirely.
- **Craft concise sentences.** Concise sentences help keep the reader's attention. Preferring shorter, direct sentences over complex sentences that span multiple lines can aid the reader's understanding while maintaining the reader's attention.
- **Keep the content simple.** The more complex the legal topic, the simpler the writing should be. Eliminate content obstacles when possible: Ensure that technical terms and acronyms are clearly defined and that audience members are not left guessing at the meaning of terms or phrases.

The well-known benefits of using visuals in writing include:

- Retaining readers' interest;
- Conveying facts, spatial connections, or comparisons quickly;
- Breaking up blocks of text; and
- Making the overall aesthetics of an otherwise long, uniform paper more visually attractive.

The key is to ensure that each graphic representation, regardless of the form it takes, furthers the argument and complements the text. Visual representations should never undercut your argument or your credibility with the audience. *See generally* Steve Johansen & Ruth Anne Robbins, *Art-iculating the Analysis: Systemizing the Decision to Use Visuals as Legal Reasoning*, 20 J. Legal Writing Inst. 57 (2015).

- **Use visuals.** These might be charts, pictures, tables, graphs, or any other demonstrative information that conveys in one or two images the same information that might take many pages or paragraphs to explain.

- **Use examples or analogies.** When real-life occurrences illustrate the problem, do not hesitate to use them as examples. Likewise, hypothetical situations or analogies can be useful tools to help readers understand a problem and its implications.

10.5 Drafting a positional policy paper

A positional policy paper begins with a basic premise: An issue of note has arisen on which a client wishes to take a formal position and then convey that position to the general public. Some clients are aware of policy papers only in concept, while some have no familiarity with policy papers at all. Others might draft policy papers internally on business topics or related matters and simply outsource their legal policy papers. A client who needs a policy paper might not *know* that a policy paper is needed to convey a position. In many instances, that client might simply ask for assistance in analyzing a newly proposed statute or regulation or a recent court decision. Your response to this request might be determining how the proposed statute, regulation, or recent decision affects the client as well as what position the client should take on the issue. The client might not specifically request that the analysis be in the form of a "policy paper" and might instead leave the determination to your discretion, as the lawyer. In other instances, sophisticated institutional clients are more likely to directly request a policy paper as the end product.

Regardless of how the topic of a policy paper arises, by making its position known, a client (particularly if a business or company) generally wishes to convince the public that its position is correct. In the minimum wage example discussed earlier, the client may want to explain its position as to why an increased, decreased, or non-existent statutory minimum wage is most appropriate and how that position is supported by the evidence. In crafting that explanation, you should not be the center of attention as the author. Rather, the paper should be drafted in such a way that it merely trains readers' thoughts and analysis on the substantive issues addressed in the paper.

Because policy papers vary significantly from client to client, there is no one-size-fits-all option for drafting or formatting a policy paper. Positional policy papers do, however, often share many of the same characteristics and basic components from client to client. In general, the goal and structure of a positional policy paper is to convince the reader that the client's position is correct and that the audience should likewise adopt that position. Rather than overt advocacy, however, policy papers are intended to present information in a convincing but relatively objective manner. Below is a table describing a step-by-step approach to drafting a positional policy paper, followed by a description of each step in further detail.

A step-by-step approach to drafting a positional policy paper

Step 1: Describe the issue on which the paper takes a position.

Step 2: Define the client's position on the issue.

Step 3: Provide an overview of the current state of the law at issue.

Step 4: Evaluate and analyze the position taken using supporting data.

Step 5: Analyze and rebut other interpretations of the same data.

Step 6: Conclude.

First, the policy paper will set out and describe the issue on which the paper takes a position and provide a short summary of that position. For example, "An ongoing debate disputes whether higher taxes are good or bad. This paper addresses the issue of taxation on businesses and the legal ramifications of taxes, particularly [describe any particular issues to be addressed]." Of course, the discussion should be as detailed and explanatory as possible while maintaining brevity.

Second, the paper should define the client's position on the issue, preferably taking a clear, unequivocal position that aligns with the client's values, goals, and interests. In a positional paper, this section is, in many respects, the most important part of the paper, and it should be structured accordingly. The position should be described in an objective, straightforward, non-argumentative way. The subsequent sections will delve into analysis and review relevant statutes, regulations, and related points and compare data that might not be favorable. Those points do not need to be addressed in describing the client's position.

The sample below, an introduction to a positional policy paper, analyzes the merits of a judicial selection system and explains how the system is problematic. The paper explains the system in which the state legislature selects judges to fill vacancies. The paper then works to persuade the audience that legislative selection of judges (a process used by only two states) has additional problems and would not alleviate issues the state faces with its judicial elections system. Notice how, in the excerpt below, the writer clearly sets out Step 1 by describing the issue and Step 2 by defining a position on the issue.

Sample Introduction to a positional policy paper[4]

Media reports suggest North Carolina's legislative leaders may soon propose replacing its system of electing judges with a system in which the state legislature selects judges to fill vacancies. The contours of the proposal are not yet public, including whether legislators will grant themselves exclusive authority to appoint judges, or whether they will incorporate a commission to recommend candidates. Whatever the proposal, it will be a marked shift from North Carolina's current system of electing judges. This brief outlines some significant concerns raised by legislative appointment systems.

The Brennan Center has long documented the problems surrounding judicial elections — **big spending by opaque outside groups, conflicts of interest for judges who decide cases affecting their campaign supporters, and evidence that judges change their behavior on the bench** to avoid being the target of big spending or attack ads in future elections.

There is little evidence that a legislative appointment system would combat those issues. The lack of evidence is in part because legislative appointment is the rarest form of judicial selection in the country. Twenty-one states hold nonpartisan or partisan judicial elections, fourteen states use what is popularly referred to as "merit selection," in which the governor makes initial appointments from a list recommended by a nominating commission, followed by periodic retention elections, eight states use gubernatorial appointment systems, and five states use hybrid systems. There is extensive research analyzing judicial elections and merit selection, the most common systems of judicial selection. Only two states, South Carolina and Virginia, currently empower their legislatures to appoint state high court judges to their first full term on the bench, and there is little study of those systems. Rhode Island previously used legislative appointments until scandals led to the abandonment of that system in 1994.

However, the evidence that does exist from South Carolina, Virginia, and Rhode Island suggests that legislative appointments are unlikely to alleviate the problems associated with judicial elections and may further undermine judicial independence and integrity in critical ways. While there are good reasons to be concerned about how judicial elections are operating in North Carolina, legislative appointment systems present unique and understudied problems. Further, the specific details of how a legislative appointment plan is implemented, along with other factors such as a state's political culture, are crucial to understanding the likely impact of a move to legislative appointments. These factors should be seriously considered before adopting a legislative appointment system in North Carolina.

Below we outline several common problems that have arisen in legislative appointment systems, based primarily on news accounts and some scholarly research.

Notice that the first paragraph identifies the issue and describes it in depth. The second paragraph describes the problem with the current system of judicial elections so the reader can understand the problems with the current system. This structure will help the reader better understand the writer's ultimate position.

Notice how the author follows Step 2 here by clearly explaining the position to be taken in the paper and by specifying which evidence will support the position.

The third paragraph provides an overview of how different states grapple with the issue of judicial selection. By showing that only two states allow selection via the state legislature, the writer is foreshadowing the position she will be taking in the paper.

By summarizing the evidence from the few states who allow for legislatures to select judges and showing how that process does not alleviate the unique problems that exist in North Carolina, the author further sets up her ultimate position.

Third, the paper should provide an overview of the current state of the law, regulations, or the other main issue and topic of the paper, summarizing and explaining the importance and effects of the issue:

- What does the current law do?
- How does it affect the audience?
- What is the law's overall importance?

Fourth, the paper must thoroughly evaluate and analyze the information that you are presenting. Typically, policy papers are loaded with data to support the conclusion. Using the minimum wage example discussed previously, a typical policy paper addressing this issue would likely analyze and discuss detailed information including the number of individuals making minimum wage, minimum wage amounts based on jurisdictions, the economic spending power of individuals making varying minimum wages, the economic benefits of increased or decreased minimum wages, and the costs to employers. All of this information would (or should) be supported by scientifically proven data that can be used to draw reasonable inferences used in the policy paper. The paper should analyze this information to reach the client's objectively supportable conclusion and should explain how the data led to that conclusion. For example, assuming the relevant data demonstrate that a higher minimum wage leads to increased spending among minimum wage earners and that increased spending leads to better economic results for the surrounding economy generally, a business client might be in favor of a higher statutory minimum wage. The policy paper should provide a clear path of its analysis to allow readers to follow along.

Fifth, the paper should also analyze and rebut other interpretations of the same data. For instance, if the client's position is that a statutory minimum wage increase is good for businesses and the economy and that the statute should be amended, the policy paper should use the data it cites to explain both why an increase is justified and why a decrease is not justified. The data should be used to rebut these differing views and opinions or to otherwise frame them in such a way that the client's position is the more viable option, where possible. Almost inevitably, some of the data or other information will reach conclusions that do not support the client's positions. You must address the data head on, as any intelligent audience will have a healthy sense of skepticism and expect there to be competing data on most points, and omission of the data and related information would likely lead the audience to conclude that the policy paper is intended to intentionally mislead them.

Identifying the contrasting facts and data affords a number of benefits, including having the opportunity to address them first, before an unfriendly critic of the client does so, and building credibility with the audience by acknowledging that there are multiple sides to the story. By taking the opportunity to address opposing facts and data, you have the chance to cast them in the appropriate light—explaining how the results do not apply, the methodology was flawed, or the data can be interpreted differently. Similarly, by acknowledging the existence of alternative sets of data reaching different conclusions, you build credibility with the audience and come across as an honest and objective guide for them.

Sixth, and finally, the positional policy paper should have a formal conclusion, reiterating the initial short analysis and conclusion and tying a finishing bow on the policy paper.

After handling each of these points, you will have a positional policy paper.

10.6 Drafting an analytical policy paper

An analytical policy paper, like a positional policy paper, is a fairly basic piece of writing. In fact, most practicing attorneys, law students, and professors are likely familiar with it, though possibly by a different name. In effect, an analytical policy paper is much the same as an objective client memorandum. While the main goal of a positional policy paper is to identify a position for a client and to convey that position to the general public, the goal of an analytical policy paper is to analyze one or more issues for a client, often explaining to the client, rather than the public, how the issue would affect the client.

For example, while a positional policy paper might require a client to explain to the public why a higher statutory minimum wage is beneficial to the business community and the economy generally, an analytical policy paper might precede it, analyzing the effects of both lower and higher statutory minimum wages on the client to help it decide what position to take. Of course, like a memo on a particular issue, the client might also simply want an overview or analysis of the issue or issues for its own internal operations, with no intention of taking a public stance. In practice, many attorneys find that clients requesting a "white paper" most often want a policy paper of the analytical variety, mostly to explain how a statutory or regulatory change will affect their businesses.

Regardless of a client's reasons for requesting an analytical policy paper, the structure will be something of a combination between a client memorandum and a positional policy paper. Below is a step-by-step approach to drafting an analytical policy paper, followed by a detailed explanation of each step.

A step-by-step approach to drafting an analytical policy paper

Step 1: Identify and describe the issue to be addressed.

Step 2: Provide a short summary of the writer's conclusions.

Step 3: Provide an overview of the current state of the law.

Step 4: Provide an overview of the proposed changes to the law.

Step 5: Analyze how the proposed changes affect the law and the client.

Step 6: Conclude.

First, the policy paper should identify and describe the issue or issues to be addressed for the client.

Second, to the extent the issue or issues have a readily identifiable "answer"—such as how exactly an increased or decreased statutory minimum wage would affect the client—the policy paper should provide a short answer or short analysis, providing an initial summary of your conclusions. This short answer should be concise but should also provide enough information that, if the client decided not to read further, it would answer the question.

Third, the paper should provide an introductory overview of the current state of the laws, regulations, or issue to be addressed in the paper. If the client's questions concern minimum wage, this section should provide a general overview of applicable minimum wage laws; if the questions relate to changes in insurance coverage for employees, the section should provide an overview of the insurance requirements and so on. The excerpt below provides an example of an effective introduction, providing a succinct and easy-to-understand overview of the paper:

Sample introduction to an analytical policy paper[5]

In contemporary market democracies, law reaches deeply into many aspects of daily life. Thousands of Americans every day find themselves facing troubles that emerge "at the intersection of civil law and everyday adversity," involving work, finances, insurance, pensions, wages, benefits, shelter, and the care of young children and dependent adults, among other core matters. Though these different types of problems affect different aspects of people's lives and concern different kinds of relationships, they are defined by a central important quality: they are justiciable. They have civil legal aspects, raise civil legal issues, have consequences shaped by civil law, and may become objects of formal legal action.

This Paper reviews what we know about the civil legal needs of the public, focusing on the U.S. context but drawing on research from peer nations as well. In so doing, the Paper reveals some key gaps in our knowledge. Across a range of studies, we have good evidence that:

- Experience with civil justice situations is common and widespread, affecting all segments of the population. Many involve "bread and butter issues" at the core of contemporary life, affecting livelihood, shelter, or the care and custody of dependents.
- Populations that are vulnerable or disadvantaged often report higher rates of contact with civil justice situations, and greater incidence of negative consequences from these events.
- Most civil justice situations will never involve contact with an attorney or a court.
- The most important reasons that people do not take their civil justice situations to law are:
  (1) They do not think the issues are legal or consider law as a solution; and
  (2) They often believe that they understand their situations and are taking those actions that are possible.
- The cost of legal services or court processes plays a secondary role in people's decisions about how to handle the civil justice situations they encounter.

Paradoxically, despite the stylized facts we often deploy in our arguments and advocacy, we do not know the answers to some of the million dollar questions. To be specific, we do not know:

- How many civil justice situations are actually civil legal needs;
- How many civil legal needs go unmet; and
- How civil legal needs affect the people who experience them and society at large.

Note how the author clearly establishes the purpose of the paper, plus the issues for which answers are known and those for which answers remain unknown.

Fourth, the paper should provide a thorough overview of the proposed *changes* to the applicable statutes or regulations, describing how those changes would modify the status quo.

Fifth, the paper should address exactly how the proposed changes would affect the client and its interests. In some instances this section and the preceding section might be combined into one discussion of both the changes and how they will affect the client, but to facilitate ease of reading, many authors choose to create distinct sections. To the extent that any facts (e.g., data) support this analysis, they should be included in this section. In addition, because an analytical policy paper is intended to provide an objective overview of information rather than a subjective persuasive view, this section should also include potentially negative data—the data that might reflect information unfavorable to the client but that the client needs to know to make an informed decision on how to proceed. Because data and scientific research are often the defining characteristics of a policy paper, it is particularly important that relevant data, research, and other scientific information be included in the analysis of how proposed changes might affect a client. Indeed, the inclusion of such data and research is the main distinction between an analytical policy paper and a memorandum drafted for a client's review. As with positional policy papers, the analytical policy paper should provide a clear path of its analysis to allow readers to follow along.

Sixth, and finally, the analytical policy paper should have a formal conclusion, reiterating the initial short analysis and conclusion.[6]

Policy papers need not be mystifying or intimidating. In many ways, they resemble the types of work that law students get as soon as they begin law school. With logical structure, clear analysis, and effective writing skills, you can confidently produce any kind of policy paper assignment.

Notes

1. We would like to thank Lewis & Clark Law graduate Daniel Fan for his excellent research and writing contributions to this chapter.

2. Purdue Online Writing Lab, *White Paper: Purpose and Audience*, owl.purdue.edu (last visited Jan. 7, 2019).

3. Al Kemp, White Paper Writing Guide: How to Achieve Marketing Goals by Explaining Technical Details 6, 9, 71–72 (2005).

4. Douglas Keith & Laila Robbins, *Legislative Appointments for Judges: Lessons from South Carolina, Virginia, and Rhode Island*, Brennan Ctr. Just. (Sept. 29, 2017) (citations and footnotes omitted) (direct quote; quotation marks omitted).

5. Rebecca L. Sandefur, *What We Know and Need to Know About the Legal Needs of the Public*, 67 S.C. L. Rev. 443, 443–44 (2016) (citations and footnotes omitted) (direct quote; quotation marks omitted).

6. *See generally* Kemp, *supra* (discussing white paper writing); Purdue Online Writing Lab, *supra* (same).

Chapter 11

Op-Eds

11.1   Why write an op-ed?
11.2   Trust and discourse: Elements of a successful op-ed
11.3   Drafting the op-ed

An Opinion Editorial (op-ed) is a short article expressing the personal views of the author on a specific issue that is submitted to a news media outlet for publication. Authors write op-eds on a diverse array of topics—political debates, the correct interpretation of a criminal law statute, drafting strategy for sports athletes, or even the effectiveness of plant-based products on removing stains. Regardless of the topic, op-eds are primarily written for two reasons:

- To garner attention on an issue of which many readers are unaware; and
- To convince readers that the author's argument offers the best way forward.

Op-eds are readily accessible in a variety of forms. For example, internet news aggregation sites such as Real Clear Politics[1] present viewers with a long list of op-eds written by authors across the political spectrum. This compilation allows users to gather information from a variety of sources to create an informed opinion. Similarly, printed newspapers often feature op-eds opposite the editorial page, the place where a paper's editorial board states its opinions, to provide readers an additional perspective on controversial topics. In addition, some news media outlets and papers feature op-eds online that can be freely accessed by their site's subscribers and the public.

11.1 Why write an op-ed?

The professional and personal benefits of writing an op-ed go far beyond simply raising awareness about an important topic. Through pointed criticisms of congressional bills, insightful comments about underreported statistics, or a unique perspective on a "settled" issue, legal writers (whether law students, practitioners, or academics) can shift the course of dialogue.

Beyond affecting discourse, successful op-eds also help authors attain recognition and establish trust with the public. By writing well-researched opinions for popular media outlets, authors promote their credibility on future issues and bolster readership of their other scholarship pieces. After all, millions more people read op-eds published in online newspapers than scholarship printed in academic journals or books. This wide release introduces the author to the viewing public as a knowledgeable person with the credentials needed to help address specific problems.

11.2 Trust and discourse: Elements of a successful op-ed

Consider reviewing the earlier chapters in this book to identify potential topics (Ch. 1), to obtain research tips (Ch. 2), to craft an effective thesis (Ch. 3), and to hone your analysis by developing persuasive arguments and using supporting data (Ch. 4).

Creating a successful op-ed, like other pieces of legal scholarship, starts by choosing a topic relevant to a news outlet's readership. From there, meticulous research must be completed to identify relevant arguments and data before drafting. Additionally, maintaining a strong narrative voice that demonstrates civility toward readers holding differing opinions is key to effectuating any change. (You may want to preview Chapter 13, *Creative Works*, for a more in-depth discussion regarding the use of narrative voice.)

11.2.A Topic selection

Relevance: To foster public dialogue, various groups should be connected to the subject matter.

Timeliness: Challenged by the news cycle, which constantly changes.

Like any other piece of legal scholarship, creating a successful op-ed begins with topic selection. When choosing a topic, consider two primary aspects: relevance and timeliness. For the piece to foster a public dialogue, various groups must feel connected to the subject matter including you as the author, the media outlet running the editorial, the viewing public, and the news cycle at large. Choosing a timely topic is also challenged by the fickle and fleeting cycle of information; the news cycle is constantly changing, and what is relevant today may be stale in a week. Timeliness is further complicated by our obligation to be credible and effective—the op-ed should be accurate, precise, and solidly grounded with credible research and data.

To find a topic, start by combing through the week's news stories for issues that are personally interesting. Maybe there is a story on a new bill proposed by the legislature advocating the aerosolization of chemical byproducts into the atmosphere to reduce the amount of waste in landfills, but you believe such a policy would be detrimental to local ecosystems. From there, conduct research to see if information exists supporting that thesis. For instance, if writing an op-ed about the aerosolizing of chemicals, this might include determining whether similar bills have been passed in other states and, if so, whether environmentalist groups have compiled any statistics concerning its detrimental effects on the environment.

One consideration affecting your choice of topic is where the piece may be published; from the outset, consider which media outlet might publish the piece. For example, an environmentally conscious news outlet like the *Environmental News Network* might be interested in publishing a pollution-related piece. Broader considerations about the topic also merit your attention, including the scope of your topic and the demographics of the outlet's readership. For example, the outlet's readership could be too narrow, or the op-ed might be intended to reach readers who do not typically read about environmental issues. Thus, if your topic has appeal beyond a narrow readership, you might consider an outlet that has a larger national readership or one that draws readers from a variety of fields.

11.2.B Evidence and how to use it

For op-ed pieces, you will want to support your main assertions, but because a great deal of the piece flows from your own opinion, you will not need to cite with the frequency needed in a brief or law review article. In law school, like many other areas of education, students are told to provide evidence for all of their claims or risk losing precious points. Providing legal authority and a citation after just about every sentence is commonplace in most legal writing. Although writers should support their positions by using statistics, expert opinions, and other data, this model may be adjusted when writing an op-ed because the writer's opinion interests the reader far more than a laundry list of facts and numerical data.

Detailed evidence from credible sources provides the foundation for a successful op-ed, but citations to such evidence should be used judiciously. Overwhelming the reader with too many specific facts may obscure both the analysis and narrative voice. Readers know they are reading an opinion and therefore expect to be presented with a strong narrative voice taking a definitive, yet respectful, stance on an issue. This strong narrative encourages readers to think critically about the writer's stance and maybe even research the issue in more detail themselves; this additional thought and research may lead the reader to the discovery of additional information that will support or critique the writer's position.

The types of evidence used in an op-ed vary depending on the piece's purpose. Expert opinions from well-respected academics and professionals bolster a piece's credibility by showing that the author's position aligns with that of other scholars. Evidence from non-partisan entities provides readers with defined numbers and percentages to convey the gravity of a situation. Furthermore, incorporating analogies and examples can help relate stories to readers' own life experiences.

• Expert opinion

An expert opinion is simply the views or researched thoughts of someone who is considered an authority in a particular field. That person could be a government official, a professor, or someone with decades of experience. By quoting them or citing their scholarship, writers leverage the experts' credibility; their words help convince readers that the writer's opinion is not from the fringe but is something that has support from other intellectuals.

For example, the head of a government agency, such as the Department of Environmental Quality, might be an expert whose opinion would be influential for the earlier example concerning the environmental impact of the aerosolization of landfill chemicals into the atmosphere. Before using an individual's opinion, always look to see if the expert has taken a stance against a proposed policy or has expressed any concern about pending legislation. When choosing an expert, it may be helpful to avoid partisan organizations or lighting-rod politicians. These individuals could have a corrosive effect on readership, since many readers could have dubious views of the expert's credibility. If the op-ed is meant for a bipartisan audience, consider using political figures who have shown a willingness to bridge the partisan divide. Investing time to find an expert respected across the political spectrum encourages skeptical readers to engage with the text and reconsider their positions.

• Statistics

Hard data gathered from a reliable source can be a powerful tool to help persuade readers. These data strengthen an argument by acting as a higher authority; if third-party data validate the writer's concerns, readers tend to view the scholarship credibly. However, always thoroughly check the source of the statistic, especially since certain websites or agencies may have a history of dubious data plagued by polling errors. Some sources even have a nefarious intent to misinform readers and cause them to unwittingly adopt conspiracy theories or unsupported assertions. In the last several years, many websites that deliberately publish false facts have, with good reason, come under increased scrutiny from the federal government.

Usable statistics come in a variety of forms. Polls from organizations such as Gallup, Rasmussen, Pew Research, and similar non-partisan organizations are particularly influential in political pieces. For example, if a 2020 poll indicated that 45% of Americans worry about climate change "a great deal," the results of this poll could be used to show readers that Americans care about the environmental impact of certain chemicals.

The results of empirical studies conducted by experts might also bolster a piece's credibility. Empirical studies are like polls in that they extrapolate results from a smaller population and then apply them to a much larger group. However, their scope extends beyond opinions. Empirical studies attempt to derive the effect of one or more variables on another to better understand a phenomenon. For example, a study noting the socioeconomic status of individuals living within five miles of landfills that aerosolize chemicals might help show whether the poor would be disproportionately affected by the proposed legislation.

- **Analogies and examples**

Writers often attempt to help their readers understand a large issue by providing an analogy or example that illustrates the issue on a smaller scale. Using an analogy or an example is particularly helpful if the audience has had limited exposure to the issues in the piece. However, overusing analogies can be dangerous because they risk obscuring the main point. Lawyers win cases for clients by analogizing current issues to something already decided in prior cases. The link sometimes requires some logical reasoning on the part of the judge and might ultimately be distinguished in the court's opinion. Conversely, op-ed analogies should be so clear that they can only be interpreted one way. The analogies are meant to provide context and clarification—not to be a topic for debate. Therefore, the analogy should be an accurate reflection of the point to be made.

Examples can also be powerful additions to an op-ed because they show the reader the real-world effects of a policy. An example might tell the story of a specific person's experience dealing with a biased policy or situation beyond their control. For instance, after the longest government shutdown in U.S. history in January 2019, dozens of personal stories were published about the shutdown's harsh effects. These stories showed readers the costs—which often extended beyond financial trauma—of our legislators' inability to find a compromise to reopen the government.[2] Including these real-life examples helped authors advocate for reopening the government immediately and impressed upon readers the need to contact their legislators about the situation.

Consent is important when using someone's personal narrative in a publication. Writers should never confuse someone's willingness to share an individual personal story with that person's consent to having that story published. Writers must always ask for the source's permission to have the story told publicly for a specific cause before writing the piece. Sources might also be asked if using a pseudonym in the piece to hide their identity would make them feel more comfortable. This simple step helps build the author's credibility as someone who respects their sources of information.

11.2.C Maintaining a strong, authoritative voice

Op-ed authors present their views to a readership eager to learn more about a particular issue. This format requires more than expert opinions, statistics, and examples; it requires a commanding narrative voice that informs but does not offend, because no one likes being demeaned for their beliefs or being made to feel unintelligent because they approach an issue in a certain way. This is not to say that an op-ed should not debunk contrary opinions (some of which might not rely on the best facts); rather, it should do so courteously and civilly. To convince readers, an author must appear knowledgeable without seeming pompous.

Regular contribution to the discourse on a topic is one way to build a strong narrative voice. If readers are used to hearing from someone routinely, they are more likely to view their points as credible. Therefore, op-eds might be tailored to advocate for improvements to a single area of the law. This could relate to environmental policy, social justice, or immigration reform, for example. Whatever the topic, using germane news events in an op-ed builds a strong narrative voice that carries into newly written pieces.

• Emotion

Effectively harnessing emotion is the key to maintaining a strong narrative voice. Excellent op-ed writers have an emotional attachment to their topics that drives their work and helps maintain quality. Therefore, statements (or images) appealing to a reader's emotions can be valuable additions to an op-ed.

However, do not let emotional appeals overshadow hard facts. Evidence of hard facts builds credibility, while emotion evokes readers' sympathies to convince them that the issue is worthy of their time. Too much emotion may alienate the reader. Therefore, rather than stand alone, emotional appeals should supplement data and expert opinions in an op-ed.

• Civility

When writing, be mindful that the tone of the piece does not devolve into incivility. In today's political world of fake news and alternative facts, both sides of debatable issues often fail to maintain a civil discourse. Further, politicos can exacerbate conflict and polarize the debate. The rash bravado and one-liners of similarly minded politicians and pundits often entertain rather than inform. These actions limit the potential to build consensus and effect change by making persuadable individuals feel insulted or demeaned. Therefore, always consider whether the tone of an op-ed furthers the piece's objectives by asking the following questions:

- Does it make jokes about some readers' beliefs that may be considered offensive?
- Are radical claims presented with limited or no support?

If the answer to either of these questions is "yes," consider softening the language to remain non-partisan and promote a more diverse readership. An echo chamber often appears to validate opinions, but instead, it merely isolates them from public discourse.

Excerpt from an op-ed

Oregon's new death-penalty law is not retroactive.
It's how the law works.[3]
By Stephen Kanter and Aliza B. Kaplan
Kanter is emeritus dean at Lewis & Clark Law School. Kaplan is a law professor and Director of the Criminal Justice Reform Clinic at Lewis & Clark Law School.

Recently, we've seen some controversy emerge over Senate Bill 1013, the new law that sensibly narrows the definition of aggravated murder. Currently, aggravated murder is the only crime in Oregon for which someone can be sentenced to death.

The Oregon Department of Justice recently released an opinion that says the new law applies to pending cases, and to cases where death penalty convictions and sentences have been overturned but no new death sentence has been imposed. Prosecutors — who largely opposed the bill during the legislative session — cried foul, claiming they'd been misled. They're now demanding the Legislature "fix" the new law.

This call is perplexing and potentially damaging. As law professors who closely tracked the legislative process and supported and testified for SB 1013, the DOJ opinion aligns with our understanding of SB 1013's language, intent and impact. Changing SB 1013 now, as some prosecutors are suggesting, would have serious unintended consequences.

Like most Oregonians, we believe accountability in our criminal justice system is paramount. People who are guilty of crimes must be held accountable for them. And if there are errors in how cases have been tried, people accused of crimes deserve due process to be sure that they are not inappropriately sentenced to death and innocent individuals are not executed.

SB 1013 was professionally and carefully drafted in alignment with those values, and the new law is not retroactive. That means it does not reverse the convictions or sentences of people on Oregon's death row.

If the new law were retroactive, it would mean that even those with valid death sentences affirmed through appeals could request a new trial or sentencing under SB 1013. Legislators rebuffed that approach by rejecting a different bill that expressly sought that outcome. Instead, they passed SB 1013, which allows death sentences to stand when original convictions and death sentences are valid.

Although the authors are criticizing a stance on a legal issue, notice that they maintain civility and do not engage in ad hominem attacks against any particular group. Legal communities are often quite small, so when writing in a public form like an op-ed, be mindful that any zeal to persuade not result in incivility.

But SB 1013 does — and should — apply to death row cases that are over-turned on appeal because the old trial or sentence is ruled unconstitutional or un-fair. That's not retroactivity — that's retrial or resentencing to correct serious errors. Moreover, a reversal of a death sentence (where the conviction remains valid) does not mean release, it means life in prison, often without the possibility of parole.

Hard numbers provide a tangible example of the underlying harm the bill seeks to correct. These hard numbers both sup-port the assertions and persuade the reader that any potential adverse result is minimal in comparison to the harm.

This isn't an issue of semantics; rather, it's how the law works. When someone is re-prosecuted after a reversal, current laws at the time of retrial or resentencing will apply.

The "fix" some prosecutors are asking for would effectively take away due process rights that everyone deserves, even those accused of a very serious crime. Unfortunately, the death penalty is too often unconstitutionally applied, and sometimes, innocent people are sentenced to death; **Since 1973, over 156 people have been released from death rows in 26 states because of innocence.** Nationally, at least one person is exonerated for every 10 who are executed. When the stakes are this high, it is critically important that defendants receive a fair trial and sentencing proceeding.

Notice how the authors appeal to emotion in a subtle way by assuring readers that the bill maintains safety while simultaneously being more just.

Finally, we cannot let this debate distract from the numerous benefits of SB 1013. **By clarifying when the death penalty can be applied, SB 1013 will make prosecutors' jobs easier.** They won't be forced to make as many difficult discre-tionary decisions, or allocate scarce resources toward expensive capital trials where a death penalty sentence is not likely to be obtained, or is likely to be overturned if it is obtained. Instead, our state can focus our finite public resources on effective violence prevention measures including mental health treatment and addiction re-covery programs, victim services, and public defense. These are expenditures that are more likely to have a positive impact on the safety of our communities.

....

Our communities will be safer, and our criminal justice system more effective because of SB 1013. The law should stand as adopted.

11.3 Drafting the op-ed

Like the types of legal writing discussed in law school, successful op-eds follow a defined format. Following a "hook"[4] or lead that piques the reader's interest, op-eds generally contain an introductory paragraph stating a claim about a contemporary topic, body paragraphs providing context and background, the author's perspective, and possibly a qualifier paragraph acknowledging divergent perspectives. Finally, the piece usually concludes with a takeaway paragraph or conclusion that ties the piece together and challenges the reader to rethink prior assumptions in light of the information in the editorial.

11.3.A Providing a lead or hook

Op-eds often use a lead or hook, that is, the pithy statement that captures the reader's attention. Short sentences are best, and relevance to the news cycle is vital. The title can also provide a good lead into the story if it inverts a traditional perception or features a witty phrase. When looking for a compelling lead, you may want to consider the following as a starting point: an ironic phrase, a pop culture reference, a personal or social anecdote, a news reference, a major new study, or a startling statistic that can be explained through thorough analysis.

11.3.B Introduction

The introduction is a bridge between the lead and the thesis. It should provide the reader with necessary background about your claim in a simple and concise manner. The overall thesis statement comes at the end of the introduction and should declare the writer's position on the issue. That declaration should be firm; it could be as simple as "the legislature's position on X is wrong for the state because Y."

Consider the following introduction taken from the op-ed, *Return NC to a Democracy Through Fair Redistricting,* by Christine Coughlin and Adam Messenlehner, which was published in *The Raleigh News and Observer.*[5] The op-ed argues that gerrymandering (i.e., manipulating the boundaries of an electoral district to favor one political party over another) is undemocratic; thus, to ensure fair representation, redistricting should be done by an independent, non-partisan commission. In reading below, consider how the introduction provides context about the differing definitions of a mandate and how narrow interpretations have been used to defend ultra-partisan tactics (like gerrymandering).

Excerpt from an introduction

Since the election, there has been much talk about **mandates**. While staying true to one's political philosophy is appropriate, the concept of **mandate** should be interpreted broadly so that fundamental concepts of democracy and the people come first. The problem with using a narrow interpretation of "**mandate**" is that it leads to ultra-partisan tactics, which, in turn, negatively affect the functioning of a democracy.

Following the 2016 election, media pundits were debating the concept of voter mandates; thus, the term mandate was used repeatedly to "hook" readers interested in that topic.

11.3.C Body: Evidence and analysis

The main paragraphs of an op-ed present the reader with the author's perspective as well as relevant divergent perspectives via an analysis of the data, experts' opinions, and examples to support the thesis. While the body should be factually specific and use the relevant evidence, citing multiple polls and expert opinions will overload readers with too much information, while also obscuring the analysis.

On the next page is an excerpt from the body paragraphs of the *Return NC to a Democracy* op-ed referenced above:

Excerpt from the op-ed's body paragraph

Here, the authors ac-
knowledge that gerry-
mandering is not limited
to one political party.
This recognition pro-
motes civility and may
enable individuals with
divergent viewpoints to
come together.

The data in the paragraph
clearly identify the
authors' perspective and
the social problem resulting from gerrymandering.

Both parties used strategies such as "packing" together individuals to form a super-majority in a few districts, thus eliminating their electoral influence in the surrounding area, and "cracking," or dividing a certain group of people who tend to vote a certain way across multiple districts despite geographic proximity, to reduce their electoral strength.

Although North Carolinians recently voted for GOP control of the state legislature, the size of their majority is inconsistent with election results. **In 2014, GOP state senate candidates received 53.81% of the popular vote whereas the Democrats received 45.29%. However, those same votes gave the GOP a super-majority of 68% of the total state senate seats. Similarly, in the 2014 North Carolina house races GOP candidates received 54.12% of the popular vote, but won 62% of the chamber's legislative seats.** This wide discrepancy between the votes received and the seats won effectively stripped thousands of North Carolinians of their legislative vote.

Gerrymandering also resulted in fewer voting districts in which voters were able to choose between at least two viable candidates. In 2016, 76 out of 180 (45%) incumbent state legislators ran with no major party opposition. Voters in those districts effectively lost their vote and had to resign themselves to representation by someone they may not have supported. The lack of two viable options at the ballot box is not limited to districts with incumbents; the vast majority of North Carolina's state house and senate districts were classified as noncompetitive during the election cycle. Choice is a cornerstone of democracy; without viable alternatives, how can we hold our elected officials accountable for their actions?

In this section, the authors present statistics that show readers how gerrymandering leads to legislative representation that does not accurately reflect vote tallies. The wide disparity is noted for the reader and then analyzed further in subsequent paragraphs. The rhetorical question at the end of the section also highlights a major problem caused by gerrymandering that the authors plan to discuss later in the op-ed.

11.3.D Conclusion

The concluding paragraph should restate the author's opinion on the issue, while also advocating a way forward—in other words, the key takeaway. This solution is important because readers tire of seeing pieces that merely promote awareness of a particular issue. People want to be told what they can do to effectuate change. Think of this section as a call to action, keeping in mind that most readers cannot pass a law or mandate change. However, they might be able to lobby their legislators to pass a bill, engage in peaceful protests demanding change, or alter their purchasing habits. Any suggestions should be simple and should note for readers that lasting change often necessitates incremental steps. Further, the last sentence of an op-ed should provide readers with a way to foster discourse about the issue that extends beyond the op-ed. Consider the conclusion of the *Return NC to a Democracy* editorial:

Excerpt of a conclusion section

North Carolina legislators' **mandate** should be to place the interests of citizens ahead of ultra-partisan politics. One way we, as citizens, can promote this ideal is to write our legislators and ask them to pledge their support for nonpartisan redistricting and the creation of an independent redistricting commission. If legislators refuse, North Carolina voters should band together to vote self-interested members out of office before reapportionment in 2020. Standing up to these partisan tactics by calling our elected officials' offices and later voting out the ultra-partisans during the next election cycle should remind politicians that fundamental concepts of democracy and the people need to come first. If voters are willing to set aside partisanship in the interest of fair representation for all North Carolinians, why should we accept less from our legislators?

Here, the authors offer a solution and tie up the main points of the opinion. The authors return the piece to the "mandate" discussed in the lead of the op-ed, thereby linking the two sections. They also advocate writing to state legislators and banding together to vote out ultra-partisans as ways to effectuate change. These suggestions offer a tangible path forward for the average voter seeking to end partisan gerrymandering. This proposed solution extends the discussion beyond the awareness stage, thereby showing readers their role in advancing meaningful change. Finally, the readers are left with a discussion question at the end of the piece, which works to continue the conversation beyond this op-ed.

Because attorneys are often at the forefront of new ideas involving change in topics of law, politics, or even social culture, they are often in a position to alert others to a new problem or issue of interest and to advocate for a solution. Op-eds provide a way for writers to use their voices to effect change or at least to promote awareness of a problem. You might find this form of writing to be an interesting and fulfilling way to change the narrative on a topic that matters to you. Even without changing the narrative, it also provides an opportunity to remain engaged in a particular area and to increase your visibility as a leader in the field.

Notes

1. REAL CLEAR POLITICS, realclearpolitics.com (last visited Jan. 13, 2020).

2. For stories about the government shutdown, many newspaper and other sources are available for consultation. *See, e.g.,* Christina Caron & Mihir Zaveri, *Federal Workers, Some in 'Panic Mode,' Share Shutdown Fears on Social Media,* N.Y. TIMES, (Dec. 27, 2018); Heather Long et al., *'This Is Ridiculous': Small-Business Owners Can't Get Loans as Shutdown Enters Day 20,* WASH. POST (Jan. 10, 2019).

3. Stephen Kanter & Aliza Kaplan, Opinion Editorial, *Oregon's new death-penalty law is not retroactive. It's how the law works.*, THE OREGONIAN-OREGON LIVE (Aug. 20, 2019).

4. The term "hook" is used in many types of writing genres. You may be familiar with the use of the term in the memorandum of law where it means the legal point for which a case illustration will stand. *See* CHRISTINE COUGHLIN, JOAN ROCKLIN & SANDY PATRICK, A LAWYER WRITES 116–17 (3d ed. 2018).

5. Christine Coughlin & Adam Messenlehner, Opinion Editorial, *Return NC to a Democracy Through Fair Redistricting*, RALEIGH NEWS & OBSERVER (Feb. 9, 2017).

Chapter 12

Social Media and Blogs

12.1 Social media

12.2 Blogs

12.3 Responsible and professional use of social media and blogs

---

The goal of social media is to facilitate communication and interaction and to convey and receive information. Because social media is constantly evolving, the definition of what qualifies as social media likewise constantly evolves. "Social media," as defined by Merriam-Webster includes "forms of electronic communication (such as websites for social networking and microblogging) through which users create online communities to share information, ideas, personal messages, and other content (such as videos)."[1]

Now, you might say, "Great, but why is this relevant to academic and professional writing?" Social networking is key to today's professional discourse. According to the 2019 ABA TechReport, 94% of respondents under the age of forty indicated that they use social media for career development and networking.[2]

But career development and networking may be just the tip of the social media iceberg—social media also may play a key role in legal scholarship. As Professor Jennifer Romig explains, "using social media can really help people to find their thesis in the first place if they invest in following good accounts in their area of interest."[3] We agree! Following experts with common interests can spark ideas for your scholarship by keeping you apprised of the latest developments in the field and the newest published works. It can also help others learn more about you, your professional interests, and your work.

But first, a word of warning. When using social media and blogging, be vigilant of the applicable ethical and professional rules of conduct. Be intentional to avoid any copyright or trademark violations, to seek permissions when necessary, and to provide proper attribution. Social media users also must take care to remain professional in every post, reply, or other interaction. Remember, incidents of unprofessional behavior on social media can easily go viral and cause widespread harm to your personal and professional reputation.

12.1 Social media

A diverse array of social media is available to students, practitioners, and academics. Indeed, these platforms connect individuals with similar interests by providing numerous forums for content and communication. As membership increases on a particular social media platform, so too does the value of joining that platform. Millennials and Generation Z are prolific consumers of social media content. According to Pew Research, 94% of Americans between the ages of eighteen and twenty-four have a Facebook account, and 71% of that same demographic use Twitter.[4] However, adults outside those demographics also use the platforms. A majority of Americans over the age of fifty have a Facebook account, and roughly 40% of Americans between the ages of thirty and fifty maintain an Instagram account.[5] In addition, Pew also notes that every platform examined in its surveys has seen an increase in use since 2012, with a significant percentage of responders checking their account more than once per day.[6]

These next subsections examine some of the more common social media platforms that offer legal professionals a way to direct short bursts of content toward viewers.

12.1.A LinkedIn

Many lawyers use the LinkedIn networking platform to increase their professional network size, communicate with coworkers and other colleagues, store modified versions of their resumes, and advertise their skillsets. According to the 2019 ABA TechReport, LinkedIn is "the most popular social media platform for both firms and individual lawyers."[7] But many law students and lawyers fail to optimize their use of LinkedIn by not taking advantage of some of its features.

Like most social media platforms, LinkedIn permits users to register and use the site and its related app for free. This use is generally referred to as the "Basic" account option and merely requires users to register their name and contact information.[8] Using LinkedIn's free account option, many users have access to all they will ever need to make the site worthwhile; users can create their own profiles, connect with other professionals, and share or re-share posts or other articles.[9] For users seeking a greater return from their social media platform, LinkedIn also has a paid registration option.[10]

So, what relevance does LinkedIn have to scholarly and professional writing? LinkedIn can be a powerful way to share information about you

Tip:

Make sure that your social media accounts are both truthful and accurate. In *Office of Disciplinary Counsel v. Magee,* No. 137 DB 2015 (2016), the Pennsylvania Supreme Court suspended the license of an attorney, based in part on a LinkedIn account that represented that the attorney was licensed to practice in Pennsylvania when he was not, in fact, a member of the Pennsylvania bar.

or your writing by posting an "update." An update often consists of a short message to the author's connections, an announcement of a new development in the law or a "share" of an article, blog, or other publication.[11] Similarly, practicing attorneys can post an "update" regarding their recent court successes or the closing of a deal, for example.[12] However, and we cannot stress this enough, whenever publicizing any type of client interaction, be sure to maintain client confidentiality and abide by all applicable rules of ethics and professionalism in the state or jurisdiction in which you are practicing.[13]

In short, a LinkedIn page is a great way to establish a user's credentials and is often one of the first results when searching for an individual using a search engine. Therefore, maintaining a detailed, accurate, visually appealing profile and actively engaging with connections by providing useful "updates" can be beneficial for students, practitioners, and academics.

12.1.B Twitter

Unlike LinkedIn, Twitter is not limited to or geared towards working professionals; rather, it is intended to be used by anyone and everyone seeking to share a message or gain information in short bursts. Twitter offers users the opportunity to communicate directly with followers— who can include friends, colleagues, or anyone else—with limited characters. Initially, Twitter posts (referred to as "tweets") were limited to a total of 140 characters, but that limit was increased to 280 characters in 2017. Such limitations require posters to carefully craft each tweet to make a narrow and easily understood point.

After writing the text of a post, authors often add "hashtags" to the

Expert Tips for Networking and Professional Development:

We interviewed a leading expert in law and social media, Professor Rachel Gurvich of the University of North Carolina School of Law, to obtain her tips on using Twitter for networking and professional development. (Note that many of Professor Gurvich's common-sense tips are also applicable to other social media platforms.) Here's what she recommends:

1. Research to find interesting areas of the law that are being discussed on Twitter. Determine which areas interest you or which would be most professionally advantageous and identify and follow experts in those areas. You may want to start by following some helpful informational accounts such as ABA for Law Students (@ABALSD); ABA Young Lawyers (@ABAYLD); or your state's Bar Association account.

2. Find out which faculty members at your law school are active on social media. Follow those faculty members and watch how they engage with other scholars and law students.

3. Find hashtags affiliated with topics that you may be interested in learning more about and check out the posts under those hashtags. (If you're not sure where to start, you might consider hashtags like #AppellateTwitter; #PracticeTuesday; #LadyLawyerDiaries; #LegalWriting.)

4. Review and listen to the relevant social media conversations in your areas of interest, paying particular attention to the posts of those who are most active in those areas. This will allow you to observe and understand the norms and conventions of online discourse in the relevant community.

5. Dive into the conversations in a respectful and appropriate manner. If you follow the norms and engage professionally, you will likely find other users welcoming—and even eager—to interact with law students and young lawyers.

6. Remember that social media generally, and Twitter, in particular, can be a powerful platform to convey your personality and your intellectual curiosity. This tool can help you get to know others and help others get to know you. Don't be afraid of injecting appropriate warmth, personality, or humor, as long as your posts are professional.

7. If you think you might regret a tweet in the future, or if the tweet is such that you would not want a family member, professor, or future client to see it, do not post it.

end of the post. A hashtag consists of the pound symbol—"#"—followed by a trendy word or phrase that identifies the topic or subject matter of the tweet. These hashtags both readily identify what the tweet is about and link the tweet with others that include the same hashtag. In fact, when a hashtag is used by a large number of Twitter users, it may begin "trending." Users can also search Twitter by specific hashtags.

In addition, Twitter allows users to follow groups of other users based on specific categories.[14] Similarly, Twitter chats, which are recurring discussions about specific topics, connect users with similar interests across continents. The host might initiate the conversation by setting a topic or asking a series of questions related to the topic, generating multiple, sortable responses. Each participant includes the designated hashtag at the end of each related tweet, creating a running list of all questions and responses and thereby allowing users to search the hashtag to view all questions and responses in their feed.

Many lawyers and law students use Twitter to network; some even claim that "Twitter's highest use is as a professional development tool," primarily due to the ease with which information can be spread through Twitter.[15] Unlike other forms of social media, Twitter provides an opportunity for those in the legal field to engage with each other in a less formal atmosphere but also provides more ability to categorize and search for information of interest. In fact, at least one appellate state-court judge has encouraged judges, lawyers, and non-lawyers alike to engage through social media to discuss various matters of import to those demographics.[16] The textbox contains some expert tips to use if you are considering developing a professional presence on Twitter.

> **Expert Tips for Promoting Your Scholarship:**
>
> Professor Gurvich's tips on using Twitter to promote scholarship are as follows:
>
> 1. Work to gather a following on Twitter *before* you start promoting your work so that when you do have a piece to share, it can reach a broader audience that includes followers who are motivated to read it. You do not want to become engaged on Twitter only when you are promoting your own work; doing so will both read as self-serving and decrease the likelihood that your work will reach new audiences.
>
> 2. Pay it forward by reading and engaging with other scholars' work. In addition to helping with networking and professional development, paying it forward will reap dividends when you're ready to promote your own work.
>
> 3. When promoting your work, include bite-size excerpts from the piece or otherwise indicate how the piece may relate to current events or timely legal or social issues to pique readers' interest in clicking on the link and reading your article.

Given its reputation as a social media platform where anyone can make an opinion heard, Twitter may, at times, be overlooked by legal professionals or dismissed as merely a social networking site. Indeed, Twitter has sometimes been called "deceptively simple."[17] Accordingly, many users, particularly professionals, might underestimate Twitter's ability to help spread legal scholarship. Do not fall into this trap. Twitter can be an effective platform to promote large pieces of scholarship and engage broader audiences. For example, an academic might advertise an article on Twitter, along with a short post providing a link to the article, or the editor of a law journal may use Twitter to publicize an upcoming guest speaker or academic symposium. Like most other social media platforms, Twitter allows users to link to third-party resources, such as written scholarship that might be hosted on the Social Science Research Network (SSRN). In sum, Twitter can be a powerful and rewarding platform for networking, researching, and promoting scholarship for users who use a thoughtful and intentional strategy.

12.1.C Facebook

In the realm of social media platforms, Facebook is now an elder statesman, having been around since 2004 and open to the public since 2006.[18] Many people use Facebook for personal reasons, whether it is to share a humorous meme they found on a friend's wall or to give others an update about their vacation to the Bahamas. However, if you simply scroll through Facebook posts, you will see how many organizations, companies, and academic institutions use Facebook to promote new products, advertise discounts, and display images of new merchandise.

Many law firms maintain Facebook pages that provide information related to their practice.[19] A firm's ability to maintain such a page might lead more potential clients to choose them over competitors by giving those potential clients more insight into a firm's attorneys and operations. Firms can provide a glimpse into the daily lives of their employees in a less formal atmosphere than those that clients usually see; firms can then show the "human" side of a business relationship and cultivate client relationships in a way similar to common "business development activities."[20] Given these opportunities, most firms would likely benefit from the use of Facebook pages in the business context.

Unlike Twitter, Facebook does not have a defined character limit, but the most effective entries are often short because brevity allows posters to get the message across without losing readers with shorter attention spans. These posts appear on an individual's "home page," the first page visible after the individual logs onto the Facebook account, and the page made available to other "friends" (i.e., connections) on the site. Facebook's extensive reach makes it a useful form of social media to network; share interesting articles, blogs, and opinions from others; and promote your own work.

12.1.D Instagram

Like Facebook, Instagram is extremely popular and, in fact, has made significant inroads in the social media market. Part of Instagram's appeal is its emphasis on the visual—the platform was designed to display photos and videos on smart phones. The Pew Research survey discussed above found that 71% of Americans from age eighteen to twenty-four use Instagram, while more than half of Americans from age twenty-five to twenty-nine do the same.[21] Although many users look at exclusively recreational content, more than twenty-five million business profiles exist for the purpose of marketing products or services to consumers.[22] The Instagram platform offers practicing attorneys and firms the opportunity to connect with young professionals as they seek to hire and retain the best talent.

Instagram accounts typically feature bold images (remember, make sure to consider copyright implications with images) and less text than a Facebook post or tweet; thus, while many Instagram posts contain some writing, they are unlikely to be a substantive source of academic information. However, these photograph-centric posts might contain legal news updates or links to third-party sources for more substantive discussions of legal scholarship. (Again, however, make sure that you adhere to copyright rules.) Text is often surrounded by background images that draw the reader's eye, thereby encouraging that reader to learn more.

One thing is for certain: Social media platforms will continue to proliferate, providing a rare opportunity for legally trained intellectuals bold enough to jump in headfirst.[23] While social media holds great promise for networking and professional development—as well as for researching, publishing, and promoting scholarship—these online opportunities also come with potential long-term personal and professional consequences. To that end, whether a law student, practicing lawyer, or tenured law professor, be exceedingly careful of anything you post.

12.2 Blogs

Blogging, while a form of social media, merits its own separate sub-category.[24] A blog is defined as "a website containing a writer's or group of writers' own experiences, observations, [or] opinions."[25] Blogs cover a wide breadth of topics and may feature images and links to other websites where readers can find more detailed information. An effective blog builds a ladder to persistently critical and innovative thinking by offering a trove of easily accessible information to which readers respond. Blogging, along with other types of social media writing, have created what Professor Andrea Lunsford terms "life writing,"[26] the success of which depends on garnering attention and thoughtful comments or "notes" from viewers.

Blogs emerged in the early 2000s as "personal web logs" and were generally used for personal communication and writing to expand connections through the web. While some authors used blogs as a means of personal expression, many companies and professionals used blogs for marketing purposes. Presenting dynamic information in shorter and more concise blog posts seemed easier for the readers to connect to rather than longer static web information that rarely changed. Readers visited blogs more often than they visited static webpages and often left comments.[27] This trend has continued. While the number of general blogs may be decreasing from its heyday, blogs are still "important to those invested in specific subjects.[28] According to the blogging platform WordPress, every month, users produce 41.7 million posts and readers leave more than 60.5 million new comments.[29]

While blogs with personal topics, such as food reviews and recipes, still frequently appear, some professionals use blogs to stay current in their specialties, including in law. Since attorneys need to stay on top of news and current trends in their areas of practice, blogs are often powerful tools both to host and to follow. (Blogs that focus on the law are sometimes referred to as "blawgs";[30] however, for the purpose of this chapter, we use the term "blog.")

Unlike searching for information, blogs filtered through "Really Simple Syndication" (RSS) feeds (a type of software or web application that collects similar web content such as blogs, podcasts, and news articles so they can be viewed together) can be a powerful way of both disseminating information and having information delivered to you.[31] RSS feeds allow readers to quickly view similar content published by the website. Feeds can be divided topically, thematically, or using other designation criteria. Many websites and bloggers use RSS feeds to advertise upcoming posts or link current information with similar past discussions.

Understanding how to navigate blogging while simultaneously maintaining professionalism and topical focus helps students, academics, and practitioners disseminate pieces of their scholarship as well as their well-researched opinions to a wider audience. The professional blogs discussed here are different than the social blogs maintained by someone's brother on the best bodybuilding exercises or those run by a social "influencer" on some cultural hot topic; legal blogs demand clear focus, logical progression, and source attribution. In an online world burdened by "fake news" and "alternative facts,"[32] readers want to learn something new from trustworthy authors—who are experts—presenting thoroughly balanced opinions.

12.2.A Creating a blog

Choosing a blogging platform and formatting the page is the first step to creating a successful blog. Many options exist, and each has its own advantages and disadvantages. After selecting a blogging platform, carefully consider how the blog will appear to readers using both computers and mobile devices. First-time blog writers frequently overlook the aesthetics of blogging and instead choose to spend the bulk of their time writing the post. However, the blog's visual appeal—its formatting, layout, and ease of use—will determine whether online users take the time to read the blog or simply skip over it.

• **Common platforms**

Three of the most common platforms used by legal professionals are WordPress,[33] LexBlog,[34] and Google Blogger.[35] Each platform affords bloggers the opportunity to share their work with readers, but each platform also has some distinctive features that need to be considered before selecting one over the other. At the outset, be intentional about which platform you select for your blog because changing platforms can affect readership. For instance, a law student who started using WordPress to post about the future re-escalation of the war on drugs under one presidential administration may later want to switch to LexBlog to better direct the blog toward legally trained readers. However, the transition may cause the author to lose search engine rankings, so it is helpful to think long-term about which platform best meets your needs.

• **Templates**

After selecting the appropriate platform, the next step is to build your individual blog. Templates are preformatted layouts that enable blog owners to add content to an established design. Choosing a template that will enhance your message and appeal to your audience is vital.

Also, unlike traditional journal articles where the formatting and layout are dictated by the publisher, blogs afford the author incredible choice. When choosing a template, think both about appearance and functionality. Depending on your proposed blog's purpose and audience, take some time to look through the different templates offered by a platform to see which best matches your needs and your future audience's expectations. The following graphic explains common blog templates.

Two-Column Blogs	One-Column Blogs	Magazine Templates
This type is the most common type of blog because it allows writers to offer additional information on the same page as their blog posts. It features a wide column of text and a sidebar with further content or references. The blog posts appear in the main column in reverse chronological order.	This type of blog features a single column of content, with no sidebars (a part of the blog's layout usually used to give visitors quick access to important material) on either side of the content. The blog posts appear on the home page in reverse chronological order and look similar to traditional books or academic journals.	The homepages of magazine templates resemble the layouts of magazines, newspapers, and other popular online news sources. Photos, videos, and short pieces of text are meant to encourage the reader to click on specific content and thereby gain access to the interior pages of the blog.

By way of example, SCOTUSblog, a popular law blog focusing on topics concerning the U.S. Supreme Court, is a two-column blog.[36] On the main page, a running list of blog posts by contributing authors appears on the left side of the screen, while the right sidebar provides broader information that may interest readers. This sidebar includes information about the Supreme Court's calendar, a list of featured posts, and a means to navigate the blog's archives. As the reader goes to different sections of the website, the left side displays the corresponding information and the right side remains constant. This format allows readers to use the sidebar to find specific information relevant to their practice.

12.2.B Writing a blog post

After formatting your overall blog, the next step is to start working on your first post. Writing a blog tends to be a much quicker exercise than the other types of scholarly and professional writing described in the other chapters. Unlike formal legal writing, when blogging, a writer has leeway to "explore style and voice much more freely."[37] Therefore, the writing style is more colloquial. Even so, you will want to keep certain strategies in mind when blogging.

Below is an excerpt of a blog post that provides advice to legal employers seeking to hire excellent writers (hint: all legal employers want to hire excellent writers). This post is part of Professor Abigail Perdue's blog titled *Teach Law Better*, which is a site designed to exchange innovative teaching ideas and experiments in the law school classroom. Following the excerpt, we explore in more detail the characteristics of effective legal blogs.

Expert Tips for Bloggers:

Professor Jennifer Romig, a leading expert in social media for lawyers, developed an advanced legal writing course in blogging and social media in 2014 and has taught the course annually at Emory University School of Law. Her recommendations are:

1. Check out what other bloggers have written on your topic. It is better to link to another post and give credit, rather than to unintentionally say the same thing someone has already said.

2. State your thesis early in the post—such as bringing attention to a new law or case or drawing connections between developments—because online reading attention spans can be very short.

3. Use a conversational style throughout such as by using links instead of footnotes and by avoiding formal language such as "this post proceeds in three parts."

4. Do not go too far with the conversational voice; avoid clichéd language such as "Must. Read. This. Post. Now."

5. Use frequent headings and subheadings, and make sure they are marked as such in your blogging software (not just bold type in a pasted word-processing version) because these coded subheadings will raise the post's profile in search-engine results.

Wanted: Law Students Who Can Write
By: Professor Abigail Perdue

It's that time again—the part of the semester when nervous students anxiously buzz around the hallways decked out in black, pinstripe suits and power ties. They carry fancy leather-bound portfolios and practice "firm handshakes" to make a good first impression during on-campus interviews. But too often when I speak to potential employers, I hear the same refrain: *Law schools need to do a better job of teaching strong writing and editing skills.*

Notice the short descriptive title.

The author uses vivid description to paint a picture in the reader's mind and generate interest in the post.

The author uses a colloquial tone and interjects short, snappy sentences to keep the tone conversational.

I agree. Legal writing, analysis, editing, and research are fundamental skills at the heart of effective lawyering. No person can be a competent attorney without them. And even when we do our best to prepare students for the practice, we should always strive to do better. But as budgets tighten and the number of core faculty shrink at law schools across America, law professors in general, and legal writing professors in particular, often find themselves between a rock and a hard place expected to do much more for students with far fewer resources at their disposal.

This begs the question: What can *legal employers* do to identify and attract the best writers? Perhaps they should *change the way that they hire.*

Self-assess: The first step is for legal employers to thoughtfully self-assess. *Reflect upon* **why** *you are recruiting.* What are your short-term and long-term needs? Which qualities do you require in applicants? Why are these particular qualities necessary to achieve success in this specific role and environment? Legal roles, work environments, and employer expectations differ, and accordingly, so do the attributes necessary to succeed therein. Thus, you will not find a custom fit if you use generic hiring criteria. *Take the time to decide what you need and want.*

Next, reconsider **whom** *you are recruiting.* Do practicing attorneys actively participate in the applicant screening process, or is it primarily handled by Human Resources personnel who have not practiced law? Do you currently use generic criteria like the law school's rank, the applicant's class rank, law review membership, or grade point average to automatically "filter" applicants, or is your vetting process more holistic and thoughtful? Consider hiring applicants based on more than academic achievement (or proxies thereof). Instead, weigh recommendations, experience, character, and personal qualities like resilience, work ethic, and positivity more heavily.

Finally, rethink **where** *you are recruiting.* Do you recruit at the same schools each year using the same criteria? Have you investigated each school's writing and clinical programs, experiential offerings, hiring processes, and bar preparation programs before agreeing to recruit there, or did you base your decision primarily on the law school's geographical location or latest ranking in *U.S. News and World Report*? Do seasoned, experienced core faculty teach the experiential and other writing-intensive courses that are perhaps most relevant to preparing students for the practice?

Request a writing sample or incorporate a writing exercise. Ask applicants to provide an edited or original writing sample. Peruse it carefully. Alternatively, require applicants in the final phase of the interview process to participate in a timed writing exercise where they craft a short legal analysis of a discrete legal issue or revise a legal document. These measures will help you distinguish between applicants who are genuinely capable of independently producing high-quality work from those whose written materials were heavily vetted by others.

Hire from law schools that adequately value and invest in Legal Writing and Research. If you seek applicants with strong writing, research, analytical, and editing skills, then actively (or only) recruit at law schools that place a premium

See how the author chunks relevant information into topics to organize the material and make it easier for the reader to remember points and find relevant information.

on legal writing and research. *Assess the rank, reputation, and quality of the law school's LAWR Program, rather than relying exclusively on the law school's latest overall ranking.* Select schools that award at least two credit hours per term or more to LAWR. Schools that afford the same weight to experiential courses like LAWR as to other exam-based courses send a clear message to students that writing and skills-based courses are just as important as courses that focus primarily on learning black-letter law. As a result, students are likelier to invest more time and effort into honing their research and writing skills. If they know that their LAWR grade will impact their G.P.A. and class rank as much as their other courses, they will likely take LAWR more seriously and probably become stronger writers, analysts, researchers, and editors as a result.

....

• Topic

Legal blogs usually have a niche focus somewhere in the law. This focus is akin to finding an original point to make in a sea of other scholarship for a law journal article, only with a sharper focus and narrower reach. Writing a blog about criminal justice reform to reduce incarceration rates is too broad, but emphasizing the specific ways to provide non-violent offenders with access to gainful employment may make the blog an attractive resource. The niche focus will likely increase the blog's exposure to the target audience.[38] Furthermore, authors are more likely to keep up with a widely read blog than with one that receives limited views, few comments, and no mention in other academics' social media posts.[39]

Authors should subscribe to an RSS feed or use a news aggregator to grow their professional network by locating other bloggers who focus on similar topics. RSS feeds will also help you figure out what else is being written in your area of interest. This information, in turn, will help you narrow and delve deeper into a specific topic that is appropriate for your intended audience.

Some academics blog about journal articles that they have recently published. For example, the excerpt above was derived from Professor Perdue's earlier paper *Mind the Gap: Nine Easy Ways for Legal Employers to Identify Strong Applicants*, which appeared in the June 2017 edition of *The Practical Lawyer*. In drafting the post, the author obtained permission from the prior publisher, cited the prior paper, and used a hyperlink so the readers could access the prior piece. Remember, even if you are the author of the original paper, if it is published, the publisher may hold the copyright.

• Title

Many excellent blog posts start with a clever title that grabs the reader's attention. Academic blogs are no different. However, a careful balance must be struck between relevance and creativity. The title of a blog post will serve as keywords for search engines trying to steer readers to useful content. Consider the following:

- Make the title engaging to the legal reader by generating a sense of urgency or needed action;
- Keep the title sufficiently descriptive so that the reader understands the post's contents;
- Create a short, simple, bold title;
- Include at least one keyword that would come up in an online search for the topic; and
- Provide unique information in the title.

Examples of effective blog post titles

Name of the entire blog, author, and date	Title and topic of the individual blog post	Technique used
The Appeal, Sarah Lustbader, November 12, 2019	**Title:** *You can be sentenced, even if you were acquitted* **Topic:** Reviewing the concept of relevant conduct whereby a criminal defendant's sentence may be increased by consideration of uncharged, dismissed, or acquitted conduct.	An intriguing point about the issue that makes the reader want to learn more.
Teach Law Better, Abigail Perdue, October 19, 2018	**Title:** *Listen Up: The Advantages of Audio Commenting* **Topic:** Embedding audio comments into student papers for enhanced feedback for students and increased efficiency and ergonomics for faculty.	Play on the phrase "listen up" followed by the traditional use of a colon and a description of the related topic.
Jotwell, Juliet Stumpf, November 14, 2019	**Title:** *Crowd-Sourcing Decolonization* **Topic:** Review of an article that questions the justifications countries use for excluding economic migrants.	Interesting use of a modern term being applied to an unusual and controversial topic.
Bojack.org, Jack Bogdanski, November 10, 2010	**Title:** *We'll clean up our room … tomorrow* **Topic:** Opinion piece on letters sent by Congress to the IRS pledging to rectify alternative minimum tax legislation.	A short, simple title that intrigues the reader.

Creative titles can help separate an individual's work from the multitude of scholarly blogs that bombard readers. Therefore, always remain mindful of the title's power to persuade viewers to both read and disseminate a blog.

• Text

Blogging follows a general format; however, that format is much looser than other traditional forms of legal writing discussed in this book. Every blog post should contain a thesis, supporting facts, and usually, a visual that (1) captures the reader's attention or (2) illustrates the blog's idea.

As previously mentioned, blog posts are short pieces of writing that are meant for popular consumption. The text should flow much like a conversation with a colleague or a peer. The opening sentences should be clear and draw the reader in, similar to the pithy yet relevant nature of the blog's title. Sentence structure should not be complex, and the supporting details for the thesis should appear within the first three sentences.

> **Expert Tip:**
>
> According to Professor Romig, while legal blogs may have an informal tone, lawyers need to take care not to write a post that may hurt (or could be claimed by opposing counsel to hurt) a client's legal position. When blogging, be cognizant of the tension between writing freely versus writing to inform while maintaining a healthy revenue-generating law practice in the same practice area where you may be blogging.

Authors should avoid complex vocabulary or words that may be unfamiliar to the average reader. For example, a legal professional may understand that the term *subpoena duces tecum* is a summons ordering a non-party in litigation to produce documents and other tangible evidence that will be used at trial. However, laypeople with no legal training may not have seen this phrase before. They may think it means something else, be annoyed that they must look up its definition, or worse, stop reading the blog entirely. To avoid this problem, authors should provide definitions or use simple metaphors to explain complex words or concepts that most people will not have encountered.[40]

• Visuals

Viewers are drawn to colorful pictures and graphics and expect them in today's online sources. Whenever you think about using a visual, the first issue that should pop up in your mind is copyright or possibly trademark. Visuals can add great value to your blog posts once you have researched and determined that they can be lawfully used.

People increasingly read blog and other social media posts on their smart phones. When looking through such a post on a phone, the reader may see only a small image if one is featured. Thus, a visually appealing or intriguing visual—one that can be seen clearly on a small screen—can interest a reader.

In their article, *Art-iculating the Analysis: Systemizing the Decision to Use Visuals as Legal Reasoning*, Professors Steve Johansen and Ruth Ann Robbins explain that "the term 'visual' encompasses graphs, charts, diagrams, maps, pictures, [and] photographs."[41] However, instead of categorizing them by design, these scholars suggest that visuals should be categorized by their functions as follows:

- **Organizational visuals**, such as a chart, taxonomy, or bulleted list, present information hierarchically, by level, or by relationship.
- **Interpretive visuals**, such as a flow chart or pie chart, can help readers understand difficult or ambiguous concepts.
- **Representative visuals**, such as photographs and other types of pictures, convey the same information as a text but use the image to "anchor the information through what educational psychologists call dual-coding of texts and images."[42]

Representative visuals are most commonly used for blog posts, but you should take some time to consider what type of visual would be best for your post and conduct careful research to find a suitable visual that you can legally use. You may be able to find one through Creative Commons[43] or Unsplash,[44] both of which provide for free distribution of some copyrighted works or images. If you are obtaining an image from Google Image, you can use the advanced search function for "free to use, share, or modify, even commercially" to see what visuals may be available for public use.[45] If you are uncertain about copyright or ownership for a visual, consider running a reverse image search on a site such as tineye.com to uncover available ownership information. Always verify that an image is available for public use or take the necessary steps to obtain permission and appropriately attribute the contribution.

Another option (particularly if you are interested in using organizational or interpretive visuals) is to create your own image. Many platforms, such as Canva[46] and the like, can assist in creating useful visuals. And, of course, you can always use your own photo or other visual creation—your creativity may be rewarded with increased readers!

• Citations

Blogs require citations for any specific facts, figures, or thoughts pulled from another source.[47] Blogs are similar to op-eds (see Chapter 11, *Op-Eds*) because they are both short pieces of writing that mostly focus on the author's opinion, but blogs are expected to have more citations. Citing is done in a variety of ways, depending on the source of the information. Words or phrases taken directly from a source should be in quotation marks with the author noted at the end of the sentence, along with a web link to its source. A statistic should also be cited by providing a hyperlink to the publishing source. As another example, for a polling statistic generated by

Tip:

Always remember to acknowledge background sources. Your failure to do so can be seen as an ethical violation. Rule 8.4(c) of the Model Rules of Professional Conduct prohibits attorneys from engaging in "dishonesty, fraud, deceit, or misrepresentation."

Gallup, the author might mention Gallup's name in the sentence and turn that reference into a hyperlink to its homepage. Similarly, references to other students' and academics' blog posts in the piece should be cited with hyperlinks to their blogs. Doing this both identifies the sources to readers and allows them to learn more about the topic.

In sum, blogs offer an easy way to quickly convey specific and important content to the public without disclosing the personal information adorning sites such as Facebook, Twitter, and LinkedIn.

- **Publicizing your blog on social media**

Once you have written your blog, remember to share a link to your post on other social media platforms such as Twitter, LinkedIn, Facebook, and Instagram. As one social media expert explained, "Your blog is where people meet you. Your social media channels are where they seek you out.[48] In other words, readers are likely to seek out further information about a writer after reading a thought-provoking blog post.

You may also want to tag the individuals that you cited, or email them a link to the blog post, so they can see how you relied on their work.[49] This courtesy not only acknowledges the important work of other scholars but makes it more likely that other scholars will read and perhaps rely on your work in the future.

12.3 Responsible and professional use of social media and blogs

Just as important as knowing *where* to publish scholarship or any other written works on social media and blogs is knowing *what* can be published. Perhaps unsurprisingly, many ethical considerations arise when posting on social media and blogs, especially for legal professionals. For example, many state bars have stringent rules or regulations governing the information that attorneys or law firms may share on social media and blogs. While fewer regulations may apply to law students, numerous practical considerations arise; for instance, students should consider whether their social media posts might be harmful to their employment prospects upon graduation. Attorneys and prospective attorneys alike should be familiar with the "best practices" stemming from their jurisdiction's governing rules and concepts *and* from ABA proposals and guidelines. Since blogs and social media posts extend beyond the boundaries of a jurisdiction, a legal professional should be award of "best practices" for both, regardless of whether a rule is in effect in a particular state.

Numerous examples make clear that lawyers who post on social media and blogs must take ethical rules and principles into consideration before posting a LinkedIn update, making a Facebook post, tweeting, or otherwise disseminating information via a blog post or other social media platform. It is vitally important that attorneys, law students, and academics ensure that they do not run afoul of state bar ethics rules and that they do not mislead readers, prospective clients, or both.

Excerpt from *Seduced: For Lawyers, the Appeal of Social Media Is Obvious. It's also Dangerous,* by Steven Seidenberg (ABA Journal)

"Sean W. Conway thought he was writing an ordinary blog post. He never suspected he would wind up facing ethics charges.

'I felt completely within my rights as a citizen, exposing what I thought was an injustice,' he says. It seemed to the then-35-year-old defense attorney that a Florida circuit court judge was methodically depriving criminal defendants of their right to a speedy trial.

....

On Oct. 30, 2006, he put 11 paragraphs on JAABlog, where attorneys discuss issues concerning the Broward County Court. 'I thought the most appropriate thing was to expose what [Alemán] was doing,' he says.

Conway's blog post did that — and more. After asserting that Alemán was trying 'to make defendants waive their right to a speedy trial,' the post excoriated the judge. It called Alemán — who died of lung cancer on Dec. 2, 2010 — an 'evil, unfair witch,' 'seemingly mentally ill' and 'clearly unfit for her position and knows not what it means to be a neutral arbiter.'

Conway chose his invective deliberately. 'I wanted to protect people, and the only power I had was my words, so I was going to use the most powerful ones I had.'

The Florida Bar, however, concluded that he had violated five ethics rules, including Rule 4-8.2(a) (making false or reckless statements regarding the qualifications or integrity of a judge) and Rule 4-8.4(d) (engaging in professional conduct that is prejudicial to the administration of justice). Conway argued that his actions were protected by the First Amendment, but the Florida Supreme Court rejected this. In the end, Conway acquiesced with a public reprimand and a fine of $1,250."

Remember, too, that attorneys generally remain subject to bar regulation regardless of the specific capacity in which they might publish a particular piece. Practicing attorneys have been sanctioned in numerous incidences as a result of their social media publications. For example, one Florida attorney prepared a social media exposé regarding a judge's actions that he purported were depriving criminal defendants of their right to a speedy trial. (See sidebar.) After calling the judge at issue an "evil, unfair witch," "seemingly mentally ill," and "clearly unfit for her position," the attorney was sanctioned by the Florida Bar, despite his contention that the publication was protected by the First Amendment.[50]

Such cases are altogether too common. While practitioners, students, and academics should not permit the rules to chill free speech, the rules and potential professional ramifications of social media and blog posts necessarily require thoughtful consideration of two things: the subject matter of any post and the manner in which the subject matter is presented. You do not want to jeopardize your professional reputation by testing where free speech ends and ethical violations begin. Some simple rules that everyone can follow are: (1) avoid cathartic, insult-laden posts; and (2) always add appropriate disclaimers in an obvious place to make clear that posts do not constitute legal advice, the practice of law, or formation of any attorney-client relationship.[51]

In the next few sections of this chapter, specific situations are explored in which ethical and professionalism concerns may arise with respect to social media and blog posts.[52]

12.3.A Client confidentiality

ABA Model Rule 1.6 provides that, "A lawyer shall not reveal information relating to the representation of a client unless the client gives informed consent, the disclosure is impliedly authorized in order to carry out the representation or the disclosure is permitted" under certain limited circumstances.[53] Everyone knows that attorneys have an obligation of confidentiality towards their clients, and most of us understand that this obligation means not publicizing a client's personal information or other information related to the case. One concern, however, is that many individuals mistakenly believe that this rule is limited to attorney-client *privileged* information.[54] The rule "applies not only to matters communicated in confidence by the client but also to all information relating to the representation, whatever its source."[55]

This rule has become increasingly important in the digital age because (1) many, if not all, states have adopted this rule in some form,[56] and (2) lawyers who blog or otherwise post on social media have increasingly begun to discuss their clients' cases openly both while those cases are pending and after they have been completed. In light of the increase in attorneys discussing their clients' cases, including on LinkedIn or blogs, the American Bar Association issued Formal Opinion 480. In that Formal Opinion, the Standing Committee on Ethics and Professional Responsibility concluded: "Lawyers who blog or engage in other public commentary may not reveal information relating to a representation that is protected by Rule 1.6(a), including information contained in a public record, unless disclosure is authorized under the Model Rules."[57] This opinion is broad in scope and includes situations in which a lawyer describes a client's "hypothetical" situation "if there is a reasonable likelihood that a third party may ascertain the client's identity or legal situation."[58]

12.3.B Attorney advertising

Other rules likewise limit one of the most prolific types of attorney communications: advertisements. Model Rule 7.1 states: "A lawyer shall not make a false or misleading communication about the lawyer or the lawyer's services. A communication is false or misleading if it contains a material misrepresentation of fact or law or omits a fact necessary to make the statement considered as a whole not materially misleading."[59]

Although this rule was initially intended to address advertising, it also applies to *all* communications about the lawyer and the services offered by that lawyer.[60] For example, Model Rule 7.1 can be interpreted as expected to apply to attorney biographies published on websites, attorney advertisements on television or other media, and direct attorney solicitations to clients, where they are permitted. It may even apply to LinkedIn endorsements by others. Be aware that Model Rule 7.1 is also subject to a broad interpretation that might include false or misleading statements in scholarly publications or similar works, at least to the extent that such statements implicate the attorney or the services that the attorney provides.

12.3.C Duty to be truthful and accurate

This rule relates to many of the points discussed throughout this book but also serves as a reminder that any scholarship or publication should present information truthfully and accurately. As discussed earlier, in Section 12.2, Model Rule 8.4(c) prohibits attorneys from engaging in "dishonesty, fraud, deceit or misrepresentation."[61] Model Rule 4.1(a) likewise prohibits lawyers from knowingly making a false statement of material fact to a third person.[62]

These rules do not mean that articles and posts cannot reflect the author's opinions, but it does favor ensuring that scholarship presents a full view of a given issue, as opposed to solely adopting one perspective with no discussion or analysis of another potential perspective. Keep in mind that puffery—exaggeration reasonably expected about the quality of a product—is permissible about subjective claims but not about objective facts.[63] Accordingly, in the context of firms and attorneys who have a social media presence, posts should not be too hyperbolic and should give prospective clients an accurate and realistic understanding of the firm, any attorney, and any accompanying services.

The bottom line is that you should be careful with puffery because its legal definition lacks clarity and its invocation by defendants has become a hallmark of false advertising cases.[64] If a post—whether about your scholarship or professional legal services—misrepresents objective facts, it should not be posted under any circumstances. The reputational and career risks far outweigh any potential immediate benefits.

12.3.D Technology

Aside from rules regulating the scope of what communications in social media might include, many states have also adopted a variation of Comment 8 to Model Rule 1.1 (governing an attorney's competence and ability to perform the job), which provides that, "[t]o maintain the requisite knowledge and skill, a lawyer should keep abreast of changes in the law and its practice, *including the benefits and risks associated with relevant technology,* engage in continuing study and education and comply with all continuing legal education requirements to which the lawyer is subject."[65] Consistent with Comment 8, several states, including North Carolina and Florida, have implemented rules requiring CLE courses specifically related to technology and technology training.[66]

Generally, this rule demonstrates the importance that the ABA and state bars now attribute to technological proficiency for attorneys; these organizations recognize that social media is one of the next significant issues to be addressed in the practice of law, and they also recognize that, while many attorneys are advanced users of social media, others lack any proficiency whatsoever with technology generally or social media specifically. By implementing this rule, the ABA formally places the burden on licensed lawyers to ensure they are technologically competent to remain in compliance with existing ethical obligations. Therefore, consult the relevant rules in your jurisdiction before publishing any scholarship or approving advertising.

12.3.E Unauthorized practice of law

In addition, take steps to ensure that a post does not become the "unauthorized practice of law." Social media and blog posts can be the subject of disciplinary action by a state bar when the information provided crosses the line from general advice on a legal topic to specific legal advice based on a particular set of facts. Law students should be particularly aware of this rule since they are not yet licensed to practice. As a rule of thumb, general legal information that educates the public as a whole may be allowed but specific advice about a single case or factual situation usually is not. However, be intentional with content, especially if your post is disseminated to multiple jurisdictions in which you are not licensed; states vary widely on what constitutes the definition of "practicing law."[67]

Problems in this area can arise in different ways. For instance, a lawyer who is licensed to practice law only in Kansas would not want to publish a blog post that discussed Illinois state laws in such a specific manner that an Illinois reader may think the post constituted legal advice.[68] Yet another facet of this prohibition on the unauthorized practice of law concerns attorney representations on social media sites such as LinkedIn or Twitter. Lawyers must take care not to misrepresent that they are licensed to practice law in a state where they are not, in fact, licensed.[69] Again, unlicensed law students should take special care not to run afoul of any prohibitions.

Furthermore, many other rules and regulations[70] either do or could relate to different aspects of social media and the practice of law. The takeaway, however, is to be careful, intentional, and professional in all of your posts, and always add an appropriate disclaimer.[71]

Conclusion

Social media platforms and blogs are powerful tools that legal professionals in all areas of the profession may use. The days of willful ignorance and dismissal as a millennial fad are over. As all age groups of society continue to flock to various types of social media platforms, lawyers should be prepared to use these platforms to network, increase their professional visibility, publish and promote their scholarship, and connect with other experts in the field in real time. As technology grows, we all must adapt. As social media continues to proliferate, all lawyers and law students stand to benefit if they can harness its far-reaching potential.

Notes

1. *Social Media*, MERRIAM-WEBSTER ONLINE (2019). Thank you to Professor Ellen Murphy and Professor Mary Susan Lucas, Wake Forest University School of Law; Professor Jennifer Romig, Emory University School of Law; and Professor Rachel Gurvich, University of North Carolina School of Law, for sharing their expertise with us, along with their helpful comments and suggestions on this chapter. We would also like to thank Adam Messenlehner for his important contributions to this chapter.

2. Catherine Sanders Reach, *2019 Social Media and Blogging,* ABA TECHREPORT (Nov. 20, 2019) (85% of lawyers aged 40–49 also report using social media for career development and networking).

3. Interview with Professor Jennifer Romig, Professor of Practice, Emory University School of Law (Nov. 24, 2019).

4. Aaron Smith & Monica Anderson, *Social Media Use in 2018*, pewresearch.org (Mar. 1, 2018).

5. *Id.*

6. *Id.*

7. Reach, *supra*; *see also* DENNIS KENNEDY & ALLISON C. SHIELDS, LINKEDIN IN ONE HOUR FOR LAWYERS 1 (2012).

8. *Id.* at 9–10.

9. *See id.*

10. LINKEDIN, linkedin.com (last visited Jan. 13, 2020).

11. KENNEDY, *supra*, at 52–54.

12. *Id.*

13. *See, e.g.*, FINDLAW, *Starting a Law Firm Blog: Ethical Considerations*, findlaw.com (last visited Dec. 31, 2019) [hereinafter "*Starting a Law Firm Blog*"].

14. *See* Danielle Elefritz, *"From Frisbees to Flatulence?": Regulating Greenhouse Gases From Concentrated Animal Feeding Operations Under the Clean Air Act*, 48 ENVTL. L. 891 (2018).

15. *Id.* at 45–46.

16. Stephen Louis A. Dillard, *#Engage: It's Time for Judges to Tweet, Like & Share*, JUDICATURE, Spring 2017, at 11–13.

17. JARED CORREIA, TWITTER IN ONE HOUR FOR LAWYERS 44 (2012).

18. *Id.* at 51.

19. *See* KENNEDY & SHIELDS, *supra*.

20. CORREIA, *supra*, at 52.

21. *See* Smith, *supra*.

22. Sarah Eshiwani, *Instagram for Law Firms*, martindale.com (Mar. 8, 2018).

23. *See, e.g.,* FINDLAW, *From Novelty to Necessity: Pragmatic Social Media for Law Firms,* findlaw.com (Aug. 9, 2016).

24. The vast majority of academics studying social media agree that blogging is a form of social media. *See* Maxim Wolf et al., *Social Media? What Social Media?,* semanticscholar.org (last visited Jan. 18, 2020). However, disagreement persists in the blogging community at large.

25. *Blog,* dictionary.com (last visited Jan. 13, 2020).

26. Jennifer Murphy Romig, *Legal Blogging and the Rhetorical Genre of Public Legal Writing,* 12 LEGAL COMM. & RHETORIC: JALWD 29, 36 (2015).

27. *See, e.g.,* Rick Burnes, *Study Shows Business Blogging Leads to 55% More Website Visitors,* hubspot.com (last visited Jan. 18, 2020).

28. Farah Mohammed, *The Rise and Fall of the Blog,* daily.jstor.org (Dec. 27, 2017) (noting that general blogs are no longer as influential and members of the general public "are more likely to turn to Twitter or Facebook for a quick news fix or take on current events"); ABA TECHREPORT 2018, LEGAL BLOGS AND SOCIAL MEDIA, americanbar.org ("In 2018, 24% of firms reported having a blog, down from a high of 31% in 2017.").

29. *About Us,* wordpress.com, (Nov. 18, 2019).

30. *But see* Benjamin Zimmer, *Blawgs Phonolawgically Speaking,* LANGUAGE LOG, itre.cis.upenn.edu (Jan. 24, 2006) (analyzing complaints about the term "blawg" and noting that "if there are any concerns about misconstrual, one can always opt for the more orthographically distinct bLAWg.").

31. HARVARD LIBRARY, *Research Guide for CES Visiting Scholars,* guides.library.harvard.edu (Feb. 6, 2019).

32. *See generally* S.I. Strong, *Alternative Facts and the Post-Truth Society: Meeting the Challenge,* 165 U. PENN. L. REV. ONLINE 137 (2017).

33. WordPress, wordpress.com (last visited Jan. 1, 2019).

34. LexBlog, legblog.com (last visited Jan. 1, 2019).

35. Google Blog, blog.google (last visited Jan. 1, 2019).

36. SCOTUS BLOG: SUPREME COURT OF THE UNITED STATES BLOG, scotusblog.com (Jan 13, 2020).

37. Romig, *supra,* at 65.

38. *Id.* at 56 (explaining that readers of public legal writing are saturated with options and are, therefore, impatient and less likely to keep reading unless the piece is informative and gratifying); *see also* Mohammed, *supra* (explaining that with the prevalence of social media sites such as Twitter and LinkedIn, there has been a decrease interest in general blogs but "[b]logs are still important to those invested in their specific subject."). For further reading on student scholarship created online from the beginning, Professor Romig recommends students consult Jack Goldsmith's article on the well-known Lawfare blog, *Successful Online Student Legal Writing* (Oct. 27, 2016).

39. *See, e.g.,* ABA Journal Web 100, *Best Legal Blogs of 2018,* abajournal.com/blawg100 (compiling a yearly list of the best legal blogs).

40. *See* Romig, *supra,* at 62 (citing CHRISTOPHER JOHNSON, MICROSTYLE: THE ART OF WRITING LITTLE (2011)) ("Metaphor aids thinking because it 'activates rich patterns of reasoning'; metaphor aids persuasion because '[a] good metaphor leads people to make the inferences you want them to make.'").

41. Steve Johansen & Ruth Anne Robbins, *Art-iculating the Analysis: Systemizing the Decision to Use Visuals as Legal Reasoning,* 20 J. LEGAL WRITING INST. 57, 66 (2015) (citing LINDA LOHR, CREATING GRAPHICS FOR LEARNING AND PERFORMANCE: LESSONS IN VISUAL LITERACY 13, 16–22 (2d ed. 2007)); *see generally* Ellie Margolis, *Is the Medium the Message? Unleashing the Power of E-Communication in the Twenty-First Century,* 12 LEGAL COMM. & RHETORIC: JALWD 1 (2015).

42. *Id.* at 67 (citing A. PAIVIO, IMAGERY AND VERBAL PROCESSES (1971)).

43. Creative Commons, creativecommons.org (last visited Dec. 31, 2019).

44. Upsplash, upsplash.com (last visited Jan. 1, 2020).

45. *See* Google Advanced Image Search, google.com (last visited Jan. 1, 2020).

46. Canva, canva.com (last visited Jan. 1, 2020).

47. Romig Interview, *supra*; *see also* FindLaw, *Starting a Law Firm Blog: Ethical Considerations*, findlaw.com (last visited Dec. 29, 2019) (stating that "[a]ttorneys have an ethical code to uphold which also applies in cyberspace.... Even though it's a less formal method of writing, blogging still requires attributions.").

48. Mack Collier, *The Key Difference Between Your Blog and Other Social Media Channels That Most Companies Miss,* MackCollier.com (Jan. 25, 2016).

49. Interview with Professor Jennifer Romig, Emory University School of Law (Dec. 27, 2019).

50. Steven Seidenberg, *Seduced: For Lawyers, the Appeal of Social Media is Obvious. It's Also Dangerous*, abajournal.com (Feb. 2011).

51. Jennifer Ellis, *A Guide to Social Media Disclaimers for Lawyers*, good2bsocial.com (Nov. 16, 2017) (encouraging attorneys to "make certain that you check with your jurisdiction(s) to make certain that your disclaimers are correct").

52. For an excellent discussion of the ethical issues that may arise when considering a law firm blog, *see Starting a Law Firm Blog, supra.*

53. MODEL RULES OF PROF'L CONDUCT r. 1.6(a) (AM. BAR ASS'N 2017).

54. Note that, in some situations, the identity of a client may be subject to the attorney-client privilege. *See, e.g.,* N.Y. STATE BAR ASSOC. ETHICS OPINION 1088 (Mar. 31, 2016).

55. MODEL RULES OF PROF'L CONDUCT r. 1.6(a) (AM. BAR ASS'N 2017) cmt. 3.

56. *See, e.g.,* N.C. R. PROF'L CONDUCT 1.6(a) ("Confidentiality of Information").

57. ABA Comm. on Ethics & Prof'l Responsibility, Formal Op. 480 (2018).

58. *Id.*; *see also* Holland & Knight, *ABA Clarifies Lawyers' Confidentiality Obligations Regarding Online Public Commentary*, hklaw.com (March 14, 2018).

59. MODEL RULES OF PROF'L CONDUCT r. 7.1 (AM. BAR ASS'N 2018). Students should also be aware of Model Rule 7.2, which concerns the costs of advertisements, attorney recommendations and referrals, and specialists. *See* MODEL RULES OF PROF'L CONDUCT r. 7.2 (AM. BAR ASS'N 2018).

60. *Id.* cmt. 1.

61. MODEL RULES OF PROF'L CONDUCT r. 8.4(c) (AM. BAR ASS'N 2018).

62. *Id.* at 4.1(a).

63. Archishman Chakraborty & Rick Harbaugh, *Persuasive Puffery,* 33 MARKETING SCI. 382, 382–83 (May–June 2014) (discussing the definition of puffery and its use as a defense in fraud cases).

64. Roger Colaizzi et al., *The Best Explanation and Update on Puffery You Will Ever Read,* 31 ANTITRUST 86, 86–87 (Summer 2017) (discussing the ongoing legal debate related to the boundaries of puffery).

65. MODEL RULES OF PROF'L CONDUCT r. 1.1 cmt 8 (AM. BAR ASS'N 2018) (emphasis added).

66. 27 N.C. ADMIN. CODE 1D.1500(c)(17) (requiring technology training); FLA. R. PROF'L CONDUCT R. 6-10.3(b).

67. *Starting a Law Firm Blog, supra.*

68. *Id.*

69. *Id.*

70. *See, e.g.,* MODEL RULES OF PROF'L CONDUCT 4.2 (communication with person represented by counsel), 4.3 (dealing with unrepresented person). These rules, for example, could implicate incidental communications with represented parties via social media, such as "liking" a party's post on Facebook or other social media.

71. *See* Ellis, *supra*; *Starting a Law Firm Blog, supra.*

Chapter 13

Creative Works

Defining "creative writing" in law school[1] can be an elusive task because of the diversity of forms and topics encompassed within the genre. However, most scholars agree that creative writing is a piece of writing, whether fiction, poetry, or creative non-fiction, which highlights the author's imagination and ingenuity. Effective creative writing often addresses societal struggles, proposes innovative solutions to problems, or simply tells a story that readers can relate to and learn from through an imaginative lens.

As lawyers, creative writing affords us a unique opportunity to craft stories that encapsulate real narratives and issues not fully understood by the public or politicians responsible for crafting policy.[2] Through well-written fiction, poetry, and creative non-fiction, we can address how an honor roll student might turn into a heroin addict, how an impoverished person may gain access (or not) to legal services, or how an environmental policy might affect future generations. In turn, these narratives—whether fictitious or real—can foster a dialogue that sheds light on legal issues and solves real struggles in contemporary society. Although creative legal writing may come in many forms such as essays, poetry, non-fiction, or fiction, this chapter will focus on basic considerations for creating quality fiction writing with legal underpinnings.[3]

13.1 Conceptualizing a story

Starting the story is the hardest part of creative writing for many people. Some individuals describe a serendipitous moment where the idea for their next story simply appears in their head. For others, reading over published stories triggers an interest or idea that they want to explore in a way that is different from the author they are reading.[4] Once you have an idea for the story, you will need to transform the story in your head into a story on paper. Whether inventing a fictional story or writing an essay about a personal experience, outlining different plots and diagramming character development can help convert your thoughts into the tangible pieces of an excellent story. Some authors use a visual aid, such as a storyboard (a graphic organizer that can help a writer plan the narrative arc of the story), to help in the process. These fragments are then combined to create the first draft of your creative vision for a plot and characters.

13.2 Finding your inspiration

Like any other genre, topic selection is the first step to creative writing. Writing a good story requires selecting the appropriate theme or societal struggle to address. If the piece is for a class, consider the topics the class has been exploring throughout the semester. For example, a health law class may have investigated the legality of physician-assisted suicide through the court cases surrounding euthanasia advocate Dr. Jack Kevorkian. These cases may inspire a fictional story or creative essay about someone's own struggle with choosing physician-assisted suicide in light of their family's religious beliefs against it.

Just as in academic writing, preemption is an important consideration in preparing creative writing stories. You may have seen an episode of a popular TV drama where a drunken doctor attempted to operate on a patient, forcing the nurse to decide whether to intervene at the risk of losing her job, or a movie about a policeman walking into a diner only to slowly realize that he had inadvertently interrupted a robbery in progress. These storylines might have left an impression on you, causing you to wonder, "Why didn't I think of that?" and influencing you to write an eerily similar storyline with a few alterations. Many writers inadvertently start writing about a popular storyline they saw in the media, only to realize near the project's completion that it bears an uncanny resemblance to the creative piece that inspired it. Resist such a temptation. Just as in academic writing, a storyline is plagiarized if it uses the same idea without dramatic changes to the plot, characters, themes, and motivations.

Even though you may not copy or use the works of others without proper attribution, you do not need to ignore the works of others. Seeing strategies other writers have used effectively to develop their storylines is vital to becoming a better writer. They may have employed a certain technique to develop an effective surprise ending or described the scenery with eloquently precise language. To be a stronger writer, notice what strategies other authors employ and think about when and why those strategies were used.

13.3 Crafting the fictional story

With a general topic to serve as the premise of your story, the next step is to begin building the story. Start building the story by asking some general questions: Who is the protagonist? What is the protagonist's background? What is the obstacle the protagonist must overcome? How will the protagonist evolve as the story progresses? Generate questions such as these for the characters in your story and then answer them—but answer the questions just as if each character was being interviewed by a journalist for a biographical novel. The answers can serve as the foundation for the story's general outline.

For example, assume that you choose the topic of physician-assisted suicide referenced earlier in the chapter. You have decided that an elementary school teacher named Mary will be the focus of the story. First, consider the questions you would ask her if you were the doctor looking to perform the procedure. Maybe, for example, you want to know details about her condition, a timeline for her diagnosis, or the effect familial relationships have had on her life. These questions should be numerous (oftentimes writers have more than one hundred questions), and the answers need to be detailed enough so that you know who Mary is as a person. These questions and answers create Mary's identity. Repeat this process for all characters in the story.

Next, explore the setting of the story. Will it be at Mary's home? Are any of her family members living there with her? Will scenes take place in other locations? Do not choose a setting that appears exotic or captivating just because you think it will be what a reader wants. Rather, stay true to your characters and the setting in which you see those characters living and working. You might choose to let the setting be an inherent part of the plot.

After completing questionnaires for each character, start outlining the story. Weave together the characters' answers with the setting that you have identified. Generally, a more detailed outline provides a better foundation for a successful story.

Alternatively, like some writers, you could create an outline using only short descriptions of the story's scenes. For instance, maybe the opening scene features Mary being diagnosed with stage-four colon cancer. When developing this style of initial outline, identify key components of each scene by asking these questions: Who is the narrator? What will the characters wear? What are the essential pieces of dialogue that need to take place for the story to progress?

Once the outline is finished, condense it into an easily readable document. Ensure that scenes flow from one to the next. This outline will serve as the foundation of the story and the draft you are about to produce. With these ideas firmly recorded, check the outline structure against the components of a story, which are outlined below.

13.4 Weaving traditional parts of a story into your outline

While formulating the storyline for your creative piece, think about the traditional components of fictional writing. Like any other piece of scholarship, creative writing is made up of a series of components placed in a specific order. If you think back to high school English, you may have filled out a chart (or occasionally a bell-curved diagram) containing the following labels: exposition, rising action, climax, falling action, and resolution. Indeed, these are the pieces to a successful story, and each must logically flow into the other. Below is a brief description of each component and its relative length.

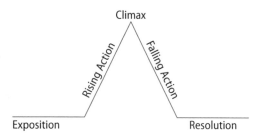

13.4.A Exposition

Every story starts by setting the background, introducing the conflict and characters, and highlighting specific things that will later become symbolic. Consider the short story *The Lottery*, by Shirley Jackson.[5] The reader is introduced to a crowd that is gathering in a small village for an annual lottery. Tessie Hutchinson (the protagonist), her family, and Mr. Summers (the head of the lottery) are introduced. The conflict is also identified when Tessie realizes that the paper her husband took from the lottery box has a mark on it. Setting the context in the exposition should be approximately 20–25% of the overall story.

13.4.B Rising action

The rising action builds the story up to its eventual climax by providing details, some subtly, that are or will become important. In *The Lottery*, the rising action is when the members of the entire Hutchinson family are called up to the lottery box by Mr. Summers to redraw their slips of paper after Tessie claims that her husband was not given enough time to draw the piece of paper that he wanted.[6] The rising action is the major portion of your story and may be as much as 50% of the overall piece.

13.4.C Climax

The climax is the central moment of the story. The goal as a writer is to pique the reader's interest and drive the reader toward the resolution. When the story is written well, readers will want to get to and through the climax quickly so that they can reach the resolution. The climax usually occurs near the end of the story and is separated from the resolution by no more than 15% of the story. The climax of *The Lottery* occurs when Tessie selects a paper from the box bearing a black dot indicating she has won the lottery.[7]

13.4.D Falling action

The falling action portion should be short and steer the narrative directly toward the resolution. Before adding new or interesting facts that change a character's development or the overall trajectory of the story, consider whether doing so would create a second climax, and thereby create a second rising action. The falling action of *The Lottery* features Tessie screaming that the process is not fair, just as the other villagers gather stones and form a circle around her.[8] This section should be, at most, 10% of the story.

13.4.E Resolution

The resolution section provides a solution to the central conflict of the story. It delivers a promise to the reader by providing some sense of finality. That promise does not mean that all questions are answered; on the contrary, many creative pieces of writing leave lingering questions for the reader to answer. For example, the resolution of *The Lottery* features a twist disrupting the reader's assumptions that lotteries are good events in which the winner takes a prize. In this story, the prize for young Tessie Hutchinson's win means that she is selected for stoning.[9] Although the author explains that Tessie is stoned, and she implies that Tessie is killed, other questions are left unanswered. The author does not explain the purpose or the origins of the lottery, nor does the writer explain the resolution for the other characters in the story.

The traditional components of a story will give your storyline ideas a solid structure. Although that structure may be somewhat flexible as it melds with your own writing style and creative story ideas, you will still want to create strong fiction that has these component parts.

13.5 Other considerations for the creative writer

Creative writing demands different considerations than a typical comment, note, or other piece of scholarly writing. Those forms require writing a piece based upon careful research of existing scholarship, but with creative writing, you are creating something entirely new. Characters are assigned identities, plot points are subtly conveyed for the reader's enjoyment, and a narrative voice is designed to seamlessly propel the story along. To that end, vocabulary usage, discreet clues, and proper narration are vital to building a successful story.

13.5.A Vocabulary

Choosing the correct vocabulary for both the narrator and the characters is an overlooked part of creative writing. Characters, like people, talk a certain way based upon their background, education, life experiences, geographic region, etc. An auto mechanic who dropped out of high school to earn money to support his siblings will not talk like an astrophysicist with a Ph.D. from Cal Tech. Consider the following statement made by Joe, a factory worker who has received no formal education, about the state of his life:

> "My prosaic life affords me no fulfillment. Each day, I traverse the streets of the city after work thinking what could have been had I only leveraged my skillset into a lucrative career in mechanical engineering," Joe said.

On the surface, this dialogue seems plausible; it explains how Joe feels about the current state of his life clearly. However, would Joe really talk that way? If Joe is a factory worker without a formal education, it is unlikely he would use a string of terms like "prosaic," "traverse," or "leverage." Such a long, drawn-out sentence with deep undertones and symbolism would not likely represent how Joe would actually describe his situation to a friend, colleague, or family member. When writing dialogue, instead of writing how you would speak, stay true to the characters and make sure their words reflect who *they* are and not who *you* are.

Carefully considering vocabulary usage for narration is just as important as vocabulary usage is for characters. As in the example with Joe, some writers think using large words to articulate sophisticated imagery makes their writing more meaningful. The opposite is usually true; in creative writing, just like in legal writing, simple is usually better. Everyone has read a paper or narrative that used so many complex words and images that reading it to the end became a burden. For example, that paper might be a three-page description of a butterfly's wings as seen by a small child through a window. The paper appeared well written, used several complex images to describe the wings, and required a great deal of time to perfect. Nevertheless, it was a chore to read and understand. If a reader is turned off by the complexity of the vocabulary, how can you expect to adequately convey the story's underlying message and foster a useful dialogue? Choose simple words. Do not use "edifice" when you mean "house."

An increased likelihood of error is another problem with utilizing complex vocabulary in narrative. Consider the following sentence using the word "clandestine," the meaning of which is frequently misunderstood:

> The sparrow's clandestine wings sparkled with beaded dew as they soared toward the rising sun.

Clandestine is a beautiful-sounding adjective that appears to convey an almost divine beauty on its noun. Unfortunately, it actually means "marked by, held in or conducted with secrecy: surreptitious."[10] Therefore, rather than create a positive image, the author has inadvertently described a sparrow's wings as somehow illicit. When writing, use familiar vocabulary to avoid some of these common misconceptions.

13.5.B Show, don't tell: The art of subtlety

"Show, don't tell" is a maxim that creative writing teachers bore into their students' skulls from the first day of class. That maxim, incidentally, applies to legal writing as well as fiction writing. A successful writer must make a reader feel a certain way or identify a central conflict without explicitly characterizing what every character thinks and feels. Good writing often requires the reader to interpret such thoughts and emotions. Furthermore, effective writing often requires that readers use their own thoughts, feelings, and experiences when understanding the characters and the plot. Compare the next two examples and identify which one you think is more intriguing and why.

Example 1: Mary sat there and worried how her children would react if she travelled across state lines for physician-assisted suicide.

Example 2: As the doctor spoke in a quiet voice, Mary sat with a half-smile on her face. Yet the nurse noticed how tightly Mary clenched one hand around her IV pole while repeatedly rubbing the palm of her other hand back and forth across her pants. Mary locked eyes with the doctor, the same half-smile on her face, but the smile no longer reached her eyes. "Do you know someone?" she asked, "someone that — who could help me when I am ready?"

Showing, rather than telling requires an artful dance of narration and dialogue. Here, Mary may have a conversation with a doctor about her options and express hesitant interest in physician-assisted suicide but ultimately appear timid. The narrator may describe Mary's discomfort by highlighting her sweating palms or fidgeting that the nurse's aide noticed. These subtle clues "show" the reader that something is making Mary uneasy, thereby hinting at the conflict that will be developed throughout the story.

To a person exclusively familiar with academic writing, this technique may seem bizarre and nonsensical. In comments, notes, and academic papers, we are always told to clearly articulate our thoughts and identify our addition to existing scholarship. To be subtle is to be evasive, and to be evasive is to seem unknowledgeable. Why then do we use this strategy for creative writing? Well, it is because the goals of formal legal scholarship and legally based creative fiction are fundamentally different.

Remember those long discussions in high school English trying to understand a character's inner thoughts, why they took a certain action, or the symbolism of a certain object? If the author instead chose to simply come out and tell the reader the answers through narration or dialogue, readers would have been cheated out of these discussions. The goal of creative writing is to make the audience think about what the symbolism means, what is hidden behind the words, and what broad point concerning society the author is trying to make. Curtly informing the reader "you are supposed to think this way" robs the reader of divergent interpretations and deprives the story of its most important function: fostering a complex and lasting dialogue.

13.5.C Choosing the narrator

Choosing a narrator is an important part of creative writing that writers often fail to consider. In grade school, most students probably learned about the three common types of narration: first person, third-person limited, and third-person omniscient. However, selecting the type of narrator does not by itself create successful narration—the gender and voice of the narrator must also be considered and carefully tailored to the story's needs.

• Voice

The narrator is never the author of the story. Mark Twain may have written *The Adventures of Huckleberry Finn*,[11] but his characters and the narration that accompanies them take on an identity of their own. Similarly, the narrator in your story is not you but is instead a carefully chosen voice to best convey meaning upon the narrative.[12] Think carefully about the type of voice you want to use and the perspective from which the story should be told. Below are the most common forms of narration, with brief descriptions of their central characteristics.

Common forms of narration

Type	Explanation
First Person	With first-person narration, a single person tells the story using the pronoun "I" or other first-person pronouns. The person may be the main character of the story or someone with a connection to the main character. This narration may be biased toward the main character and the narrator's actions may feature internal monologues not known by the other characters in the story.
Third-Person Limited	Third-person limited narration associates the third-person narrator with a single character. This narrator gets to know the inner thoughts of only one character but not the other characters in the story.
Third-Person Omniscient	The most common form of narration, third-person omniscient narration, confers omniscient authority on the narrator, allowing the narrator to know each character's inner thoughts and to enjoy unlimited control over the story. The narrator may reveal as much or as little to the reader as the narrator chooses.

- Gender

Some student writers find that they unconsciously use narrators of the same gender as they identify themselves. Next time you read a collection of creative short stories, however, look to see if this holds true. Choice of gender is often the biggest barrier to distinguishing the narrator's voice from that of the "invisible" author. While you may want to write from the perspective of the gender in which you identify (in fact, choosing your own gender may give you the ability to accurately convey information from first-hand insight), consider whether the story could be told more effectively or compellingly from the perspective of a different gender, in a non-binary manner, or even with an undisclosed gender. Remember, the narrative voice is not *your* voice but is instead a source of the report (a possibly biased factfinder or unreliable purveyor of information) who conveys the story's themes to the reader. A well-chosen narrator can provide readers with a clear story while also provoking questions that might not have deducible answers. So, think about your narrator and choose the voice that best accomplishes these objectives.

13.6 Bringing in the law: What makes the piece a creative legal work?

Opportunities to write creatively in law school are becoming more common. Courses on a wide range of topics now afford students the opportunity to write a creative story on a legal issue as either a class assignment or a final exam. Often, submission of the piece as the final exam is contingent upon substantial footnotes linking portions of the story to case law or contemporary policy debate. While the annotations need not answer every question presented in the story, they may, however, encourage the reader to think more deeply about the underlying legal background to the conflict presented by the story. The growing presence of opportunities for creative writing provides students the opportunity to diversify their scholarship while also broadening legal readership to individuals who rarely read academic journals.

13.6.A Citations

Footnoting is likely the defining feature of creative legal writing prepared for a law school class. The footnotes carefully link elements of the story to established case law and provide the reader with the background surrounding the legal debate.[13] For instance, the earlier example in this chapter describing Mary's desire for physician-assisted suicide may feature numerous references to legal cases surrounding the legality of the practice. Specifically, a scene in which her doctor tells her that only a handful of states have legalized the practice would feature detailed footnotes describing how physician-assisted suicide has been legalized those states. These footnotes should contain any relevant statutes, as well as illustrations of seminal cases and any important secondary sources.

Finding supporting research to non-legal information is synonymous with citing to legal sources and should be done with creative legal writing. Even though most of the story is original, do not skip this step. Well-written creative legal scholarship typically brings in statistics or real-world figures that highlight the problem being discussed. For example, citing to a source explaining the story of Dr. Jack Kevorkian and the statistics about the number of physician-assisted suicides taking place in the United States each year may help the reader understand the scope of the issue in your fictional story. The presence of sources in the footnotes connects the fictional story to reality, thereby raising awareness of the topic and fostering widespread debate.

Law students today have a variety of opportunities to write creatively in law school and the possibilities are continuously growing.[14] As previously noted, some law schools have begun offering courses that provide students the chance to write creatively; others offer discussion groups that read, critique, and discuss law students' short stories. A legal education can enhance your creativity and provide you with endless opportunities to use narrative techniques to explore creative legal works. Who knows, law school may heighten your creativity, and you may find yourself becoming the next popular writer of legal fiction like Scott Turow or John Grisham.

Notes

1. We would like to thank former Wake Forest Law student, Adam Messenlehner, for his excellent research and writing contributions in this chapter.

2. Arthur Austin, *Evaluating Storytelling As a Type of Nontraditional Scholarship*, 74 NEB. L. REV. 479, 507–27 (1995); Nancy Levit, *The Theory and the Practice— Reflective Writing Across the Curriculum, 2008 AALS Annual Meeting Panel Discussion: Writing Across the Curriculum: Professional Communication and the Writing that Supports It*, 15 J. LEGAL WRITING INST. 253, 253–78 (2009); Carol McCrehan Parker, *What Will I Do on Monday, and Why Aren't We Doing It Already?: Reflecting on the Value of Expressive Writing in the Law School Curriculum, 2008 AALS Annual Meeting Panel Discussion: Writing Across the Curriculum: Professional Communication and the Writing that Supports It*, 15 J. LEGAL WRITING INST. 279, 286 (2009).

3. *See* CREATIVE WRITING: A WORKBOOK WITH READINGS 17–70 (Linda Anderson ed., 2006); CREATIVE WRITING: WRITERS ON WRITING, (Amal Chatterjee ed., 2013); STEVE MAY, DOING CREATIVE WRITING (2007); Austin, *supra*, at 479; Daniel A. Farber & Suzanna Sherry, *Telling Stories Out of School: An Essay on Legal Narratives*, 45 STAN. L. REV. 807, 807–56 (1993); Jennifer Jolly-Ryan, *Bridging the Law School Learning Gap Through Universal Design*, 28 TOURO L. REV. 1393, 1393– 1442 (2012); Levit, *supra*, at 253–78; Philip N. Meyer, *Confessions of A Legal Writing Instructor*, 46 J. LEGAL EDUC. 27, 27–42 (1996); Parker, *supra*, at 279–92; Gary L. Stuart, *Lawyers As Creative Writers*, Ariz. Att'y, December 2008, at 12; Stacey A. Tovino, *Incorporating Literature into a Health Law Curriculum*, 9 J. MED. & L. 213, 213–56 (2005).

4. *See, e.g.*, AMRA PAJALIC ET AL., CREATIVE PROCESS 99–104 (ClickView, 2016).

5. Shirley Jackson, *The Lottery, in* THE LOTTERY AND OTHER STORIES, 291– 302 (Farrar, 1991).

6. *See id.*

7. *See id.*

8. *See id.*

9. *See id.*

10. *Clandestine*, WEBSTER'S DICTIONARY, merriam-webster.com (last visited Oct. 7, 2019).

11. MARK TWAIN, THE ADVENTURES OF HUCKLEBERRY FINN (Charles L. Webster & Co., 1885).

12. ANDERSON, *supra*, at 101.

13. Austin, *supra*, at 515–23.

14. *See, e.g.*, WAKE FOREST UNIV., *Awaken*, awakenwfu.com (last visited Jan. 7, 2020) (publishing creative legal works involving law and bioethics).

Chapter 14

Submitting and Publishing Your Work

Congratulations—the writing process is complete! Now what? Now is the time to begin the publishing process and find a permanent home for the article, book, or other writing. This chapter examines potential publication options and provides tips on submitting and marketing articles to generate interest from various law journals, book publishers, internet sites, or other media outlets engaged in publishing legal writing.

As with most other kinds of writing, the "where" of publishing depends largely on "what" you are publishing. As might be expected, the final publication source is determined by the specific type of writing being published. Law review articles are generally published in law journals or law reviews, which might be operated by a school or a professional, third-party organization. Professional articles—those intended for distribution to a professional audience—are most likely to be published in a legal publication run by a state or national bar association such as a magazine, book, or online forum.

Regardless of the form of a scholarly writing, the submission and publication process can be broken down into three steps. First, the main consideration will be *where* to publish the writing. Second, after determining where to publish the writing, consider *how* to go about having the writing published. Third, and finally, consider *when* to publish the writing so that the intended audience can best access it.

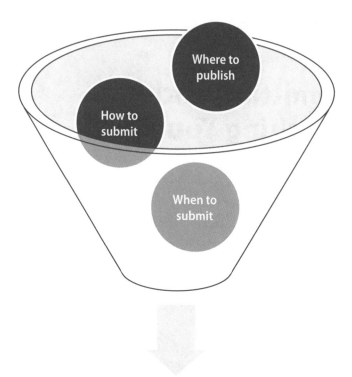

Submission and Publication Process

14.1 Publishing law review and law journal articles

In determining where and how to publish scholarly writing, writers must consider a number of questions. Often, these questions boil down to your familiarity and connections with a publisher or publication, such as the following:

- Do you have a relationship with a publication that might increase the chances of your scholarship being published?
- Does your article lend itself to a particular kind of publication, like a specialty journal?
- Does a particular journal require that submissions be made through a designated submission platform?

For most scholars, their current law school (for students and professors) or their alma mater (for practitioners) will often be the starting point. However, ensuring that a piece of scholarship is published requires determination and a willingness to be flexible with where and how the scholarship is published.

14.1.A Where to publish: Considerations for students

• **Your law school's journals**

For many people in the legal field, the most likely place to publish a scholarly article will be a school-sponsored journal. Most school-sponsored journals set aside a certain number of slots in each edition to highlight their own students' or own professors' work. Most 2L or 3L staff members of a law journal are likely to be required or encouraged to write a Note or Comment to be considered for publication in their respective journals. The journals may offer publication opportunities to the student population as a whole—even if the writer is not a law review member—as well as to alumni practitioners and to current professors, among others.

For some law schools, publishing with your institution's journal is another route by which students who are not on law review may get an invitation to join.

Although many schools have just one journal or law review, other schools have multiple publications—a primary general law review and then other publications (whether law reviews or journals) that may focus on a legal specialty. When deciding, look for the journal that would fit best with your article's topic. If your article focuses on water laws, for instance, it might fit best with a school's environmental journal; however, if the topic expands to how water rights can unconstitutionally affect a segment of the population, a primary, general law review might be an equally good fit. You might also consider the reputation of each journal. Prestige is gauged by different factors such as the journal's history, longevity, readership, the school's reputation, or even how many times that journal is cited in other works, briefs, or judicial opinions.[1] Traditionally, the more "prestigious" journal will be a school's primary, general law review followed by other specialty legal publications.[2] At some schools, however, highly ranked specialty journals maintain equal levels of prestige. Regardless of the particular journal, checking all publication opportunities at your current school (for students or professors) or your alma mater (for practitioners) is a good first step.

• **Other law schools' journals**

You may also seek publication with journals at other law schools. While most school-sponsored journals do not reserve publication space for articles authored by students from other schools, many journals will nonetheless allow a student from another school to publish if the student meets or exceeds the same criteria specified for other professional authors, such as professors or legal practitioners, or

Special concerns for judicial clerks:

If you are or plan to be a clerk, always check with your judge to verify that anything you may want to publish is not prohibited by any judicial code of conduct or rules for your judge's chambers.

if the student has some unique credentials, such as a student who is a patent examiner writing about patent law or a former member of the National Transportation and Safety Board writing about aviation law.

Sometimes the "when" of publishing an article affects where it is published. Many journals have a particular desire to publish articles by practicing lawyers, so students unable to get an article published while in law school might elect to update the article after graduation and submit it for publication as a practitioner. For those intending to clerk for a judge after graduation, that one- or two-year clerkship might provide an additional opportunity to revise the article and shop it to journals. Journals may consider the submission more appealing because it is coming from a law clerk rather than a law student. Some law journals solicit articles by clerks as a way to offer future professors their first publication opportunities; these journals recognize that many clerks have more time to thoroughly research and develop their articles than full-time legal practitioners do.

 • **Specialty journals**

Specialty journals provide a third option for publication, though that option is more frequently utilized by practicing lawyers or legal scholars than by law students. As the table below demonstrates, specialty publications generally publish articles in a particular field or on a discrete legal topic. More frequently, such topics include intellectual property, the Uniform Commercial Code, healthcare law, animal law, and business law. These journals are sometimes sponsored by particular schools and may be secondary, student-run journals. In other instances, specialty journals are operated and published by professional organizations rather than schools.

Examples of specialty journals

Topic	Journal
A student-run journal focusing on law, health, the sciences, and bioethics.	*The Minnesota Journal of Law, Science & Technology*
A student-run law review geared solely to environmental and natural resources issues.	*Lewis & Clark Environmental Law Review*
A student-run law journal focused on "women's experiences as they have been structured, affected, controlled, discussed, and ignored by the law."[3]	*Yale Journal of Law & Feminism*
A law journal sponsored by the American Association of Law Schools geared toward issues related to legal education and theory.	*Journal of Legal Education*

Publication standards vary considerably depending on who is operating and publishing the journal, but in each instance, practicing lawyers and law students — particularly those with a demonstrable expertise or interest in the journal's field of specialization — are often encouraged to submit articles and to publish with such journals.

14.1.B Where to publish: Considerations for practicing lawyers

Practicing lawyers may want to consider law journals at their alma mater. Some school-sponsored journals give preference to their alumni to encourage those individuals to publish with the journal and to ensure that the journal gets a "known commodity" in the form of someone with whom the school—if not the journal itself—has familiarity. However, journals of all varieties are often much more willing to publish articles written by practicing professionals than by students who may lack a substantial academic reputation. This preference sometimes enables practitioners and professors to be more selective in determining where their articles might be published.

Practicing lawyers often find that publishing in a specialty journal that emphasizes an aspect of their own practice area provides a good outlet for publication of their article—e.g., healthcare, intellectual property, financial services, and so on. As a result, publishing in a specialty journal ensures that an article reaches a particular, highly specialized audience that has more interest in the article than would a general law journal audience.

14.1.C Journal standards

Regardless of a writer's status as a student, practicing lawyer, professor, or other individual in the legal profession, the vast majority of law journals—both student-run, school-sponsored journals and professional journals—readily disclose their publication standards and processes to potential authors. These standards might be listed in the front or back pages of a print copy of a journal and are almost universally listed on the journal's website. The standards typically include particular topics that the journal's editors have found to be conducive to publication, the length and formatting requirements for any articles to be submitted, the timeline for articles selected for publication, and the general standards expected for publishing with that particular journal.[4]

After determining where to have a writing published, the process becomes a more mechanical one of closely following instructions—something in which we all, as practicing attorneys or law students, should be well versed. Just as there are various options for publishing, each of those options typically has numerous processes and procedures that must be followed to ensure that the writing is considered for publication.

14.1.D Online law journals

Online law journals are good options for shorter articles or for time-sensitive pieces that need to be published quickly. Some articles that start out as potential law journal articles or even as professional journal articles may not get published for a variety of reasons: The author may lose interest in developing a topic further, the article may simply not be selected for publication by a law journal or professional journal, or the article may not meet various other criteria for publication. An author might simply want to publish a piece rather quickly, possibly due to a new development in the law or society. In those situations or when the author intends from the beginning for the article to be a shorter, less-formal piece of writing, an online journal may be a better option.

If the writing is fairly short—generally between 500–5,000 words, depending on the publication—and focuses on a particular practice issue or an issue of time-sensitive importance, consider whether an online-only law journal forum would be the most appropriate final publication destination. Online legal publishing forums are now ubiquitous—most, if not all, school-sponsored law journals maintain online publishing forums, as do most professional bar associations and other similar organizations. These very same organizations publish print copies of various journals, but their online forums are usually geared toward publishing pieces of interest to lay individuals and practicing lawyers. Also, the journals publish in a medium that is more easily accessible to those individuals, usually at little or no cost and often with no subscription requirements. In light of these factors, an online audience might be larger and include a wider variety of individuals than the audience of a traditional law journal or professional journal.

In addition, online forums tend to publish articles both more frequently and more quickly than traditional journals, owing in large part to the shorter articles, which require less editing. Thus, publishing in an online forum often presents an opportunity to be the first authoritative voice analyzing a recent major legal development—often several months in advance of traditional print legal journals and professional journals. So, with careful planning and a bit of luck, an author accepted to an online journal might be one of the first legal "experts" to analyze a major legal issue and to weigh in with an opinion.

14.1.E How to publish: Submission platforms

At times, the publication process requires authors to be very proactive in marketing articles, submitting them to multiple outlets for publication, and frequently following up on the status of the article in the journal's review process. Traditional methods meant that an author had to directly contact every journal with a publication request for an article. Thankfully, for modern legal scholarship, that process has evolved to a more streamlined system. One way to mitigate the effort required to market a particular piece of writing is to use online submission platforms and aggregators. The main goal of online submission platforms is to provide a central location where authors can upload their relevant writings and where publications can then review writings to determine whether any of those writings would be a good fit for them.

• ExpressO and Scholastica

Law journals often use aggregating and distribution services for managing and selecting potential articles. These services are similar to those employers use to organize and select potential job applicants—an applicant uploads materials to a central databank, and employers can peruse applicants to find the best fit for each opening. Two of the most popular services are ExpressO[5] and Scholastica.[6] Each of these submission platforms allows authors to upload and submit their manuscripts and related documents for consideration by a variety of journals, law reviews, and other third parties. ExpressO and Scholastica focus most specifically on the distribution of journal articles and provide a platform where authors can upload their manuscripts, cover letters, and other documents that might encourage law reviews and law journals to accept articles for publication. Most school-sponsored law journals and many professional journals have access to one or both platforms. Through the platform, journal editors are able to review and sort through all articles to find those related to a particular topic or issue of the journal. Because ExpressO and Scholastica can be expensive for individual authors, an institutional license both to download articles from third parties and to upload student-written articles is a particularly valuable resource. In some instances, practicing attorneys might find that law firms also maintain subscriptions to one or both of these platforms. Even with an institutional license, be aware that submissions may still come with fees, so make sure you understand the costs and your institution's policies on submissions.

Journals often have a preference for one of the two platforms, even if they utilize both, and indicate this preference on their websites. Others

Students: Get prior approval for submissions

Even if your school has an institutional subscription to an aggregating service, fees will likely accrue for each submission. Make sure that you have permission to submit your article and that you fully understand any school policies or limitations on submissions.

do not have an express preference and are willing to select articles from either platform. The best advice is, after making a list of potential journals, to review those journals' policies to determine which platform would be more beneficial for an article. After uploading one or more articles, authors simply wait for a response from a journal. Authors can then manage offers and acceptances through their accounts. Once a journal selects the article, authors then work directly with the individual law journals, following that journal's publication process.

• SSRN and LawArXiv

In addition to Scholastica and ExpressO, many other platforms are widely used to connect authors with potential publishers and to provide an opportunity for distribution of journal articles. The Social Science Research Network (SSRN)[7] is an example of one such platform and LawArXiv is another.[8] LawArXiv, a relative newcomer to the scene, is a non-profit repository for legal scholarly articles and is owned by members of the legal community. Although SSRN is more widely used as a platform for the initial publication and peer review of scientific research papers than for identifying potential law review articles, some journal editors use SSRN to identify articles or authors that might be a good fit in upcoming issues. LawArXiv, on the other hand, is dedicated to legal publishing, has open public access, and is free to use. Both SSRN and LawArXiv are intended to provide quick distribution of research through an open-access model.

• Other opportunities

Outside of online publishing-coordination platforms, the primary option that many authors continue to use for submitting their articles is the direct-to-journal option. Most journals continue to accept direct submissions, though a few accept only those articles submitted through online platforms.[9] To know the acceptable method, consult the individual journal's submission policies, as discussed above.

Most publications maintain working websites where they set out the requirements for publishing in their journals. These might include page or word limits, topic restrictions, deadlines, and most importantly, the person to whom authors should submit their draft for consideration. In addition to these online sites, some journals have an "articles editor" or similar contact person listed in their print copy journals. Even with online information, it is not always feasible to review the publishing requirements for every single journal you are interested in.

Luckily, some resources aggregate this information and provide regular updates. Two of the most frequently used and most helpful resources in identifying journal submission policies are (1) the Washington and Lee University School of Law's *Law Journal Rankings* website[10] and (2) the annually updated working paper, *Information for Submitting Articles to Law Reviews & Journals* by Professors Nancy Levit and Allen Rostron,[11] which is maintained on the SSRN website.

The first of these two resources, the Washington and Lee website, is known for its rankings of school-sponsored law journals based upon various factors. More importantly for the context of this chapter, the website also collects and compiles vast amounts of information on each journal that it ranks, including the specific publication processes, technical requirements, and often the main contact person for publication questions.

The second resource, the annual paper by Professors Levit and Rostron, does not independently rank law journals, but it does independently verify submission requirements for manuscripts, formatting requirements, and options to expedite or withdraw. This information includes the relevant articles editor or other person to contact for submissions; the relevant email addresses; the journal's preferences for use of Scholastica, ExpressO, or other options; and related information.[12] The Levit and Rostron article can be used in tandem with the Washington and Lee rankings platform because the two resources often complement each other in many respects.

An author seeking to publish might use this information advantageously in a couple of ways. First, online resources can help strategically narrow the list of journals to which authors would submit articles for potential publication, possibly by evaluating its rankings, the number of citations articles often get in the journal, and related points. In addition, these resources might help authors identify particularly informative issues or frequently cited issues; by identifying those pertinent issues, an author can then either narrow potential topics for an article or refocus the analysis of an article already in progress based on how those previous articles were received or how often they were cited. Most importantly, however, these resources are time savers; once an author has decided on a topic, drafted an article, and is prepared to move forward with publication, these resources will allow the author to streamline the marketing process for the article while simultaneously increasing the exposure that the article is likely to receive.

14.1.F When to publish: Journal publication cycles

The third and final consideration in the submission and publication process for legal writing is when to begin the publication process and when to aim for final publication of the writing. The "when" of publishing varies depending on the type of writing being published.

Nearly all law journals, including school-sponsored journals and professional law journals, publish in cycles. Some publish a specific number of issues annually or per school year, while others publish at other regular intervals, such as quarterly or monthly.

For school-sponsored law journals, the best times to submit articles for publication are frequently in late summer, around August, and early spring, around February and March. August is when law review editors generally return to school to begin working on their selection processes for upcoming issues, while February and March are when the new editorial boards are generally chosen and begin selecting articles for their next volume. For professional law journals, the best time to submit articles will vary by journal since professional journals often have publication dates that do not correspond to a school calendar. Once an article is chosen, the publication process times can vary. Some journals select articles nearly a year in advance of their final publication dates, while others select articles mere weeks prior to publication.

Online-only law journals or law forums are generally willing to accept documents throughout the year, but some do follow timelines for submissions. Because school-sponsored online journals or forums are on the same calendars as the institution's print journals, the August or February–March timelines may be equally applicable. Other online forums, those sponsored by organizations and not law schools, are not limited by the school calendar and are free to accept articles at their convenience. Most forums indicate on their websites any preferred submission dates. Websites may also indicate whether articles will be published in batches or on a rolling basis as submissions are accepted.

14.2 Other considerations: Length, abstract, cover letter, keywords, and table of contents

A few other considerations can enhance the appeal of an article and make it easier to attract the attention of a publisher. Introducing the article to a publisher with a strong cover letter can catch an editor's eye. Using an abstract to briefly summarize the main points of the article and using a succinct table of contents to map the article's subtopics make it easier for potential editors to gauge the article's fit in a publication.

14.2.A Length

Trends show that shorter articles are being published, so adhere to a publisher's length guidelines. In the early 2000s, the average length of an article in a top law review publication was 87.76 pages.[13] In 2004, the *Harvard Law Review* conducted a nationwide survey of law school faculty regarding the state of legal scholarship. Of the nearly 800 professors who completed the survey, nearly 90% agreed that law review articles were too long. Many responding professors opined that shortening articles would improve both the quality and effectiveness of legal scholarship.[14] These findings led to a joint statement by the law reviews at Duke, Berkeley, Columbia, Cornell, Georgetown, Harvard, Michigan, Stanford, Texas, Penn, Virginia, and Yale, acknowledging their role in fostering the trend of excessively long law review articles and advocating a length range of forty to seventy law review pages.[15]

Together, the survey findings and joint statement led to the implementation of stricter length requirements at many law reviews. Schools such as Yale, Harvard, and the University of Virginia have issued policies stating that their law reviews now strongly prefer articles under 25,000 words in length, which is the equivalent of fifty law review pages. Duke asserts a preference for articles that are under seventy pages (35,000 words) in length, while Wake Forest prefers articles within the range of thirty-five to fifty pages.[16] Specialty journals may have even shorter limits so as to include more articles; for example, *The Animal Law Review* at Lewis & Clark Law School prefers articles ranging from twenty-five to fifty pages, and other types of submissions, such as essays, may be much shorter. Adhering to a journal's length guidelines may give your article a better chance of being selected for publication, so make sure to check those details.

14.2.B Abstract

An abstract is a summary of an article that sets out the general topic and describes the thesis and the primary arguments. Abstracts generally consist of approximately 250 words or fewer (although be sure to consult the specific requirements for any law review to which you are submitting). Abstracts typically introduce the topic broadly at first and then highlight narrow components that draw the reader to the complexities of a paper. The goal of abstracts is primarily two-fold:

- Abstracts give the reader a preview of the main points of the article.
- Abstracts serve as a marketing tool for the article; through it, the reader, whether another scholar doing research or a law review editor looking for a submission, can see whether the article is a good fit for that person's search.

When drafting your abstract, use the same principles of good writing that you used in the article itself. A well-written abstract resembles something of an outline that clearly lays out each of the salient points made in the article; thus, it increases the reader's efficiency in terms of time and comprehension of material, which will likely make it easier for the reader to follow and comprehend the article itself. This ease of reading, in turn, allows the reader to spend less time interpreting the article, which facilitates an all-around more efficient execution of the reader's task.

Like all legal writing, abstracts should be written clearly and concisely. While other disciplines expect a scholarly article to have a comprehensive one-paragraph abstract, for legal scholarship, the author may want to consider breaking down the abstract into short paragraphs.[17] Below is the abstract from Professor Leti Volpp's article, *The Citizen and the Terrorist*:[18]

Sample of an abstract

Notice the use of a rhetorical question about political events and legal and cultural issues to spark interest in the topic generally.

Here, the abstract provides a brief overview of the article's contents.

Since the terrorist attacks of September 11, 2001, there have been more than one thousand incidents of hate violence reported in the United States. How do we understand the emergence of this violence in a context of national tragedy? This Article suggests that September 11 facilitated the consolidation of a new identity category that groups together persons who appear "Middle Eastern, Arab, or Muslim," whereby members of this group are identified as terrorists and disidentified as citizens. While the stereotype of the "Arab terrorist" is not an unfamiliar one, the ferocity with which multiple communities have been interpellated into this identity category suggests there are particular dimensions converging in this racialization. The Article examines three: the fact and legitimacy of racial profiling; the redeployment of Orientalist tropes; and the relationship between citizenship, nation, and identity.

Good organization and effective use of key words can enhance the function of an abstract. Use techniques such as signals (first, second, third) and enumeration ((1), (2), and (3)) for clarity. Also, because they are written for academic audiences, abstracts should use the same level of technical language and expertise as found in the actual article and include as many keywords that may be used in a Boolean search as practicable. Using these keywords or key phrases will assist others in finding the article in an index because the technical language likely includes keywords and phrases of a topic that a reader is researching.

Generally, abstracts take two forms: (1) a quoted portion from the article, or (2) a short paragraph noting the high points of the article. Either option can be effective if prepared appropriately. Authors who elect to use a quotation from their article as the abstract often identify a defining aspect of the article, such as a hard-hitting conclusion with flourishing language, to make the article stand out from the pack. As an analogy, think of Reverend Dr. Martin Luther King, Jr.'s "I Have a Dream" address. Rather than attempting to condense that speech into a summary, an author of a similar piece might select one or more paragraphs of the speech to serve as a stand-alone abstract.

Most commonly, however, abstracts consist of a short description of the article, highlighting the main points the article espouses and the conclusions reached. Regardless of the type of abstract, the goal is to ensure that the abstract operates as an accurate, short, stand-alone representation of the article as a whole.

Abstracts also optimize an article's scholarly influence by increasing its visibility to other researchers. Researchers who are looking for an article on a particular topic or law review editors looking for a potential submission rely on abstracts as a means of getting information quickly. According to one study, the rate of citation for law review articles that contain an abstract is roughly 1.62 times the rate of articles that do not.[19] In a sense, then, a well-written abstract is a powerful advertisement for a busy reader, helping the reader to choose one article over countless others.

Additionally, many online platforms present a field for inputting an abstract to describe the article and make it stand out to journal editors wading through thousands of submissions on the platform. Many journal editors will not take the time to read an entire article to determine if it would be a good fit for their next issue. Instead, they will rely on the title of the article, any information they can find about the author, and any abstract provided to reach their conclusions about the article. As a result, the article must be represented by a strong and well-crafted abstract.

14.2.C Cover letter

In the same vein, when marketing an article, whether through platform uploads or direct solicitations, many authors find that cover letters serve to engage editors and to convince them to consider articles for publication. In many respects, cover letters in direct solicitations serve the same purpose as abstracts for articles uploaded to online platforms and should include the following:

- An overview of the article and its thesis;
- Author background information, including relevant publications or specific credentials (which might also include a résumé or CV);
- Why the article is original, relevant, and should be published in the particular journal; and
- Word count, including footnotes.

In the same way that employers prefer individualized cover letters explaining how employees are a good fit for the specific employer, journal editors likewise expect cover letters for law journal articles to explain why the articles should be published in their journal. As a result, individualized cover letters are key. Review the following cover letter used by Professor Lawrence Cunningham in a 2008 submission, *The SEC's Global Accounting Vision: A Realistic Appraisal of a Quixotic Quest*.[20]

Excerpt of the body of a sample cover letter

The accompanying Article provides the **first comprehensive analysis of the revolutionary proposals the Securities and Exchange Commission is making to jettison traditional US accounting requirements in favor of international standards.** This subject is a matter of intense discussion worldwide in many settings. This Article offers numerous perspectives on the pending debate and examines

Here, the author provides an overview of the article, how it presents an original thought, and why the article offers an important contribution to the scholarly dialogue.

The author provides useful information about his background and credentials and why he is an expert in this area. A beginning scholar may draw from relevant life or work experience here or try to provide an overview of the author's educational background. An author may also ask a mentor or expert in the area to review the work and provide a recommendation of the work's importance or relevance that can be set out in the letter.

Here, the author pitches the potential market for the article, emphasizing its relevance to a wider audience than other academics.

challenges that must be met in the near and medium term. It synthesizes recognized issues in the discussion and extends them in several important directions that continue to be overlooked. It is intended to be a useful immediate contribution to the academic and policy discussion and furnish an assessment that will remain useful over the longer term.

My background makes me nearly uniquely qualified to provide this contribution. **My scholarship is widely cited and well known as providing a leading, informed and reflective analysis that often contrasts with commonly but mistakenly-held conceptions in pending debates.** Recent examples of this style of my work appear in some of the best law reviews in the country, including Minnesota (2007), Vanderbilt (2007), Columbia (2006), Michigan (2005), and UCLA (2004), among numerous others. This work occupies what can be called "law and accounting," which usually means encounters with numerous legal subjects including, in the case of the current Article, administrative law, comparative law, corporations, international law, and securities regulation.

I have prepared this Article to be the most thorough and realistic appraisal of the SEC's policy vision and to illuminate this debate for **a wide audience of scholars, practitioners, and policy makers within the US and abroad.**

Additional summary information appears in an abstract included with this submission. I hope you will accept the piece for publication.

Lawrence A. Cunningham

14.2.D Keywords

One overlooked aspect of publishing law journals is to develop an accurate and enticing list of keywords to identify an article. Most publishing platforms strongly encourage the use of keywords to enable editors using the service to identify articles that meet with topics in which they have a particular interest. For example, if a law journal's editors intend to publish an issue devoted entirely to real estate law, the editors are likely to use real estate-related keywords to identify articles that relate to real estate. They might search for articles discussing "deeds," "leases," "construction," "builders," "real estate," "property," and any number of other words that relate to real estate. As a result, developing a thorough and accurate list of keywords early in the publishing process (and ensuring that these words are incorporated into the abstract and the article) may better position an article for selection by a journal.

14.2.E Table of contents

A final primary point of consideration for article publishing is the table of contents. Specifically, a table of contents, like an abstract, provides an overview of the article or other written pieces, previewing its contents for the audience. In most instances, the table of contents will correspond with sections, chapters, headings, or subheadings within an article. One key to a helpful table of contents is for each line to clearly and concisely describe the contents of the section, chapter, or subsection to which it refers. Notice how the following table of contents from Professor Meghan Boone's *Lactation Law*[21] succinctly describes the topic being discussed:

Table of Contents

The considerations of drafting an informative abstract and table of contents with plenty of keywords are only a few of many considerations an author should have in publishing a journal article. If followed closely, these pieces will put an article on the right path to getting published by a journal.

14.3 Publishing bar journal and other professional articles

Practicing lawyers, students, and professors often seek to publish articles with practical appeal, with the principal goal of being published in a professional journal. As discussed in more detail in earlier chapters, professional journals and magazines share many of the same characteristics and publishing standards as school-sponsored and specialty law journals. Articles for journals and magazines, however, are generally shorter, less formal, and more specifically focused on the topics that affect practicing lawyers on a day-to-day basis rather than the theoretical topics often addressed in law journal articles. Like law journals, professional journals include a wide variety of publications, with some journals and magazines containing an array of topics distributed broadly to all lawyers admitted to practice law in a given jurisdiction and others focusing on particular areas of law that serve a more specialized practice group.

For students and newly minted practicing lawyers (and possibly even new professors) the most welcoming publication for a professional journal or magazine article might be a student or "young lawyer" edition of a local bar magazine. Many state bar organizations publish magazines or journals that are directed either to law school students or practicing lawyers who are new to the profession, which might include individuals up to a specified age or who have been practicing law for less than a particular amount of time. These publications often limit articles to those written by or directed to the student and young lawyer audience. They may specifically seek out publications by students, particularly those at law schools within the states where the journals are published.

For more senior practicing lawyers, professional journal publication options are similar to those for students and younger attorneys. A bar association's primary, all-lawyer journal is likely to remain a viable potential publication source. Outside of bar-sponsored journals and magazines, some journals and magazines are published specifically for particular practice areas and can be published by the same bar associations or by unaffiliated third-party organizations. Other organizations focused on other aspects of the legal profession likewise publish topic-specific journals and welcome articles from practicing lawyers in those fields.

Regardless of an author's status as a student, practicing lawyer, or professor, when considering potential professional journal publication opportunities, the American Bar Association's website (www.american bar.org) is a helpful resource in identifying such opportunities and their publication cycles and requirements.

14.4 Other options: Bar associations, professional organizations, and writing competitions

Even outside the scope of periodical publications by law journals, professional journals, and other such publications, myriad opportunities exist for less-traditional and more-enterprising options to publish your legal writing.

For example, many bar associations and similar professional organizations also publish regular newsletters or bulletins to highlight new developments in the law. Most frequently, these publications are not afforded the formal legal editing process and mainly are intended to distribute breaking news—or at least notable legal news events, opinions, and the like—to relevant audiences. Some such newsletters and bulletins have regular contributors cycling on and off to publish columns on a regular basis, while others have no constant contributors and welcome on-topic contributions from anyone willing to take the time to put together an article. In many cases, articles intended for practicing lawyers are more likely to reach a receptive audience when published in these frequently distributed, short newsletters and bulletins than in the more academic-focused realm of law journals.

Outside of these options, depending on its content, an article or other writing might also qualify for one of many writing competitions. Bar associations, law firms or companies, and other professional organizations often sponsor writing competitions in the hope of generating substantial theoretical and practical debate regarding a particular topic, in return for the promise of scholarship money or similar rewards for law students. Fewer organizations sponsor similar programs for practicing attorneys, but they do exist. If the article is not already accepted for publication in a law journal, professional journal, or other publication and the article is on topic and meets the competition's entry requirements, entering the article into a competition is a good fallback option. In other instances, an author might draft an article specifically for the competition with the hope of winning scholarship funding or other cash prizes. If the work wins the competition (or otherwise qualifies for publication with the sponsoring organization), it provides a further sterling credential for the author's professional résumé, regardless of whether the author is a practicing attorney or student.

The chart below identifies a number of resources that might be of assistance in seeking writing competitions and learning more about available writing competitions. (While the following links are accurate as of the date of publication, they might change over time, so you may have to check beyond these links.)

Sources to learn about writing competitions

Sources	Where to find background information
American Bar Association, Law Student Division, Awards, Competitions, Grants, and Scholarships	abaforlawstudents.com/events/law-student-competition/writing-competitions/
iCompete Writing, Suffolk University Law School	suffolk.edu/icompetewriting
Lewis & Clark School of Law, Law Student Writing Competition & Associated Scholarships	law.lclark.edu/academics/student_writing_competitions/
University of Michigan Law School Writing Competitions	law.umich.edu/currentstudents/studentservices/Pages/competit.aspx
The National Law Review, Law Student Writing Competition	natlawreview.com/NLR-law-student-writing-competition
New York Law School Law Review, Writing Competition Database	nylslawreview.com/writing-contest-database/
University of Richmond School of Law, Legal Essay Contest Catalog	law.richmond.edu/students/essay-catalog.html

14.5 Promoting your work

With all of this in mind, congratulations are in order! You have worked hard on a piece and published your work, and it is now time to promote that work and share your expertise and original ideas with the world. Although you may feel hesitant to engage in what some consider as self-promotion, try to reframe the promotion process as a way to engage with new audiences. In Chapter 7, *Law Review and Law Journal Articles*, jurist Harry Edwards was quoted to say: "A unifying focus of legal scholarship … should be making law better serve society."[22] Law can serve society only when writers expand their readership by promoting their work.

To understand best practices in promoting your work, we interviewed Professor Jennifer Romig of Emory University School of Law—one of the leading experts in the field—to get her tips.

If you want more information on where and how to promote your work, you might review Chapter 12, *Social Media and Blogs*, which discusses ways to use social media platforms like Twitter, Facebook, and LinkedIn to promote your work. We wish you well as you promote your own modern legal scholarship!

Expert Tips for Promoting Legal Scholarship:

Professor Jennifer Romig's recommendations are as follows:

1. Write a vivid, catchy, representative abstract for sources such as SSRN and blogs.

2. Create an even shorter abstract for Twitter (280 characters including shared links).

3. Learn what promotions are already in place where your article is being published.

4. Model your own promotional post(s) after the tone and content of others' promotional posts that you admire.

5. Contact your influencers (cited in your article) and share your article with them, also thanking them for their own work.

6. Contact the managers or authors of any legal blogs in your topic area and email them your article and abstract.

7. Monitor the news and re-share your article in reference to new events that re-emphasize your article's relevance.

8. Be alert to conversations on social media, such as with established hashtags and regularly scheduled chats where you could share a snippet of your article and a link in a responsive moment.

14.6 Conclusion

By making it to this point of the book, you should now be prepared to identify a topic, thesis, audience, and publication source; draft analytical scholarship, including journal articles, policy papers, capstones, and the many other types of scholarship discussed; utilize social media and other electronic sources for distributing your writing; and complete the publication process. With this knowledge and your innate abilities, you are more than prepared to begin a scholarly journey, and this textbook can be a helpful resource throughout that journey. While the chapters in this book can certainly be read together as an entire book, each chapter might also serve as a stand-alone quick reference guide to answer questions or provide guidance about the process of preparing any written piece of modern legal scholarship. We look forward to seeing your name and your ideas in print and going viral on social media. Best of luck!

Notes

1. Nancy Levit, *Scholarship Advice for New Law Professors in the Electronic Age*, 16 WIDENER L.J. 947, 975–76 (2007).

2. *W&L Law Journal Rankings*, managementtools4.wlu.edu (last visited Sept. 20, 2019) [hereinafter W&L Rankings].

3. *About Us*, YALE J. L. & FEMINISM (last visited Sept. 20, 2019).

4. *See, e.g.*, Allen Rostron & Nancy Levit, *Information for Submitting Articles to Law Reviews and Journals* ssrn.com (Aug. 1, 2019) (listing standards and requirements for submissions to a law review or law journal).

5. *ExpressO*, bepress.com (last visited Jan. 18, 2020).

6. *Scholastica*, scholasticahq.com (last visited Jan. 18, 2020).

7. *SSRN*, ssrn.com (last visited Jan. 18, 2020).

8. *LawArXiv*, lawarxiv.info (last visited Jan. 18, 2020).

9. Rostron & Levit, *supra* (listing which institutions accept direct submission requirements, such as direct submissions or through Scholastica).

10. W&L Rankings, *supra*.

11. Rostron & Levit, *supra*.

12. *Id.*

13. Matt Bodie, *Article Length Limits: Some Early Results*, prafsblawg.blog.com (July 24, 2006).

14. *Joint statement regarding articles length*, harvardlawreview.org (last visited Jan. 18, 2020).

15. *Id.*

16. To see if these policies had any effect on the actual length of law review articles, Saint Louis University School of Law Professor Matt Bodie conducted a study of the length of articles published in the Columbia, Harvard, Penn, Stanford, Texas, Virginia, and Yale law reviews. Bodie found that, for the editorial season following the implementation of the new policies, the average article length dropped twenty pages to 67.13, which still exceeded the stated preferred length limits of the law reviews. Nevertheless, it was still a considerable drop in length. *See* Bodie, *supra*.

17. Eugene Volokh, *Writing an Abstract for a Law Review Article*, reason.com/volokh (Feb. 8, 2010).

18. Leti Volpp, *The Citizen and the Terrorist*, 49 UCLA L. REV. 1575, 1575 (2002).

19. Lee Petherbridge & Christopher A. Cotropia, *Should Your Law Review Article Have an Abstract and Table of Contents?: An Empirical Analysis*, 85 MISS. L.J. 295, 320 (2016).

20. *Sample Law Review Submission Cover Letters*, CONCURRING OPS., (last visited May 14, 2019).

21. Meghan Boone, *Lactation Law*, 106 CALIF. L. REV. 1827, 1828 (2018).

22. Harry T. Edwards, *Another Look at Professor Rodell's Goodbye to Law Reviews*, 100 VA. L. REV. 1483, 1499 (2014).

Index